# Remembering
# Stalin's Victims

# REMEMBERING

A Memorial delegation attends the funeral of its strong supporter and longtime human rights advocate Andrei Sakharov. Moscow, 1989. *Courtesy Interregional Memorial Society Archives, Moscow.*

# STALIN'S VICTIMS

*Popular Memory
and the End
of the USSR*

Kathleen E. Smith

CORNELL UNIVERSITY PRESS

*Ithaca and London*

First published 1996 by Cornell University Press.

Printed in the United States of America

Library of Congress Cataloging-in-Publication Data

Smith, Kathleen E.
    Remembering Stalin's victims : popular memory and the end of the USSR / Kathleen E. Smith.
        p.   cm.
    Includes bibliographical references and index.
    ISBN 0-8014-3194-8 (cloth)
    1. Political persecution—Soviet Union. 2. Soviet Union—Politics and government. 3. Political rehabilitation—Soviet Union.
4. Dissenters—Soviet Union. 5. Political rehabilitation—Former Soviet republics. 6. Post-communism—Former Soviet republics.
7. Inter-Republic Memorial Society (Soviet Union) I. Title.
DK266.3.S54   1996
947.084—dc20                                              95-41397

There are words whose universal attraction at some moment becomes so strong and obvious that they can be considered signs of the times. For our time . . . one of these key words will be "perestroika." And if this is so, if the impulse of dynamism, change, and improvement is so strongly expressed, then it is important to think about why the word "memory" has been used with equal frequency.

—ALEKSEI LEVINSON, 1989

People say why recall the past? What is the good of remembering what has been swept away? What is the good of irritating the nation? . . . How can one ask such questions? If I suffered from a serious and dangerous disease and recovered or was cured of it, I would recollect the fact with joy. I would be disturbed by it only if I were still ill or if I had taken a turn for the worse and wanted to deceive myself.

—LEV TOLSTOI

# CONTENTS

# ILLUSTRATIONS

# PREFACE

My personal acquaintance with the former Soviet Union began in the late 1980s, just as Mikhail Gorbachev began to lower barriers to free speech. Like many other Westerners who have lived or traveled there, I was struck by the ubiquitous tales of family tragedy stemming from the millions of arrests and incidents of persecution during the Stalin era. Some young people had been raised on vivid accounts of loss or imprisonment, whereas others were only then daring to ask reticent parents or grandparents where they had been during the purges. But by the 1980s many survivors of Stalin's labor camps had, like Boris Yeltsin's father, gone to their graves refusing to discuss their prison experiences.[1] Unlike the West Germans, who have been pushed at various times by both external and internal forces to contemplate their own complicity in the Holocaust, Soviet citizens were shielded from the need to examine dark moments in their national history. Their leaders sought to minimize the persecutions and control what was said about them. But reform and remembrance are inextricably linked.

Twice after Stalin died, Soviet leaders experimented with political liberalization, and in each instance their initiatives hinged on criticism of Stalin and his style of rule. Selective condemnation of the Stalin era seemed to promise support for reformers, but during both Khrushchev's thaw and

1. Boris Yeltsin, *The Struggle For Russia,* trans. Catherine Fitzpatrick (New York: Random House, 1994), p. 98.

Gorbachev's glasnost an intentionally unleashed discourse went further than the Party leaders anticipated or could tolerate. In both periods the expectation that reformers in the leadership and in the wider society could work together broke down over the issue of coming to terms with what the Russians term "repressions." And when Gorbachev lifted the Communist Party's monopoly on association in the 1980s, social forces organized and openly attacked the legitimacy of the whole system of Soviet domination, past and present. Citizens found many grounds—economic, ethnic, environmental—on which to mobilize against and criticize the Communist Party's rule, but antistalinism proved the strongest early catalyst and the most powerful source of consensus for mobilizing to demand democracy. Dissatisfaction with half-truths about the past united individuals from all walks of life in the Memorial Society, an independent mass movement that eventually challenged the very notion that the Communist Party could be reformed.

Reform always begins with reevaluation of the political system. The breakdown of dictatorship often provides a first opportunity to express dissatisfaction with repressive policies and hence becomes the occasion for an explosion of pent-up concerns and resentment. Just as repression is an essential part of undemocratic rule, so repudiation of repression becomes an inescapable part of the liberalization of such regimes. But the settling of accounts during or after the collapse of authoritarian rule has taken many forms, from amnesties to show trials. This book addresses state-society conflict over human rights abuses in the former Soviet Union.[2] It investigates why destalinization became a double-edged sword for reformers within the leadership and a rallying point for democratic activists in the broader society.

Why were the reformers who initiated public criticism of Stalin in the late 1950s and the late 1980s unable to accept similar complaints when they emanated from below? And why did citizens risk confrontation with the Communist Party to promote recognition of and recompense for victims of Stalinism? This book looks at how people dealt with repression not psychologically but politically; that is, it examines the social demands and state policies that emerged in respect to the state-sponsored persecu-

2. Though I use the terms "Soviet" and "Soviet Union," I focus on the core republics of Russia, Ukraine, Belorussia, and Kazakhstan. I deliberately omit the Baltic republics from consideration here because of their distinct history of forced incorporation into the USSR, mass deportations, and broad ethnically based mobilization.

tions of the Stalin era. It addresses the conflict between state and society in two time periods in the USSR and compares the efforts to come to terms with past repressions there with analogous efforts elsewhere.

To illuminate the connections between prior repression and modes of liberalization, I draw on the experiences of other countries in Chapter 1 to outline a range of potential ways to come to terms with the past. I suggest that the dominance of the Communist Party and the weakness of civil society in the USSR put the Party in a strong position to preserve its privileges and institutions. But the Party's reliance on its past record for legitimation also made it vulnerable to attack from below. The order of the empirical chapters replicates the development of the state-society conflict: Khrushchev's and Gorbachev's officially supported steps toward rejection of repression are followed by "uncontrolled" destalinization, which in turn produces conflict over antistalinism at the local and national levels. Having made the case that the totalitarian nature of Soviet rule required official reformers to balance the criticism they invited against the authority they cherished and required civic activists to balance their desire for independence against their need for survival, I consider why public interest in repudiating repression declined just as the Soviet system was finally breaking down in 1991.

The battle over the Soviet past not only illuminates the dynamic interaction between elite and mass political actors during liberalization but throws light on the scars that totalitarian rule has left on Russian society and the long-term obstacles to reform it has created. The Soviet regime has been swept away and the survivors of Stalinism are dying off, but Russia has only begun to experiment with ways to break with its totalitarian past. Coming to terms with the past is a process that lacks a definitive resolution, and any outcome should be viewed as a provisional compromise rather than as a decisive victory for one faction or another. Should democracy take hold in the former Soviet republics, the choices made during the transition will certainly be subject to further negotiation.

To analyze elite politics, social mobilization, and policy battles, I drew on several types of data. In evaluating the strategies of Party leaders, I looked at official speeches and officially approved novels, films, and nonfiction treatments of Stalinism. I also relied on secondary accounts of Khrushchev's and Gorbachev's relations with historians and cultural figures who dealt with Stalinism in their works. Key to my assessment of

Khrushchev-era attitudes was a declassified report prepared by the historian Anna Pankratova for the Central Committee. Pankratova summarized listeners' reactions to a series of talks that she gave in March 1956 on the topic of reforming the discipline of history in the light of revelations about the cult of personality. For information on perestroika-era policies, I interviewed officials involved in rehabilitation at the Moscow Procuracy and the Moscow KGB. I also spoke with deputies who drafted the laws on reparations in the Russian and Ukrainian Supreme Soviets, as well as leaders at the city level who had passed laws granting privileges to victims of repression.

With the exception of personal accounts and analyses of historical themes in samizdat writings, virtually no literature exists on social responses to destalinization. Fortunately, glasnost made possible real field research on informal organizations in the Soviet Union. During a six-month sojourn in 1991 and briefer follow-up trips in 1992, 1993, and 1994, I conducted intensive interviews with Memorial activists in Moscow, Leningrad/St. Petersburg, Minsk, Kiev, Vorkuta, Syktyvkar, Murmansk, Apatity, and Sverdlovsk/Ekaterinburg. I also combined a mail survey of activists across Russia, Belarus, Ukraine, and Kazakhstan with material from the Interregional Memorial Society Archives in Moscow to gain a sense of the variations in Memorial's activities and the state's responses to them. In addition, I drew on accounts of informal organizations in the new independent press and in state-run media. Finally, I took advantage of unorthodox sources of opinion, such as letters to the press and to Memorial, museum exhibits, and exhibit comment books.

I am indebted to all the people who graciously granted me interviews and helped me with my research. In particular I am grateful to Elena Rusakova, Marina Linnik, Boris Belenkin, Karina Musaelian, Viacheslav Igrunov, Susanna Pechuro, Volia Lebedinskii, and the late Artem Feldman of the Moscow Memorial Society. I also thank Marina Glukhovskaia, Irina Granik, Elena and Viktor Balaganskii, Alessa Semukha, Izrail Reznichenko, Aralina Zakharovna, Pavel Krotov, Mikhail Rogachev, and Viktor and Svetlana Pestov for their assistance and hospitality during my travels in Russia, Belarus, and Ukraine. Adam Hochschild, Michael McFaul, and Tanya Smith all generously shared their contacts and helped me arrange interviews.

Many hours of discussion with colleagues helped me at every stage of research and writing. I am most grateful to Shari Cohen, Jane Dawson, Steve Fish, Kathie Hendley, and Nils Muiznieks for their encouragement and advice. I also thank George W. Breslauer, Giuseppe Di Palma, Gail W. Lapidus, and Reginald Zelnik for their careful comments on an earlier version of this book. The 1990 and 1992 Workshops on Soviet Domestic Politics and Society, sponsored by the Social Science Research Council and graciously hosted by Peter and Susan Solomon, provided me with further feedback.

Research and writing were supported by grants from the Berkeley-Stanford Program in Soviet and Post-Soviet Studies, the Albert Einstein Institution, and the Social Science Research Council and the American Council of Learned Societies with funds provided by the U.S. Department of State. The American Council of Teachers of Russian arranged my first research trips. The Moscow Historical Archives Institute and the Interlegal Research Center served as my institutional hosts in Moscow. Parts of Chapters 7 and 9 are excerpted by permission from my contribution to *Impunity and Human Rights in International Law and Practice*, edited by Naomi Roht-Arriaza, copyright © 1995 by Oxford University Press, Inc. I am grateful to Roger Haydon of Cornell University Press for his support for the book. Hamilton College provided funds for a typist in the last stages of editing, and my mother, Eleanor Smith, generously donated her time and word processing skills to the final push.

KATHLEEN E. SMITH

*Clinton, New York*

# Remembering
# Stalin's Victims

# I LIBERALIZATION AND SETTLING ACCOUNTS

Nikita Khrushchev ended the 22d Communist Party Congress in 1961 by calling for the removal of Stalin's corpse from its place of honor beside Lenin in the mausoleum on Red Square. At the same time, recalling the murder of several prominent old Bolsheviks, he urged construction of a monument to "comrades who became victims of arbitrariness."[1] Khrushchev tended to describe Stalin's victims loosely as a few thousand loyal Party members and honest nonparty people, but those killed or imprisoned in the purges between 1934 and 1953 actually numbered in the millions and included people from all walks of life and all political backgrounds. The Party leadership quickly orchestrated Stalin's interment under a plain marker next to Lenin's mausoleum, but it did not commemorate the victims of the purges.

The Party could relegate Stalin's physical remains to a more ambiguous position in the Leninist pantheon without exploring all the consequences of his long and often brutal reign. A permanent shrine to the dictator's victims, however, would constantly evoke memories of the people's suffering under communism. A monument might even have served in lieu of real grave sites as a place for survivors and victims' families and friends to gather spontaneously, to mourn, remember, and perhaps draw lessons from the past. Reform-minded Communists wanted to displace Stalin in

1. *XXII S"ezd Kommunisticheskoi Partii Sovetskogo Soiuza, 17–31 Oktiabriia 1961 goda: Stenograficheskii otchet*, 3 vols. (Moscow: Gospolizdat, 1962), 2:587.

order to justify political liberalization, but they had no interest in acknowledging the extent and complexity of the political persecution that had occurred under Soviet rule. Thus Khrushchev tried to duck messy questions of accountability by covering up the physical traces of both Stalin and his victims.

A quarter of a century later a new reformer came to power and found that the past would not stay buried. When Mikhail Gorbachev eased censorship in the late 1980s, the issue of earlier state-sponsored repressions immediately resurfaced. But this time an independent group of citizens organized around the idea of commemorating the victims of political persecution. They proposed not only a monument but a research center to investigate and document the sources of the terror. The Memorial Society's call for a movement to acknowledge the suffering of common people drew thousands of citizens into hitherto unknown territory— the public realm. And the group's competition to select a design for a monument revealed popular understandings of the purges that diverged sharply from the official version.

Given its source and sensitive subject matter, the proposed memorial became the subject of intense conflict among reformers, revolutionaries, and conservatives. Both in the 1950s and in the 1980s, Soviet politicians worried about whether memories of past repressions could be evoked to support reform or whether they might provoke a revolution. A monument would be perceived as setting the tone for interpreting the purges, and that tone might be sorrowful, angry, despairing, critical, proud, or hopeful. It might depict rifts in society or try to promote reconciliation. It might continue to heap the blame for past abuses on Stalin personally or it might challenge the whole Communist regime. Indeed, concepts for a monument suggested in 1988 ranged from somber tombs to triumphal statues of brave survivors, from a respectful model of Lenin being trampled by Stalin's sycophants to a design that joined a swastika with a hammer and sickle.[2] The problem of finding some artistic form to capture the complex and controversial purges epitomizes the difficulty of coming to terms with the past.

No single dominant formula for redressing past repression has emerged—one can neither fully make amends to victims nor fully punish perpetrators. Memories of grave violations of human rights may create a

2. "Memorial zhertvam stalinskikh repressii: Proekty i predlozheniia," *Dekorativnoe iskusstvo*, no. 3, 1989, pp. 10–15.

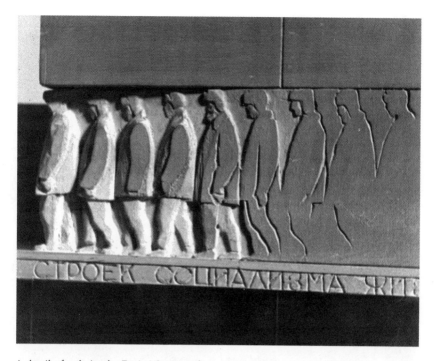

A detail of a design by Dmitri Smirnov for a monument to victims of Stalin's terror. The inscription reads: "Having laid down their lives in constructing the foundations of socialism, they are rehabilitated post-humously." *Courtesy Interregional Memorial Society Archives, Moscow.*

constituency hungry for democracy and sensitive to any compromises that might weaken a state governed by law. But unearthing past atrocities, while convincing some people that the results of democratization are worth the risks and uncertainties along the way, may so alarm members of the old regime that they threaten to disrupt the very process of reform.[3] Digging up past crimes may thus be a double-edged sword for reformers, creating pressure for more radical change on the one hand and for preservation of the old system on the other.

Societies have approached the task of coming to terms with their pasts in a wide variety of ways. Both the demands and the remedies that arise in efforts to settle accounts are shaped by the nature of the antecedent regime

3. Guillermo O'Donnell and Philippe C. Schmitter, *Transitions from Authoritarian Rule: Tentative Conclusions about Uncertain Democracies* (Baltimore: Johns Hopkins University Press, 1986), pp. 31–32.

and the path of reform. Before we investigate the specific course of attempts to come to terms with the past in the USSR, it is useful to examine the experiences of other countries that have weighed possible policies in respect to past injustices. Then we can begin to analyze the dynamics of the Soviet situation by examining which past in particular is being confronted, and by weighing two key aspects of the context for policy making: the source of the reform initiative and the climate for social mobilization.

## COMING TO TERMS WITH THE PAST

Tearing down old monuments and building new ones, stripping away honors and restoring tarnished reputations are all elements of coming to terms with the past symbolically. Public commemoration, whether through monuments, plaques, or grave markers, offers a form of compensation for the stigma attached to political prisoners and their families. But symbolic change is only one means of acknowledging past abuses. Perhaps the most common demand from below is for official truth-telling. Information on past abuses may surface from many sources, but many victims seek a government-supported investigation because it can serve several objectives at once. By informing relatives of the fates of the missing, a formal study can offer a form of reparation; by releasing official documentation of repression, it can offer historians invaluable sources for investigation and directly shape public consciousness; finally, if it discloses the identity of perpetrators, it may act as a surrogate for a court.[4]

Nonpenal sanctions in addition to public exposure may be applied to people who engaged in torture, ordered abuses, or collaborated with the secret police. In Austria, for instance, the denazification process included fines for those deeply involved in Nazi activities.[5] The government can also strip perpetrators of their privileges and pensions. And it can engage in "lustration," or purification, by removing offenders from their posts and banning them from public office or other responsible positions in the future. Outrage over past injustices may lead to witch hunts or extrajudi-

---

4. Naomi Roht-Arriaza, ed., *Impunity and Human Rights in International Law and Practice* (New York: Oxford University Press, 1995).

5. Frederick C. Engelmann, "How Austria Has Coped with Two Dictatorial Legacies," in *From Dictatorship to Democracy*, ed. John Herz (Westport, Conn.: Greenwood, 1982), p. 144.

cial reprisals, but these extreme responses generally result from a breakdown in order, not a deliberate policy choice.

Material and social reparations for survivors or the families of those who perished are often suggested as further means of achieving justice. Though it is impossible to put a price tag on human suffering, some governments have offered compensation for lost wages or, as in the case of the U.S. government's restitution to Japanese-Americans interned during World War II, uniform lump-sum payments. Similarly, the government may provide medical treatment and therapy for victims who still suffer the aftereffects of torture or other abuse. It may also reinstall victims in their old jobs if they worked in the public sector or otherwise help them return to professional life. Moreover, as part of restoring survivors to their rightful places in society, the state may need to reinstate citizenship rights and academic degrees, and give back confiscated property and fines improperly levied. In cases of forced resettlement, such as occurred with many indigenous peoples in North America and South Africa and with a dozen ethnic groups in the USSR, the property at issue consists of large tracts of territory, including land that has been repopulated and improved in the meantime.

Reparations generate controversy because they cost a great deal of money. Many people argue that society as a whole should not be taxed to pay for the policies of a previous nonelected government; but the responsible agencies may no longer be in existence or may refuse pay. And in some cases irremediable disputes may arise over indivisible assets, such as a lost job that has been given to someone else or confiscated property that has changed hands legally since its seizure.

Finally, victims may seek justice through the courts. Individuals can sue for damages or the state may prosecute the people they deem responsible for illegal acts, from those who tortured prisoners to those who ordered them to do so. The leaders of a new government may even seek to put the founders of the old regime on trial for having seized power illegally. Paul Connerton notes that a trial of the old regime is "not like those acts of justice which reinforce a system of retribution by setting its governing principles once more into motion"; in such a trial "the continuing struggle between the new order and the old will be definitively terminated, because the legitimacy of the victors will be validated once and for all."[6] Trials of

6. Paul Connerton, *How Societies Remember* (Cambridge: Cambridge University Press, 1989), p. 7.

any sort can go beyond punishment to reinforce public acknowledgment of victims. They may also confirm democratic principles by demonstrating that no group is above the law. Judicial measures, however, are almost always features of established democracies, not of societies in transition, because institutions that can call these public servants to account must first have been reconstituted.

Obviously, the characterization of imprisonment and torture of political opponents as abuses of human rights constitutes a threat to the perpetrators. Destruction or withholding of documents and other evidence, refusal to testify before courts or commissions, and threats against witnesses are all tactics that victimizers have employed to cover up their crimes. When, as in Argentina, the offenders are active-duty military officers, they can even respond to attempts to prosecute them with violent attacks on the new system.

The opposite of prosecution is amnesty. The outgoing regime may enact a "self-amnesty" law before leaving office or may make a reprieve a condition of relinquishing power peacefully. In cases such as El Salvador, where civil strife coincided with state-sponsored repression, negotiation of a transition may even be based on mutual forgiveness. Sometimes the new democratic government itself grants pardons or limits prosecutions in order to defuse tensions with hardliners. Thus Argentina's President Raúl Alfonsín moved from a commitment to prosecute broadly to the *punto final* law, which set a time limit on filing complaints.

Granting of amnesty creates controversy because some people see it as fostering a culture of impunity and many believe that only the victim has the right to forgive. But when civic groups in Uruguay managed to force an amnesty law to a nationwide referendum, a majority of voters chose to uphold it, thus subordinating individual grievances to the perceived public good of national stability. As the Uruguayan president put it: "What is more just—to consolidate the peace of a country where human rights are guaranteed today or to seek retroactive justice that could compromise that peace?"[7]

Argentina tried and convicted the leaders of its military dictatorship; Chile's old dictator still heads the military and has blocked attempts to prosecute persons accused of human rights abuses. The Czechs developed a broad program for screening persons who collaborated with the secret

7. Lawrence Weschler, *A Miracle, a Universe* (New York: Pantheon, 1990), pp. 233, 168–69.

police from high office; meanwhile, one Polish government lost a vote of confidence when it proposed to open old secret police files. Why do some countries bury the past while others expose it? The answer lies somewhere in the mix of past suffering and present reform.

## THE SOVIET PAST

Where does one begin to describe the excesses of Soviet rule? Lenin endorsed terror and violence against opponents during the civil war and against rebellious Bolshevik forces in the Kronstadt uprising of 1921. Stalin broadened and deepened the use of violence with forced collectivization of the peasantry, show trials of the political elite, and mass arrests of perceived "enemies" from all walks of life. Some of the people imprisoned without trial were deliberately targeted by Stalin himself, but most of them were the victims of centrally mandated arrest quotas, malicious informers, or public hysteria over "spies" and "wreckers." People arrested by the secret police were uniformly threatened and tortured to extract confessions of political crimes. Ultimately, with or without signed confessions, suspects were sentenced to execution or to long terms in brutal labor camps.

The number of people who fell victim to Stalin's repressions is a subject of controversy both within the republics he ruled and abroad. In all cases of persecution one encounters the difficulty of measuring its scope and impact. One may attempt a body count of the dead and missing, but an enumeration of fatalities may create a misleading picture. Between 1973 and 1979, for instance, approximately thirty people disappeared or died in official custody in Argentina for every one who did so in Uruguay; yet when the two countries' populations are considered, Uruguay had a higher rate of incarceration for political reasons—one in every five hundred citizens was arrested and one in fifty was detained for interrogation, and often tortured.[8] Indeed, in the Soviet case estimates are complicated not only by the scale of the purges and the time elapsed since they ended, but by the tremendous diversity of lethal and nonlethal forms they took. The Stalin period witnessed not just arrests of individual "enemies of the

---

8. Alfred Stepan, *Rethinking Military Politics: Brazil and the Southern Cone* (Princeton: Princeton University Press, 1988), p. 69; Robert K. Goldman and Cynthia Brown, *Challenging Impunity: The Ley de Caducidad and the Referendum Campaign in Uruguay* (New York: Americas Watch, 1989), p. 9.

people" but mass deportations of whole ethnic groups, resettlement and forced labor for "wealthy" peasant families, and by some accounts a deliberately engineered famine.

At the low end of the scale, KGB representatives in 1990 began uniformly to cite the number of people unjustly sentenced between 1930 and 1953 as 3,778,234, with 786,098 executed. Two years later, however, a representative of the security services gave the figure of 18 million "repressed," of whom 7 million were sentenced to death. Russian scholars with new access to archival data have calculated the total number of prisoners in Gulag camps and colonies as growing from 510,307 in 1934 to 2,468,524 in 1953. These figures, however, do not reflect the number of executions or the death rate among camp inmates, nor do they tell us how many new prisoners entered the system each year. And one can add to the number of people in labor camps and colonies the number of those living in some form of exile.[9]

Each of the millions of arrests had repercussions in society. In the 1930s, Soviet authorities frequently charged the original victim's wife with the crime of failing to report her husband's counterrevolutionary activities (generally men were the primary targets). The police often deposited young children in orphanages if no relatives were on the spot to shelter them. But relatives also suffered by association: if they escaped arrest and exile to a distant region, they were likely to lose their jobs and apartments. As the children of victims grew up, they faced discrimination in access to higher education and jobs. Mass repression also created an overall climate of fear and anxiety. In 1937 the secret police terrorized whole communities in their drive to meet centrally determined goals. Huge segments of both rural and urban society fell victim as the NKVD strove to overfulfill its quotas. Pervasive fear produced social atomization, suspicion, and self-censorship. And whereas some dictatorships have driven opponents into exile abroad, Soviet citizens lacked the option of flight.

In the decades after Stalin's death the form and scope of human rights abuses changed. The Soviet government ceased to persecute individuals at random, but it did not permanently or consistently relax its wholly negative attitude toward pluralism. Nor did it relinquish its monopoly on

---

9. Natalya Gevorkyan, "What's behind the KGB's Figures?" *Moscow News,* 11–18 March 1990, p. 31; Vera Tolz, "Ministry of Security Official Gives New Figures for Stalin's Victims," *Radio Free Europe/Radio Liberty Research Report* (1 May 1992): 8–10; Edwin Bacon, "*Glasnost'* and the Gulag: New Information on Soviet Forced Labour around World War II," *Soviet Studies* 44, no. 6 (1992): 1071.

expression and association. It harassed, spied on, and imprisoned or exiled anyone who challenged its ruling principles. Even during the
Khrushchev thaw, when authorities released millions of political prisoners, the secret police continued to persecute nonconformists and
dissidents.[10]

The Soviet Union also employed novel but effective forms of constraint
in the post-Stalin period to coerce cooperation from the mass of the
populace. Criminal prosecution was still to be feared, and at the same time
the state encouraged fear of less drastic but more easily applied sanctions
in the workplace. It also encouraged a mood of futility and despondency
by disregarding any and all complaints. General passivity thus resulted
largely from coercion, not from a "social contract" under which people
renounced independent political activity in exchange for a steady rise in
their standard of living. After all, the state as universal employer could
mete out rewards and punishments at its pleasure: it could promote
workers and give them cash bonuses, or it could label them as troublemakers and fire and blacklist them.[11] As Jacques Rupnik put it, "Within
this system, police repression is replaced by the personnel office, the police
officer by the personnel officer."[12] Vaclav Havel adds that participation in
rituals of conformity, enforced in part through immense networks of informers, made all citizens collaborators in maintaining the regime.[13]

All nondemocratic regimes limit some aspect of regular, meaningful
competition for posts in government, often by limiting civil and political
liberties such as freedom of expression and association. But one must
distinguish between authoritarian and totalitarian regimes. Totalitarian
regimes are best defined not by the number of their victims or even their
use of lethal repression but rather by their efforts to eradicate pluralism
from their societies.

In a totalitarian regime the party-state is "the sovereign," and it uses its
monopoly on power to penetrate all aspects of social, economic, and

10. Ludmilla Alexeyeva, *Soviet Dissent: Contemporary Movements for National, Religious, and Human Rights,* trans. Carol Pearce and John Glad (Middletown, Conn.:
Wesleyan University Press, 1985), pp. 272–74.

11. Krzysztof Nowak, "Covert Repressiveness and the Stability of a Political System:
Poland at the End of the Seventies," *Social Research* 55 (Spring/Summer 1988): 179–208.
For an alternate view see Peter Hauslohner, "Gorbachev's Social Contract," *Soviet Economy*
3, no. 1 (1987): 57.

12. Jacques Rupnik, *The Other Europe,* rev. ed. (New York: Pantheon, 1989), p. 238.

13. Vaclav Havel, "The Power of the Powerless," in Havel et al., *The Power of the
Powerless* (London: Palach Press, 1985), pp. 35–37.

political life.[14] Ironically, the party-state's claim to embody the will of the people becomes the justification for its suppression of all independent association. As David Ost observes, "If civil society is only a breeding ground for noxious particular interests, it *needs* to be suppressed, in order that *universal* interests can be achieved. Thus, there is room for neither the organizational representation of particular societal interests, nor an independent political public sphere."[15] Ost is describing, of course, an ideal type. People may hold as wide a variety of values in a totalitarian society as anywhere else, but only the officially sanctioned values may be expressed; all others are outlawed.[16] After Stalin's death the Communist Party no longer employed terroristic methods, but the principle of Party domination and the practice of suppressing efforts to form an independent civil society continued.

As for authoritarian regimes, they too may persecute their political opponents and constrain free expression and association, but they preserve the market and generally permit the functioning of some religious organizations, trade unions, private charities, student clubs, professional associations, and other autonomous institutions. Though such organizations are often weakened by laws against subversive activity, infiltration by informers, and censorship, they can remain foci of public life and alternate sources of legitimation for citizens' values. These groups may even take on the task of defending human rights. In Argentina the families of political prisoners could file writs of habeas corpus, even if they rarely produced any positive results, and mothers of the "disappeared" worked with human rights groups to publicize government abuses and even engaged in public protest under the uneasy watch of the dictatorship.

A significant product of the totalitarian state's antipathy to diversity is its deliberate destruction of historical memory. In the absence of authoritative autonomous experts, the party-state uses its control over the flow of information to promote its own ideologized version of the past,

---

14. Ferenc Feher, Agnes Heller, and Gyorgy Markus, *Dictatorship over Needs* (New York: Oxford University Press, 1983), p. 157. These authors' conception of totalitarianism should not be confused with the classic Friedrich and Brzezinski model, which—while emphasizing the role of terror in the USSR and describing many of its consequences, such as atomization of society and strict censorship—was static and descriptive, not analytical or predictive.

15. David Ost, *Solidarity and the Politics of Anti-Politics* (Philadelphia: Temple University Press, 1990), p. 29.

16. See Feher et al., *Dictatorship over Needs*, p. 147.

and to erase all conflicting conceptions. As a consequence, Jacques Rupnik writes, "the totalitarian regime destroys the basic criterion of truth. Since truth changes in accordance with the needs of the rulers, a lie can become the truth, or rather the notion of truth disappears."[17] In Soviet-style regimes "the production of history takes on tremendous significance," Rubie Watson points out, because "one of the primary justifications of communist rule is its inevitability."[18] But the key role assigned to history in efforts to legitimate the leadership's ruling position leaves the regime vulnerable to contradictory individual recollections. Thus the struggle to remember becomes a form of opposition to Soviet-style regimes.

Given the nature of the antecedent totalitarian regime, coming to terms with the Soviet past is complicated by an accumulation of unaddressed violations of basic rights. The numbers of both victims and perpetrators are large and the line between them may be blurred. After all, dissidents were coerced into informing on one another and secret policemen fell victim to the purges. And repudiation of past repression in post-totalitarian states must address not only the resuscitation of memory but also the reform of the extensive party-state system. The sheer number of Communist Party officials, their monopoly on political experience, and the difficulty of fastening blame for suppression of political freedoms on any individual may make it harder to evict former Communists from political life. As for the actors in transition from totalitarian rule, one must expect civil society to be weak and raw and Party members to resist sacrificing their "guiding role." Unlike the military in Latin America, which could be assigned a strictly professional role in the democratic state, the Party had no barracks to which it could retreat, no role besides that of sovereign. The Communist rulers neither considered their rule to be temporary nor had any common interest other than ruling.

## The Path of Reform

The potential dynamics of settling accounts are linked not only to the nature of the chief political actors under the old regime but also to their role in liberalization and democratization. The issue of retroactive justice gener-

17. Rupnik, *Other Europe*, p. 231.
18. Rubie S. Watson, Introduction to *Memory, History, and Opposition under State Socialism*, ed. Watson (Santa Fe, N.M.: School of American Research Press, 1994), p. 1.

ally arises when barriers to free speech begin to be lifted, but modes of extrication from nondemocratic rule vary significantly. As Alfred Stepan has outlined, transitions may be driven by external forces or initiated internally by social forces or by figures within the regime. The source of the impulse for democracy and the strength of various elite actors affect both the opportunities to settle accounts and the level of interest in doing so.

The wave of democratization that swept Western Europe after World War II was triggered by external factors. Democracy was either restored from within after liberation from German occupation or imposed by American troops on their vanquished foes. In a liberated country such as Norway or the Netherlands, where dictatorship and human rights abuses had been carried out by an occupying force with the minimal assistance of local collaborators, the restored government had great credibility and authority to try collaborators.[19] Since the wartime regime was seen as a brief externally imposed aberration rather than as a failure of the nation's democratic ideals, the government had confidence in applying sanctions against war criminals. Its actions were limited only by the preexisting legal system. Where collaboration was more extensive, however, the immediate postwar period was marked by extrajudicial trials of collaborators, often ending in execution, and other forms of vigilantism. The inconsistent treatment of collaborators and the extensiveness of collaboration made the issue of settling accounts in France so painful that even today many French citizens endorse silence and forgetting.[20]

Democratization imposed by a foreign army, by contrast, often features extensive consideration of past crimes at the insistence of the occupying force. But perceptions of "victors' justice" may create popular resentment toward prosecution of war criminals and other rights violators. The occupiers' own wish to install a stable new government does not leave them indifferent to the demands for national reconciliation based on forgiveness or some form of closure. Thus the United States' desire for allies in the Cold War and its eagerness to bring the troops home led to ever-decreasing rigor in the denazification process in Germany.[21]

19. Alfred Stepan, "Paths toward Redemocratization: Theoretical and Comparative Considerations," in *Transitions from Authoritarian Rule: Comparative Perspectives,* ed. Guillermo O'Donnell, Philippe Schmitter, and Laurence Whitehead (Baltimore: Johns Hopkins University Press, 1986), pp. 66–71.

20. Henry Rousso, *The Vichy Syndrome: History and Memory in France since 1944,* trans. Arthur Goldhammer (Cambridge: Harvard University Press, 1991).

21. Frank M. Buscher, *The U.S. War Crimes Trial Program in Germany, 1946–1955* (Westport, Conn.: Greenwood, 1989).

Policies in respect to human rights violations vary in cases of externally triggered democratization precisely because the forceful destruction of once-entrenched repressive institutions allows great freedom of policy choices. New leaders may be reluctant to address controversies from the past, but with the members of the old regime disarmed, they can work from a position of strength should they decide to prosecute offenders.

In more recent decades, however, transitions to democracy have been more commonly initiated from within authoritarian regimes. Dictators rarely begin liberalization with the goal of democratization, but incremental devolution of power often combines with society-led efforts or pacts negotiated with opposition parties to produce regime turnover. The transition may be initiated by civilian political leadership, in which case leaders must craft all their policies—including any settling of accounts—carefully to avoid a military veto. Or elements in the military may lead the democratization efforts. Individuals within the military-run government may opt for democratization, but the split in the leadership is unlikely to produce a transfer of power unless social push or corporate pull comes into play. Some component of the armed forces may concur that its corporate, institutional interests would be better served by either a military-as-government or a civilian authoritarian regime.[22] A strong desire to extricate itself from the authoritarian system may create the climate for sacrifices on the part of the military-as-institution, and even for disavowal of those who created the military-as-government. Thus in Greece the military ultimately exited under harsh conditions, and the new government moved quickly to arrange multiple trials that produced substantial sentences for military officers and torturers.[23]

In all of these regime-initiated transitions, liberalization begins as a tightly controlled process, and this retention of control permits the regime's security apparatus to preserve its prerogatives. The success of repressive organs in safeguarding their privileged positions, however, is by no means assured if liberalization proceeds to democratization. Then the status of the repressive organization largely governs the settling of accounts. Has the military lost prestige and authority? Does it retain the power to intervene in politics? A democracy may renegotiate the rules of the game to annul self-amnesty laws, but only a weak or humiliated military accepts prosecution.

22. Stepan, "Paths toward Redemocratization," pp. 72–78.
23. Samuel P. Huntington, *The Third Wave* (Norman: University of Oklahoma Press, 1991), pp. 219–20.

A transition may also originate in a popular democratic movement. In the most straightforward case, the 1989 "velvet revolution" in Czechoslovakia, mass protests toppled a repressive regime. Popular unrest on the heels of the withdrawal of the Soviet threat of intervention led to the collapse of the Communist regime and to democratic elections to replace it. The primarily society-led transition in Czechoslovakia produced a rapid, but not thorough, break with the past. In a land where no independent parties had been permitted, no experienced new elite existed to take over top posts. Moreover, the old regime toppled so suddenly and peacefully that the "revolution" was accomplished without a purge or even time to ascertain who was a democrat and who was a hardliner. Nor did the velvet revolution expose those who had secretly collaborated with the security apparat. Thus the new government had to decide whether and how to purge informers while it was already operating under the constraints of due process and democratic procedure. But having empowered society, the velvet revolution created an atmosphere conducive to popular demands for retribution and lustration.

Society may also take the lead in negotiating with regime elites to reach a transition to democracy. A pact is difficult to achieve, however, because the civic leaders must have the organizational and ideological skills to form a viable coalition and the political skills to persuade their followers to accept the pact they negotiate. As part of the negotiation process, outgoing elites may force democratic parties to accept certain limits on contestation and control. In Poland, for instance, Solidarity accepted a parliamentary system in which a certain number of seats automatically went to the Communist Party and in which certain ministries remained under Communist control. A pact thus presents an opportunity for explicit or implicit understandings to be reached during the transition regarding limits on prosecution of human rights violators. Nevertheless, once democratic elections are held, the terms of the pact may come under fire and contradictory claims may be expressed through democratic channels. Thus in Uruguay and Chile the new governments have made cautious efforts at least to investigate past persecutions.

None of the paths of democratization outlined here comes with a definite mandate for policy makers to choose a particular means of coming to terms with past injustices. Yet in each situation certain constraints become clear. Redemocratization after occupation presents the fewest obstacles to a settling of accounts because of the clean break with the old regime and because blame for abuses can be placed on foreign forces. Other thoroughgoing transitions that involve the utter defeat or collapse of the old regime also allow new governments to choose from a long menu of policies. Party pacts, however, usually create specific legal obstacles to prosecution. When authoritarian forces choose to liberalize, they try to limit both the extent of democratization and any ill effects for themselves personally, or for their institutional interests. In general, any transition initiated from above provides an opportunity for security forces to protect their interests. And when the repressive bodies retain the means to reverse liberalization, aggressive policies are unlikely because both transition and consolidation are fragile.

Where does the USSR fit in this typology of transitions? Gorbachev and Khrushchev clearly initiated reform from above, though not without opposition from other top officials. But in this case the sole leader of the repressive regime was the Communist Party, with the military and secret police subordinate to it. Since the consolidated organs of repression were at the center of power and individual leaders initiated liberalization, the Soviet path to reform may most closely resemble a transition initiated by a "military-as-government." After all, the Communist Party was a strict hierarchy with ultimate control over the use of force at all levels.

To further this comparison, however, we return to the question of how authoritarian regimes differ from totalitarian regimes. On the surface the two appear similar in some respects. For instance, one could easily substitute "Communist Party" for "armed forces" in Guillermo O'Donnell and Philippe Schmitter's observation that "fundamentally at stake in this issue [of settling past accounts] is the change of the armed forces' messianic self-image as *the* institution ultimately interpreting and ensuring the highest interests of the nation—a conception, alas, even enshrined in the written constitutions of some countries."[24] But in the Soviet case, it is hard to see where the corporate push or social pull necessary to complete democratization would come from, because, as we noted earlier, the Party had no barracks to return to and the Soviet Union began liberalization with no independent social groups or genuine political parties.

Moreover, totalitarian regimes differ from military dictatorships in their basis for legitimacy. The Communist Party presented itself not only as the possessor of unmatched political insight but as the vanguard of the

24. O'Donnell and Schmitter, *Transitions from Authoritarian Rule: Tentative Conclusions*, p. 31.

inevitably victorious proletariat. As the self-appointed sole source of ideological wisdom, the Party was the natural leader of reform. But by the same token, its reform program could not embrace political competition, which would negate its guiding role. Thus, when it was faced by the decision to repress radical demands or to democratize fully, the Party had self-preservation as a powerful incentive to halt or reverse liberalization. The irony of Communist reformers' attempts to relax their dictatorship is that they expected to reap legitimation from their role as the heirs of the previous administrations without being held accountable for their predecessors' mistakes. The Party had to grapple with the contradiction between its roles as critic of the past and as sovereign in the past.

## SOCIAL MOBILIZATION

Given the lack of corporate pull present in the liberalizing one-party Soviet system, the roles of citizens in pushing reform grew in importance. But whereas grievances are always present in society, civic mobilization is rare. Collective action is a complicated phenomenon. It requires careful, sometimes costly construction by activists and some tolerance by the state. A history of totalitarian rule, with its implacable hostility toward pluralism and independent association, strongly affects both the availability of resources to nascent autonomous groups and the dynamics of concerted activity during reform.

The roots of popular mobilization often lie in new organizational resources or a broadened political opportunity structure. Reformist political leaders contribute to the potential for mobilization by adopting controversial policies and by reaching out to formerly marginalized constituencies for support in the ensuing battles among the political elite.[25] Liberalization thus changes the incentives for mobilization by lowering the risk of persecution and opening channels for citizens to influence politics. Once some autonomous social activity is permitted, new groups can exploit preexisting human, social, and material resources. The powerless thus must amass human resources and discover low-cost strategies.

Activists in totalitarian regimes lack experience, funds, and allies, yet they have one unique resource for fighting the system. Vaclav Havel and other East European dissidents pointed to a powerful weapon against

25. Sidney Tarrow, "Aiming at a Moving Target: Social Science and the Recent Rebellions in Eastern Europe," *PS: Political Science & Politics,* March 1991, p. 15.

totalitarianism—truth-telling. Like the little boy in the folk tale who broke the atomization of the crowd by shouting that the emperor had no clothes, dissidents could undermine the authority of the socialist state by articulating the nature of unfreedom and inequality embodied in Soviet-style rule and propagated through Orwellian doublespeak.[26] The Soviet regime's lingering preference for selective truth regarding emotionally charged issues such as Stalin's repressions became a weakness to be exploited by the regime's radical opponents—if they could muster the other resources necessary to express themselves.

But why and how do disenfranchised people mobilize? Movements are the result of artificially created solidarity among individuals. To achieve the sense of "we" necessary for collective action, the participants must negotiate new identities and frame issues in a way that encourages recruitment.[27] A movement's organizers must diagnose a problem, propose a solution, and recruit people to promote the suggested plan of action.[28]

Unlike most modern transitions from dictatorship, liberalization in the Soviet Union did not bring a resurrection of suppressed trade unions, parties, or clubs. Instead, the construction of collective action began with a search for common grievances, issues, and programs around which to unite. In the absence of developed alternative ideologies, potential activists had to identify core concerns that would immediately elicit strong responses. In this light, it is not surprising that recognition of the injustice of Stalinist repressions became an early litmus test to enable liberals to recognize each other. Because antistalinism involved numerous linked issues, could be expressed in many forms, and had broad institutional, legal, and ethical ramifications, it could provide the grounds for a broad political agenda. Still, one might expect that decades of sustained state-sponsored repression would rob citizens of their will to enter politics regardless of the issue.

Guillermo O'Donnell's study of repoliticization after authoritarian rule in Argentina offers some grounds for optimism. He shows that when repression forces privatization of concerns and a retreat from public life, the response to a lifting of controls may take the form of a backlash of mobilization. Having been deprived of both vertical voice (communica-

26. Havel, "Power of the Powerless," pp. 39–40.

27. Alberto Melucci, *Nomads of the Present,* ed. John Keane and Paul Mier (Philadelphia: Temple University Press, 1989), p. 20.

28. David A. Snow and Robert D. Benford, *Ideology, Frame Resonance, and Participant Mobilization,*" International Social Movement Research, 1 (Greenwich, Conn.: JAI Press, 1988), p. 199.

tion with the authorities) and horizontal voice (communication with peers), newly empowered citizens may unleash pent-up anger, as well as guilt feelings for their earlier silence, against the regime that coerced their retreat from politics. Though the idea appears counterintuitive at first glance, suppression and forced atomization, even while producing fear, skepticism, and passivity, may therefore enhance the appeal of self-expression, empowerment, and solidarity. As O'Donnell puts it, "there are some activities that gratify because of the very fact that they are undertaken; this is why some forms and moments of political participation cannot be reduced to a utilitarian calculus."[29] Survivors of Stalinism, like torture victims, may find reengagement in public life therapeutic.[30] Although mobilization is definitely still contingent to some extent on the prospects for success, the craving for horizontal and vertical voices may explain the seeming irrationality of risking mobilization after repression. O'Donnell reminds us, however, that "enhanced rebound" requires the reappearance first of some horizontal voice; people first must have time and space to interact with one another.

Control over public space falls in the domain of the state, and, not surprisingly, the dynamics of mobilization are strongly conditioned by the institutional context. In the United States, according to Frances Fox Piven and Richard Cloward, relations between social movements and authorities are subject to the "calculus of electoral instability"; that is, politicians respond to a perceived loss of constituency by acting to defuse protest movements through a combination of co-optation, timely concessions, satisfaction of moral though not material demands, and ostracism of those who spurn concessions.[31] Given their lack of electoral accountability in the 1980s, Communist politicians could not be expected to respond in this way.

Despite the upheaval in politics that allowed movements to emerge in the 1980s, state and Party leaders remained almost invulnerable to social

29. Guillermo O'Donnell, "On the Fruitful Convergence of Hirschman's *Exit, Voice, and Loyalty* and *Shifting Involvements*: Reflections on the Argentine Experience," in *Development, Democracy, and the Art of Trespassing,* ed. Alejandro Foxley (Baltimore: Johns Hopkins University Press, 1986), p. 261.

30. See Ana Julia Cienfuegos and Cristina Monelli, "The Testimony of Political Repression as a Therapeutic Instrument," *American Journal of Orthopsychiatry* 53, no. 1 (1983): 50–51.

31. Frances Fox Piven and Richard A. Cloward, *Poor People's Movements* (New York: Pantheon, 1977), pp. 3–34.

disapproval. Control of the press and of access to meeting space and other resources gave officials great leverage over civic activists. Neither the thaw nor perestroika produced a large-scale turnover of personnel or legislative oversight of the police, KGB, or courts. Thus, though Soviet reformers risked tarnishing their liberal reputations, they retained the option to use coercion rather than cooptation in their interaction with resource-poor movements. Moreover, traditionally in the USSR, state-society conflicts had not been permitted to take the form of open clashes between organized interests. The Communist Party led—it did not negotiate. Even within the elite, competing factions had long been banned. And though conflict had not been eradicated, it had been submerged and labeled abnormal.

The nature of the totalitarian regime in the Soviet Union created distinctive actors and a distinctive setting for liberalization. On the one hand, there was the Communist Party with its position as the guiding force in politics, the economy, and all aspects of organized social life. On the other hand, there was the long-abused, atomized society. Controlled reform put the Party in a strong position to preserve its privileges and institutions. Reform, however, implied admission of past fallibility and hence undermined the Party's claim to a monopoly on truth and a guiding role. Reformers in the Party had to grapple with the contradiction that they had created between the Party's image as the sole enlightened advocate and defender of popular interests and their interest in a more open society.

Reformers obviously believed they could draw a thick line between past and present administrations while maintaining legitimacy as the heirs of the existing system. But the combination of tremendous pent-up grievances and relaxation of restrictions on speech and association acted as a strong catalyst for protest centered on repudiation of repression. This issue appealed to would-be civic activists precisely because it offered victims a chance to change their status, to restore their dignity, and to amend the system that had injured them. Yet, while liberalization provided some space for a new civil society to emerge, the totalitarian state left society poor and disorganized. Moreover, it was hard to reconcile aggressive challenges from below with official reformers' vision of conflictless state-society relations. Coming to terms with the past in the USSR thus entailed a sharp reaction to mass repression, but one that was subject to the constraints of top-down reform and hampered by the lack of civil society.

# 2 KHRUSHCHEV'S THAW: SELECTIVE DESTALINIZATION

When Stalin died in March 1953, his political heirs wondered whether the Soviet people would grieve or celebrate. Publicly the people mourned and the Party's control went unchallenged. Yet despite the society's quiescence, Nikita Khrushchev chose to reform the political system; like many dictators, he believed that judicious reform could bolster the regime's legitimacy without unleashing a revolt from below. Though he boldly asserted that "criticism, even the sharpest, helps us move forward," Khrushchev recognized that information about Stalin's crimes could be used to disparage Soviet socialism.[1] Khrushchev, like many Soviet citizens, had experienced both triumph and tragedy during the decades of Stalin's dominance. Stalin had murdered Khrushchev's compatriots, but he had raised Khrushchev to a top leadership position. Khrushchev struggled to find an interpretation of the complex Stalinist past that would not delegitimize the Communist Party or its positive achievements. In defense of reform, he ultimately fought a battle on two fronts: to suppress radical manifestations of antistalinism and to convince skeptics within the leadership that the Party would benefit from self-criticism. The resulting erratic official treatment of past repressions reflected both the nature of the totalitarian regime and the balancing act required of anyone who tried to reform it.

1. *XXII S"ezd Kommunisticheskoi Partii Sovetskogo Soiuza, 17–31 Oktiabriia 1961 goda: Stenograficheskii otchet* (Moscow: Gospolizdat, 1962), 2:581–82.

Analysis of official positions in the Soviet context is complicated. Though disagreements among Party-state leaders rarely emerged into the open between the 1920s and late 1980s, one cannot assume total accord. Following Lenin's injunctions about conforming to the Party line, the political elite strove to disguise infighting behind a united front. Yet zigzags in the Party line, policy reversals, and contradictory statements by top officials reveal deep disagreements over some issues. Official attitudes may also be examined through public discourse by intellectuals, artists, and journalists.

The state's penetration of the public arena politicized all forms of expression. Since all workers—including the creative intelligentsia—were expected to serve the state in its promotion of socialism, public utterances were constantly evaluated for their *partiinost'* (party spirit) and the media were subject to strict censorship. Artists and apparatchiks did not always hold common beliefs, but officially supported expression had to be in accord with the interests of at least a faction of the Party elite. Clearly in many cases this convergence resulted from deliberate, negotiated compromises among writers, editors, and censors. During liberalization professional intellectuals became to some extent proxies for leaders on opposite sides of a growing rift. Dina Spechler labeled this phenomenon of sanctioned criticism of state policy "permitted dissent," a term that captures the balancing act involved in finding an acceptable level and form of criticism.[2]

## SILENT DESTALINIZATION, 1953–1956

In the months before his death, Stalin signaled his intention to start a new round of purges. In October 1952 the dictator created an enlarged Presidium and a smaller high-level bureau that excluded long-time top officials, among them Viacheslav Molotov and Anastas Mikoian, thus raising fears that he was preparing to replace them. Moreover, in early 1953 a number of physicians, most of them well-known Jewish specialists, were arrested and accused of murdering Party officials and of espionage. The so-called doctors' plot seemed to mark the beginning of a mass anti-Semitic campaign.

2. Dina R. Spechler, *Permitted Dissent in the USSR: "Novy mir" and the Soviet Regime* (New York: Praeger, 1982), p. xx.

Immediately after Stalin's death in March 1953, the senior members of his entourage defused and reversed these harsh new policies. They dissolved the enlarged Presidium and replaced it with a smaller one that consisted of Khrushchev, Georgii Malenkov, Molotov, Mikoian, Kliment Voroshilov, and Lavrentii Beria, among others. Having restored those members of Stalin's entourage who had fallen from favor, the new body strongly endorsed the principle of collective leadership—in effect forming a mutual protection society.[3] Publicly they retreated from Stalin's show trials as well. In April an official notice in the press announced that the case against the Kremlin doctors had been fabricated. The Party admitted that the security forces had extracted confessions from the doctors by illegal means and implicated a former NKVD minister and the head of investigations.[4] Another early measure was the release of relatives of the new leaders who had been imprisoned under Stalin, including Molotov's wife and Khrushchev's daughter-in-law.[5] These initial efforts at destalinization clearly benefited members of the apparat: they reassured themselves of their own immediate survival, corrected personal injustices, and lessened the arbitrariness associated with one-man rule.

To remove the last threat to the new collective security arrangements, the Presidium struck out at one of their own—Beria, the security chief, who allegedly was scheming to use the secret police to install himself in Stalin's place. The other Presidium members charged Beria with raising the security forces above the Party, trying to ruin Soviet agriculture, stirring up national tensions, and hampering efforts to strengthen the legal system. Ultimately, Beria was also convicted of spying for British intelligence with the goal of restoring capitalism.[6] Beria and his cohorts were also charged with criminal intrigues in the past against two old Bolsheviks; thus Party leaders planted the first suggestion that loyal revolutionaries had been victimized during the Stalin years.

The removal of Beria decreased the influence of the security forces without reforming them in any significant way. Khrushchev and the Presidium neither brought in new leaders from outside the security apparatus

---

3. Roy Medvedev, *Khrushchev: A Biography,* trans. Brian Pearce (Garden City, N.Y.: Doubleday/Anchor, 1984), pp. 54–57.

4. Sergei Chuprinin, "Ottepel': Khronika vazhneishikh sobytii," in *Ottepel', 1953–1956* (Moscow: Moskovskii Rabochii, 1989), pp. 422–23.

5. Roy Medvedev and Giulietto Chiesa, *Time of Change: An Insider's View of Russia's Transformation,* trans. Michael Moore (New York: Pantheon, 1989), p. 100.

6. *Pravda,* 10 July and 17 December 1953.

nor carried out sweeping personnel changes. The new head of the secret police, Ivan Serov, had been heavily involved in mass repressions, including the wholesale deportations of several Soviet ethnic groups during World War II. Khrushchev justified his choice by remarking, "If there are a few dubious things about [Serov], as there are about all Chekists, then let's just say he was a victim of Stalin's general policy."[7] Moreover, the closed court, exaggerated charges, and rapid executions of Beria and his colleagues were reminiscent of earlier purges of secret police under Stalin. After all, Beria was charged with being a British spy, but not with fabrication of criminal cases. A reorganization of the judiciary in 1954 and 1955 gave prosecutors greater powers of supervision over criminal investigations and made review of cases possible upon protest by the Procuracy. But as far as procedures in regard to detention, investigation, and trial were concerned, these reforms simply restored the pre-Stalin status quo.[8]

Many observers have called the period 1953–56 a time of "silent destalinization" because the official steps toward revising Stalin's repressive policies were conducted largely in secret or without explanation. Why did destalinization proceed in such a secretive and ad hoc fashion during the first post-Stalin years? Years later Khrushchev himself tried to make a case for post-traumatic stress: "Stalin was dead and buried, but . . . no one thought to rehabilitate the people who had gone to their graves branded as enemies of the people or to release the prisoners from the camps . . . For three years we were unable to break with the past. . . . It was as though we were enchained by our own activities under Stalin's leadership and couldn't free ourselves from his control even after he was dead."[9] Certainly the deeds of Stalin's entourage, whether or not they induced pangs of conscience, deterred them from reexamining Stalin-era policies. The totalitarian system had bound Stalin's entourage together with webs of complicity. As Roy Medvedev observed: "Passing the selection test into the Soviet government under Stalin depended on more than just Stalin's whim. These people worked hard to excel in his eyes and to

---

7. Quoted in Amy Knight, *The KGB: Police and Politics in the Soviet Union* (Boston: Unwin Hyman, 1988), p. 51.

8. Harold Berman, *Justice in the U.S.S.R.*, rev. ed. (Cambridge: Harvard University Press, 1963); Berman, "Soviet Law Reform—Dateline Moscow 1957," *Yale Law Review 66* (July 1957); George Ginsburgs, "Structural and Functional Evolution of the Soviet Judiciary since Stalin's Death: 1953–1956," *Soviet Studies 13* (January 1962).

9. Nikita S. Khrushchev, *Khrushchev Remembers*, trans. and ed. Strobe Talbot (New York: Bantam, 1970), p. 372.

deliver the goods that he demanded."[10] Documents released since 1989 reveal a genuine competition among Party leaders to deliver the goods during the purges—the goods in this case being "enemies of the people." Requests addressed to Stalin show regional and Party leaders petitioning for increases in arrest and execution quotas.[11]

Though he suppressed such information, Khrushchev certainly had blood on his hands. By and large, all the older members of the post-Stalin Presidium had taken part in the purges. Voroshilov, for instance, cooperated in purging the military. Mikoian signed off on execution lists and sanctioned arrests among his own staff, and in the autumn of 1937 he and Malenkov traveled to Armenia to purge the Party-state apparatus there. Lazar Kaganovich aggressively pursued policies of forced collectivization, purged the Heavy Industry and Railways commissariats, and served as special envoy to direct the purges in several regions.[12]

For the Presidium members public reassessment of the past would only stir up scandals and reawaken old conflicts, but discreet controlled reform could alter those aspects of the regime that directly threatened the elite. Since the Party remained firmly in control of the means of coercion, it acted in the months after Stalin's death to suit its own needs, not in response to threats from a restive citizenry. Not surprisingly, the Presidium began with defensive reforms, using the tried and true methods of discrediting and executing its perceived opponents. By punishing a few top figures in the secret police, it conveyed to the Party-state machine a change in policy without risking real instability by shaking up the whole security apparatus. Bound together by complicity and ambition the top leaders moved toward collective rule and personal security.

## FACING THE PEOPLE

The Presidium's disinclination to look backward, however, did not translate into total freedom to evade the consequences of Stalinism. In the years after Stalin's death, the political elite confronted the problem of how

10. Roy Medvedev, *All Stalin's Men*, trans. Harold Shukman (Garden City, N.Y.: Doubleday/Anchor, 1985), pp. viii-ix.

11. Natalia Gevorkian, "Vstrechenye plany po unichtozheniiu sobstvennogo naroda," *Moskovskie novosti*, 21 June 1992, p. 19.

12. A. N. Shelepin, "Istoriia—uchitel' surovyi," *Trud*, 14 March 1991, p. 4; Anatolii Golovkhov, "Vechnyi isk," *Ogonek*, no. 18, 1988; Medvedev, *All Stalin's Men*, p. 38.

to treat Stalin when they commemorated the past. Materials dedicated to Stalin's memory appeared in *Pravda* only up until 19 March 1953; then his name disappeared from the headlines.[13] The Party marked Stalin's death in 1954 and his birthday in 1955, but later these anniversaries passed unremarked. Such inconsistencies could only harm the people's ideological health; therefore, the leadership needed to formulate a Party line on Stalin's role in Soviet history.

Moreover, the Presidium could not ignore Stalin's most concrete legacy: the millions of political prisoners. In this respect the leadership was subject to some pressure from below. High officials were inundated by petitions for rehabilitation of victims of the purges, and they had no policy directives or mechanisms for dealing with them. Some disturbances and strikes in labor camps erupted into protracted revolts; prisoners in Kengir held off the authorities for forty days in the summer of 1954. And prisoners released from the camps brought with them scars, horror stories, and special needs for housing, employment, and medical care. The reappearance of Party figures caused confusion: should they be reinstated in the Party and restored to their old positions?

Khrushchev responded to pressure from below by initiating a study of conditions in prison camps. On 1 February 1954 the procurator general of the USSR and the minister of internal affairs and justice provided him with statistics about the number of prisoners still in camps.[14] Armed with this information, Khrushchev urged the other leaders to consider complaints about illegal repressions. Finally on 31 December 1955 the Presidium acted to investigate Stalin's terror in a more systematic but still limited way by forming a commission to study materials regarding the fates of Central Committee members elected by the 17th Party Congress in particular, and of other citizens sentenced between 1935 and 1940.

The turning point in opening up the Stalinist past to critical scrutiny came at the 20th Party Congress, when Khrushchev made his famous speech "On the Cult of Personality and Its Consequences." In a closed session on 25 February 1956—just before the congress ended—Khrushchev delivered a scathing attack on Stalin's "violations of collective leadership" and "perversion of socialist legality." He noted that, unlike Lenin, Stalin used force instead of persuasion against ideological

---

13. Iu. V. Aksiutin and O. V. Volobuev, *XX S"ezd KPSS: Novatsii i dogmy* (Moscow: Politizdat, 1991), p. 186.

14. Ibid., p. 10.

opponents and that Stalin began "mass repressions" after the exploiting classes had been largely liquidated. In blunt language Khrushchev enumerated Stalin's errors: sanction of physical force to extract false confessions; destruction of Party members who had at some point disputed the Party line; mass arrests and deportations; executions without trial or normal investigation. To a stunned audience, Khrushchev recited a few of the statistics of the terror: 1,108 of 1,966 delegates to the 1934 "Congress of Victors," along with 70 percent of the Central Committee, were arrested in 1937 and 1938. Khrushchev went on to criticize Stalin's leadership during World War II, his nationalities policy, his self-glorification, and his role in the split with Yugoslavia.

The so-called secret speech laid out Khrushchev's interpretation of the damage caused by the cult of personality and his proposals for remedying its consequences. Khrushchev made no effort to settle accounts with anyone but Stalin, Beria, and a few NKVD men; nor did he urge public exploration of the past. Khrushchev looked to the future by endorsing the theory that one must analyze negative aspects of the past to prevent their recurrence. He linked prevention of repression with a reformed and strengthened socialist regime led by the Communist Party. He confronted past repressions but diminished their scale, time span, and scope, and painted the Party as the greatest victim of the cult of personality. Not only did the terror claim many Party workers as innocent victims, but the cult "had a negative influence on the state of the Party, created insecurity, facilitated the spread of sickly suspicion, sowed mutual doubts among Communists. And it activated all kinds of slanderers and careerists."[15] Khrushchev also argued that the cult fostered *lakirovka,* or whitewashing, of reality in literature, the media, and the social sciences, producing distortions that hurt the Party's credibility.

To undo the damage caused by Stalin, Khrushchev called for active criticism of the cult of personality as alien to Marxism, and for its extirpation especially from history texts; restoration of collective leadership and traditions of criticism and self-criticism; and a return to "socialist democracy," with attention to curbing abuses of power and restoring legality. Despite his harsh evaluation of Stalin, Khrushchev praised Stalin's "sincerity" in defending the Revolution and warned that a rapid renaming

15. "O kul'te lichnosti i ego posledstviiakh," 25 February 1956, in *Reabilitatsiia: Politicheskie protsessy 30–50-kh godov,* ed. Aleksandr Iakovlev (Moscow: Politizdat, 1991), p. 39.

of cities, streets, factories, and schools might be mistaken for the start of a new round of purges. He emphasized that his reforms constituted a return to Leninist principles and demonstrated the Party's "moral and political strength." By citing tradition and the positive side of examining the Party's dirty laundry, Khrushchev strove to make destalinization palatable to those in the Presidium who nearly blocked the speech.[16]

The decisiveness and boldness of Khrushchev's discourse masked the fierce behind-the-scenes struggle in the Presidium over whether the report should be given, and if so, by whom. Khrushchev originally proposed that several rehabilitated former Party officials speak out against the cult of personality. Allegedly Kaganovich angrily rejected the notion that former convicts be permitted to pass judgment on the Party elite.[17] The Presidium opposed Khrushchev so strongly that he won the right to give his report only during the congress itself. In his first speech Khrushchev said nothing about Stalin, though he did condemn Beria and speak of having reined in state security. Supposedly Khrushchev reconvened the Presidium halfway through the congress and declared he would speak about Stalin's crimes in his capacity as an ordinary delegate if the Presidium would not sanction the report.[18]

Nevertheless, Khrushchev did endeavor to accommodate the concerns of conservatives. The 1955 commission put the problem of mass repressions within a very small time frame, so that they cast no shadow on the war and postwar years. Khrushchev also sought to create confidence in the new investigatory commission by appointing a close and devoted associate of Stalin's as its head. He evidently accepted limits in respect to timing and secrecy: the "secret speech" was delivered to a closed session of the congress after the new Central Committee had been elected, and without discussion afterward.[19] In the end, however, the speech was a strange kind of secret. Not only did 1,500 delegates, including foreign guests, hear Khrushchev's address, but the text—in slightly edited form—was read aloud at meetings of Party collectives all across the country. Thus in practice, Khrushchev exposed a wide audience to the revelations about Stalin's crimes.

16. Ibid., pp. 19–67.
17. Roy Medvedev, *Khrushchev*, p. 84.
18. Khrushchev, *Khrushchev Remembers*, pp. 378–81.
19. Nikita S. Khrushechev, *Khrushchev Remembers: The Glasnost Tapes*, trans. and ed. Jerrold L. Schecter with Vyacheslav V. Luchkov (Boston: Little, Brown, 1990), pp. 42, 85–86.

What motivated Khrushchev to denounce Stalin's crimes? His own explanation was that a cover-up would only detract further from the Party's legitimacy. One can point also to Khrushchev's obvious taste for bold reforms. Khrushchev cited the influence of his own conscience and the pressure from below resulting from the return of former prisoners with their tales of abuse and suffering. Since knowledge of the repressions would inevitably spread, Khrushchev argued in favor of preemptive damage control. Other hypotheses have focused on Khrushchev's desire to end fear among the apparat and to consolidate his own position. Yet decisive steps to end arbitrary purges had been adopted well before February 1956 without any messy disclosures of past excesses. And though Molotov, Malenkov, Voroshilov and Kaganovich perhaps had more to hide, Khrushchev could also be called to task for his complicity in the purges of the 1930s and 1940s. Khrushchev risked hurting his own reputation and the reputation of the Party to provide reformers with an ideological justification for rejecting old policies.

By criticizing Stalin, Khrushchev moved away from crude scapegoating of Beria and in effect admitted that the Party had not been totally subordinate to the secret police. Khrushchev undoubtedly shared the Presidium's concerns about the unresolved issue of accountability. At three points in his report he turned to the difficult question of personal and Party responsibility. Recalling a famous purge trial, he asked, "Why is it that now we can sort out this matter, but did not do so earlier during Stalin's life, in order to prevent the loss of innocent lives?" The reason, he said, was that Stalin had handled the case personally and kept most of the Politburo members in the dark. They did not know, so they could not have intervened. As for why Beria was not unmasked earlier, Khrushchev credited Beria with deft exploitation of Stalin's paranoia.[20]

Why, Khrushchev inquired, did the Politburo members fail to recognize the cult of personality for what it was at the time? Here Khrushchev recalled that having supported Stalin in the battles for industrialization and collectivization in the 1920s and 1930s, they had grown to admire and trust him. Finally, Khrushchev admitted that a high level of fear pervaded even Stalin's closest circle of advisers. Presidium members never knew whether a summons to Stalin might lead to a prison cell. Khrushchev candidly confessed that protesting against baseless repression was tantamount to placing one's own neck on the chopping block and admitted that Stalin had weakened the Politburo by isolating and dividing its members.[21] With discussion ruled out, Khrushchev could not be called upon to clarify the contradictions in his justification of the Party's failure to act against the cult of personality in a timely fashion. Was he unaware that the repressions were groundless or simply unwilling to protest?

Khrushchev's explanations went unchallenged, but not necessarily because the Party or the public found them satisfactory. Evidence of puzzlement can be seen in the questions posed to the historian and Central Committee member Anna Pankratova when she gave a series of lectures in March 1956 on the cult of personality and its consequences for historical scholarship. Leningrad Party officials asked Pankratova to address the topic of Khrushchev's secret speech to help Party activists, propagandists, members of the intelligentsia, and teachers assimilate the revelations about Stalin. Reactions to her talk demonstrate that this was indeed a pressing task; afterward pleas for clarification of the Party line still resounded from the audience. Leningraders beseeched Pankratova to ask the Central Committee to explain what had happened, and she was alarmed by the political "immaturity" of some of the questions addressed to her. She, too, seemed eager for further elucidation of the Party line on Stalin, for she prepared both a report and a transcript of all the queries from the audience for the Leningrad Party first secretary, the Central Committee, and Khrushchev himself.

Pankratova's listeners bombarded her with questions about the accountability of both politicians and historians. How did the "cult of personality" concept fit with Marxist theory? Could Stalin alone be responsible? How could Politburo members cry over Stalin's grave? Were today's leaders hypocrites? Who was more guilty, Stalin or those who praised him so excessively? We have no transcript of Pankratova's lecture, but her listeners' questions make it clear that she foundered in her efforts to explain historians' simultaneous roles as victims and perpetrators of the cult of personality. Pankratova admitted that by supporting Stalin and furthering the perversion of public perceptions of him some scholars had fostered the Stalin cult. Like Khrushchev, she cited fear, ignorance, loyalty, and faith in Stalin as sources of historians' acquiescence in deception.

Many members of the audience appeared to doubt that people in high

21. Ibid., pp. 63–64.

office could have failed to understand the true nature of the purges. One said: "You said that psychologically you understood long ago what this cult of personality was. What kept you from saying so earlier, when Stalin was still alive, rather than now, when you've been ordered to do it? Did you lack the will and courage to speak out against generally recognized authority? . . . Wouldn't it be better not to try to vindicate yourself?" Another put it more bluntly: "Aren't you the co-author of a series of falsifications about the history of the USSR?" Others had equally telling concerns: Why had there been no discussion of Khrushchev's report either at the congress or after it had been read out at local assemblies? Would historians who had falsified history now lose their positions? Could one still cite Stalin's works? Some revealed their shock at the unmasking of Stalin. Yet many also shrewdly observed that laying all the blame on Stalin was "the cult of personality in reverse"—if Stalin could not take all the credit for Soviet achievements, then neither could he absorb all the blame for the misdeeds that occurred under his leadership.[22]

Despite such pleas for guidance, a comprehensive, definitive Party line on Stalin and destalinization never emerged under Khrushchev. As we shall see, disputes within the leadership and efforts to "fine tune decompression"[23] during the Khrushchev era led to wide swings in official pronouncements regarding Stalin and inconsistency toward criticism of the old regime. The Party was incapable of readily absorbing criticism while retaining its authority.

## THE PRECARIOUS THAW

The first indication of a new Party line regarding Stalin emerged after the 20th Party Congress in the form of a Central Committee decree, "On Overcoming the Cult of Personality and Its Consequences." Issued on 2 July 1956, this thirty-one-page statement laid out the sources and consequences of Stalin's cult of personality in a more ideologically sophisticated but less detailed and less compelling form than Khrushchev's speech. The document constantly referred to enemies abroad who pressed the Soviet

22. A. M. Pankratova, "Dokladnaia zapiska" (report to the Presidium of the Central Committee of the CPSU, March 1956), TsK KPSS, obshchii otdel, fond 5, opis' 16, Tsentr Khraneniia Sovremennoi Dokumentatsii, Moscow.
23. The phrase was coined by George W. Breslauer in "On Criticism: The Significance of the Twentieth Party Congress," in *Il XX Congreso del PCUS*, ed. Fondazione Giangiacomo Feltrinelli (Milan: Franco Angeli, 1988), p. 119.

Union so hard in the 1920s and 1930s that the Party was forced to limit democratization temporarily. These foreign opponents, according to the decree, were now trying to take advantage of the Party's own condemnation of the cult of personality to draw attention away from the progress made since Stalin's death. Whereas foreign critics claimed that the cult of personality arose from the Soviet system itself, the Central Committee attributed it to objective historical factors—capitalist encirclement and internal enemies—and some subjective factors linked to Stalin's personality.[24] Since these subjective factors no longer existed, neither did the danger of a return to repression.

Though the July decree did not delve into the nature or scope of mass repression, it did tackle the issue of accountability. It claimed that a "Leninist nucleus of leaders" always existed within the Central Committee, as could be seen in the Party's immediate unmasking of the cult and its consequences after Stalin's death. As for the failure of this "nucleus" to speak out against Stalin during the dictator's lifetime, such actions were impossible: because of Stalin's great achievements in defense of socialism, the people would not have understood any steps taken against him; protest would have been seen as an attack on socialism.[25] Thus the Party adroitly rejected the idea of a cowardly or malicious leadership and shifted the blame to the masses, for their love of Stalin. In this manner the leadership subtly reminded Soviet citizens of their own complicity in the cult of personality. After all, Marxist theory accords the people the decisive role in history, and like the Party, they had overtly supported the cult of personality.

The Central Committee devoted a large part of its statement to constructive, future-oriented measures. But the argument that the harm caused by the cult could not have altered the nature of the Soviet social system or institutions limited the rationale for reform. The Party and the people had suffered together and worked together, and now they had together restored democracy, ended repression, and repudiated adulation of the individual. Though the leadership made the people shoulder part of the blame for Stalinism, it simultaneously praised them for their underappreciated role in socialist achievements. Thus the Party leadership gave the impression that what little institutional change had been needed was trifling and already completed.

24. *O preodolenii kul'ta lichnosti i ego posledstvii: Postanovlenie TsK KPSS* (Moscow: Gospolitizdat, 1956), p. 20.
25. Ibid., pp. 17–18.

Behind the scenes, the Soviet government also took practical steps in 1956 to alter the fates of those purge victims who still languished in camps and exile. Commissions traveled to places of incarceration across the nation to review and annul prisoners' sentences. Rapid release, however, did not generally translate into rapid reintegration of returnees into society. The Party seemed eager to avoid publicity about surviving victims lest it draw attention to the brutality and extent of the purges. With the secret speech Khrushchev decisively broke with silent destalinization, but rehabilitations, changes in the security apparatus, and many aspects of legal reform remained hidden from public scrutiny.

In view of the continued secretiveness about policy making and tight control over public discourse, official attitudes toward literary treatments of destalinization—by nature products for public consumption—become significant. One cultural analyst noted: "It is then as a window on Party politics at a crucial moment in Soviet history that the struggle between the regime and the intellectuals is worthy of study."[26] The battles over the "thaw" in literature provide the clearest view of the divisions and fluctuating attitudes toward destalinization.

Under Stalin "socialist realism" mandated that writers not only follow the Party line but shape their narratives to reflect socialist society in its ideal rather than real form. Socialist realist works propagated overwhelmingly positive pictures of Soviet life, with such petty conflicts as might be admitted to exist under socialism always resolved for the best. Writers faced not only censorship but arrest should their works be labeled "antisocialist." The purges decimated the literary community and left lasting scars on the survivors, in part because many writers had denounced their colleagues for professional advancement. In fact, after Khrushchev's secret speech, the secretary of the USSR Writers' Union committed suicide, allegedly largely because of his torment over his role in the purges. Many other members of the Writers' Union in the 1950s, however, defended their past works, and with them the genre of socialist realism and the deification of Stalin.[27] Young writers, liberals, and writers who had been repressed under Stalin brought radically different agendas to the literary

26. Priscilla Johnson with Leopold Labedz, *Khrushchev and the Arts: The Politics of Soviet Culture, 1962–64* (Cambridge: MIT Press, 1965), p. 2.

27. "Eto nuzhno ne mertvym—zhivym . . . " (interview with Eduard Beltov), *Knizhnoe Obozrenie*, no. 25 (17 June 1988), p. 7; John Garrand and Carol Garrand, *Inside the Soviet Writers' Union* (New York: Free Press, 1990), p. 52.

arena. Thus both a potential vanguard for destalinization and powerful reactionary forces existed in the post-Stalin literary community.

After Stalin's death and the relaxation of his cult, the literary journal *Novyi mir* (New World), under the editorship of Aleksandr Tvardovskii, began to champion the principles of pluralism, truthfulness, sincerity, and free speech. In effect, the journal called on writers to abandon their internal censors, so carefully nurtured during the terror, and to educate their audiences with truthful, frank presentations. But critics were expected to follow the basic tenets of *partiinost'*—they had to advance the Soviet system and be basically optimistic about the possibility of remedying the defects they discussed.

Despite the journal's political restraint, in the spring of 1954 irate members of the Party and the Writers' Union charged *Novyi mir* and its editors with what was to become a common complaint against antistalinists: promoting nihilism. When Tvardovskii failed to respond to criticism, the Presidium dismissed him in August of that year. But the Party did not take decisive steps to silence liberal writers. Though the new editor in chief, Konstantin Simonov, followed a cautious line until after Khrushchev's secret speech, he did not totally shy from printing frank articles, especially in regard to literature banned in the 1920s and 1930s and the history of World War II.[28]

Khrushchev's secret speech in 1956 gave liberals a rich new theme—the cult of personality and its consequences. An authoritative article in the writers' newspaper *Literaturnaia gazeta* on 8 May 1956 opened the debate by blaming the cult of personality for the "whitewashing" and lack of dramatic conflict in Soviet literature—while cautioning against negativism. Before a new round of liberal cultural analyses could get off the ground, however, the Hungarian uprising and a reactionary surge at home in December 1956 cut it short. In May 1957, Khrushchev sharply criticized "individual people" who "one-sidedly and incorrectly understood the essence of *partiinyi* criticism of the Stalin cult of personality." Even after Khrushchev defeated the conservative "antiparty group" in June and removed his rivals Malenkov, Kaganovich, and Molotov from the Presidium, he still faced opposition to reform from inside the Party, and so he continued his retreat from antistalinism. At a celebration of the anniversary of the Revolution in November 1957 he stated: "Having criticized the

28. Spechler, *Permitted Dissent*, pp. 3–29, 35–40.

incorrect aspects of Stalin's activities, the Party fought and will fight with all who slander Stalin, who under the guise of criticizing of the cult of personality present a distorted picture of the whole historical period of our Party's activity when I. V. Stalin headed the Central Committee. As a devoted Marxist-Leninist and steadfast revolutionary, Stalin should occupy a fitting place in history."[29] In the face of multiple offensives, Simonov not only retreated from a liberal publication policy but publicly atoned for his errors.[30]

In 1958 Khrushchev essentially called for an end to the protests against *Novyi mir* and supported Tvardovskii's return to its editorship. But that was the year Boris Pasternak, who had published *Dr. Zhivago* abroad after it was rejected by Soviet censors, was awarded the Nobel Prize. The campaign waged against him that summer again cast a pall over the literary world. Only the next year, when Khrushchev had reconsolidated his power, did the literary world dare to return to the Stalin theme. A new trend in criticism that concentrated on the past, and ultimately on the roots of Stalinism, emerged in 1960. At first writers focused on Stalin's character flaws and their impact on a single constituency—writers. Gradually, however, treatment of Stalinism broadened first to include its influence on art, the sciences, and the intelligentsia and in 1961 to accounts of arrest and terror. That fall, under the credo that full revelation of the past was necessary to discredit repressions definitively, writers even began to address such issues as collectivization and the persecution of old Bolsheviks. A whole wave of writings addressed the spectrum of victims and forms of repression that made up the purges.[31] The more aggressive approach to destalinization in the media was reinforced by an attempt to set a new Party line toward the cult of personality at the 22d Party Congress.

## AGGRESSIVE DESTALINIZATION

Destalinization in general gained momentum in 1961 after candid, detailed accounts of repressions at the 22d Party Congress. Unlike the 21st Congress in January 1959, where the question of Stalinism was not raised, the October 1961 meeting featured denunciations of Stalin's

29. Quoted in Sergei Chuprinin, "Ottepel': Khronika vazhneishikh sobytii," *Ottepel',* *1957–1959* (Moscow: Moskovskii Rabochii, 1990), p. 374, 393–94.

30. Spechler, *Permitted Dissent,* pp. 76–78.

31. Ibid., p. 138.

purges and revelations of the role played by the antiparty group in the terror. Khrushchev used the congress to consolidate reformist forces and to definitively discredit Molotov, Malenkov, and Kaganovich. Khrushchev admitted that destalinization had been rocky, but absolved himself of responsibility by arguing, "You can imagine how hard it was to resolve [questions about Stalin's part in the assassination of Sergei Kirov, the popular Party secretary in the Leningrad region, and so forth] when there were people in the Presidium of the Central Committee who themselves were guilty of abuse of power and mass repressions." Fear of destalinization, he contended, united the antiparty group and spurred them to try to "return to those times, so difficult for our Party and nation, when no one was safe against arbitrariness and repressions."[32] Thus Khrushchev tried to use the Stalin question as a weapon against members of the old regime who had challenged his personal power. Criticism served him best at moments of strength, when his authority was high.

The 22d Congress brought forth new information about the purges and emotionally charged assessments of Stalin and the repressions. The head of the Party Control Commission presented statistics on ongoing Party rehabilitations—in sharp contrast to his speech at the previous congress, where he had announced that "all Communists condemned groundlessly have been restored to Party membership, and violators of Soviet laws have been held accountable to the Party."[33] The KGB chief, Aleksandr Shelepin, stormed: "Sometimes you wonder how these people can walk the earth calmly and sleep peacefully. They should be pursued by nightmares, they should hear the sobbing and cursing of the mothers, wives, and children of the innocent comrades they killed."[34] Several touching speeches, most notably one by the old Bolshevik D. A. Lazurkina, who had been imprisoned both under the tsar and under Stalin, called for evicting Stalin's remains from their resting place beside Lenin.[35] And Khrushchev himself proposed that a memorial to his victims be built in Moscow. The regime was ready to take symbolic steps to propagate its new image.

Despite the 22d Congress's assessment that the battle against the cult

32. XXII S"ezd Kommunisticheskoi partii, 2:582–84.
33. Leo Gruliow, ed., Current Soviet Policies III (New York: Columbia University Press, 1960), p. 141.
34. XXII S"ezd Kommunisticheskoi partii, 2:404–5.
35. See the speeches of D. A. Lazurkina and I. V. Spiridonov ibid., 3:114–20.

of personality had been decisively won with the defeat of the antiparty group, some members of the establishment feared that the past had not been fully revealed and hence not fully condemned. *Pravda* published the poem "The Heirs of Stalin," in which the liberal poet Evgenii Evtushenko warned against complacency:

> We removed
> > him
> > > from the mausoleum.
> But how do we remove Stalin
> > > from Stalin's heirs?
> Some of his heirs
> > tend roses in retirement,
> but secretly consider
> > their retirement temporary.
> Others,
> > from platforms rail against Stalin,
> but,
> > at night,
> > > yearn for the old days.[36]

Evtushenko accused neostalinists of preferring full prison camps to the current fascination with poets' and writers' expressions of liberal views. He called metaphorically for trebling the guard at Stalin's grave. Evtushenko's attack on living Stalinists was approved for publication by Khrushchev himself. An aide read the poem to him during a trip to Abkhazia after Khrushchev and a local collective farm chairman had shed tears over their recollections of the purges.[37]

Similar intervention resulted in the publication of the most famous work of the thaw, Aleksandr Solzhenitsyn's *One Day in the Life of Ivan Denisovich*. In recalling his decision to champion the novel, Khrushchev wrote: "The evil inflicted on the Communist Party—on the Soviet people, on workers, peasants, and the intelligentsia—had to be condemned. The best way to condemn is to lance the boil, show the conditions under which

---

36. From *The Collected Poems, 1952–1990*, by Yevgeny Yevtushenko. Edited by Albert C. Todd with Yevgeny Yevtushenko and James Regan. Copyright © 1991 by Henry Holt and Co., Inc. Reprinted by permission of Henry Holt and Co., Inc.

37. Yevgeny Yevtushenko, *Fatal Half Measures: The Culture of Democracy in the Soviet Union,* trans. Antonina W. Bouis (Boston: Little, Brown, 1991), pp. 206–8.

people lived, and provoke anger against the one who caused it all."[38] Thus, in retrospect, Khrushchev admitted that he did not think the trauma caused by the terror had been "cured." He also revealed that he wanted to use public outrage to strengthen his reputation as a reformer. Perhaps most significant, he continued to endorse an explanation of the purges that concentrated on the guilt of a single individual rather than on the responsibility of Soviet institutions.

Solzhenitsyn's novella had the effect of a bombshell, provoking indignation from conservatives and releasing pent-up popular resentment of Stalin. The brutally realistic novel encapsulated a simple man's "almost good" day in a labor camp. Solzhenitsyn claims that he calculated that his muzhik protagonist would appeal to both Tvardovskii and Khrushchev because of their own peasant origins. Ivan Denisovich evoked further sympathy because, in the best proletarian manner, he found pleasure and fulfillment in a job well done, even in slavery. Ivan Denisovich, moreover, neither probed the roots of Stalinism nor blamed the Soviet system; he simply marveled that such a fate should befall him and his fellow citizens. An early review praised the novella for its brilliant generalizations, patriotism, and lack of sensationalism.[39]

Despite its stunning realism, *One Day in the Life* broke few taboos—unlike Vasilii Grossman's *Forever Flowing*, another short work written during the thaw, but not published in the USSR until 1989. *Forever Flowing* deals with a former political prisoner whose return to society causes friends and relatives who remained free to reconsider their own lives. Grossman raised two themes guaranteed to offend Party leaders. First, he probed various forms of individual guilt and betrayal but then reasoned that it was impossible to judge the individual without first judging the state. Second, he did judge the Soviet state, declaring it to be the incarnation of unfreedom. Grossman blamed Lenin for dreaming up the system, Stalin for building it, and Khrushchev for modernizing it.[40] In comparison with *Forever Flowing*, *One Day in the Life of Ivan Denisovich* seems remarkably tame and apolitical.[41]

38. Khrushchev, *Khrushchev Remembers: The Glasnost Tapes*, p. 198.

39. Konstantin Simonov, "O proshlom vo imia budushchego," *Izvestiia*, 18 November 1962.

40. Vasily Grossman, *Forever Flowing*, trans. Thomas P. Whitney (New York: Harper & Row, 1972), p. 80.

41. According to Solzhenitsyn, the absence of political content reflects not his political consciousness but rather a compromise he made in order to get his camp material published.

Initial positive reviews notwithstanding, the publication of *A Day in the Life* did not resolve the struggle for a Party line on destalinization. While camp memoirs poured into publishing houses and liberal intellectuals became increasingly daring and spontaneous in their critiques of Stalinism, conservatives mustered their forces for a backlash should Khrushchev falter. In late 1962 the Cuban missile crisis and other policy failures weakened Khrushchev's authority and made him vulnerable to pressure. When *One Day in the Life of Ivan Denisovich* was nominated for a Lenin prize, conservatives blasted it for failing "to rise to a philosophical perception" of the Stalin era or to reflect the fact that "the Party had gone on, building socialism."[42] Though Khrushchev did not repudiate Solzhenitsyn, he backpedaled considerably on his commitment to literary exposés of Stalinism. In March 1963 he returned to the theme of the dangers inherent in an improper interpretation of the past, arguing that negativism in art "can only plunge people into a state of despondency, hopelessness, and ennui." Seemingly withdrawing his trust in the intelligentsia, Khrushchev warned that camps, exile, arrests, and so forth were dangerous subjects that might encourage sensationalism and hurt the Party.[43] Apparently, Khrushchev had come around to the position that destalinization in its aggressive form threatened the Party.

## From Destalinization to Stagnation

The destalinization process and its inherent challenges to the Party's legitimacy were not the main causes for Khrushchev's ouster in 1964. Other policies had created greater threats to the Party apparat. Nevertheless, the change in leadership led to a gradual reversal of many aspects of destalinization. Rehabilitations came to a halt and literary conservatives convinced Party leaders that criticism of the past should be considered only one more of Khrushchev's harebrained ideas. Anti-Stalin writings were roundly condemned as "one-sided, tendentiously negative," and "ideologically disorienting," and in October 1965 the Party instructed intellectuals not to produce any more negative treatments of the 1930s or

---

See Aleksandr I. Solzhenitsyn, *The Oak and the Calf: Sketches of Literary Life in the Soviet Union*, trans. Harry Willets (New York: Harper & Row, 1975), p. 116.

42. Quoted in Johnson, *Khrushchev and the Arts*, pp. 70–72.

43. Khrushchev's speech of 8 March 1963, ibid., pp. 152–88.

works about labor camps.[44] At the 23d Party Congress in March 1966, the delegates voiced no support for destalinization; on the contrary, some Party leaders denounced past criticism of Stalin. Moreover, the Brezhnev regime partially rebuilt Stalin's reputation, stressing his role in World War II and industrialization. It also continued steps to restore the image, status, and jurisdiction of the secret police.[45]

Khrushchev and his colleagues originally approached the subject of past repressions with fear and loathing. Beyond taking rudimentary steps to protect themselves, the leaders avoided the issue of coming to terms with Stalinist purges. Despite the Party's control over the means of coercion, its leaders apparently feared that revelations of the extent and the cruelty of the purges would undermine their authority. Khrushchev, however, gambled on the potential benefits to be gained for himself and the Party by explicitly distancing his administration from the brutal and arbitrary practices sanctioned by Stalin. The purges had fostered debilitating mistrust and suspicion within the Party; now a frank denunciation of them could restore the Party's self-image and justify reform.

Khrushchev took three steps to put a positive spin on destalinization. First, he sought to put the Party and the people on an equal footing as victims and unwitting accomplices in the terror. He reminded people that they too had cheered Stalin and supported the death penalty for "enemies of the people." The ubiquity of the Stalin cult allowed reformers to try to bind society into the web of complicity. Second, he endorsed an interpretation of the purges that placed all blame for the planning and carrying out of human rights abuses on a few individuals. Khrushchev did not permit institutional explanations for the terror. Third, he tried to direct attention away from the past and toward a better future. He selectively revived destalinization to disparage his enemies, but past mistakes were to be discussed more in regret than in anger, as lessons to be learned; such discussions would not be tolerated if they served as sources of despair or "nihilism."

Unlike Party leaders who were eager to put the past behind them, some people wanted to explore the roots of the cult of personality so as better to address its consequences. But when one examined the massive scale and illegality of the purges, it became difficult to limit the blame to Stalin alone. Like Grossman, some liberals began to worry about the systemic

44. Spechler, *Permitted Dissent*, pp. 214–18.
45. Knight, *KGB*, pp. 55–62.

factors that facilitated arbitrary rule. Perhaps one did need to judge the regime first, and only then weigh the guilt of individuals. Conservatives responded to such ideas by trumpeting the dangers of allowing people to denigrate socialism. At this point, Party reformers struggled to define *partiinost'*, to distinguish between constructive and destructive suggestions. Because the Party controlled the media, however, it could tailor all interpretations of Stalinism for public consumption to match its policy of the hour.

Khrushchev's secret speech, despite its limitations, was a revolutionary gesture toward opening up the political sphere for criticism. By discrediting Stalin, Khrushchev offered protection to reformers and justification for changing the Party line; he did not, however, lift censorship or permit spontaneous criticism from below. The Party elite was too close to the bloody events of the recent past to be able to survive a real investigation of the purges. If silent destalinization offered security to the apparat, introduction of true rule of law and accountability threatened that same ruling class. But there were no public calls for prosecution or retribution. So why did the regime remain so hostile to multiple views of the past? Was it proximity to the terrible repressions or was it an inherent inability to absorb criticism and to tolerate individual views? The Soviet leaders were engaged in limited reform from above, yet they were trying to introduce an element of inverse legitimacy—that is, legitimacy based on the contrast between the new regime and the old. Inverse legitimacy is better suited to consolidation of a new regime that differs radically from the one it has displaced. And in a way perhaps unique to liberalizing totalitarian regimes, to interpret the previous leader's policies as crimes was to challenge the reformers' fundamental basis of authority: the Party justified its monopoly on power and truth by pointing to the performance of the Party throughout its history.

# 3 GLASNOST AND THE REEMERGENCE OF THE STALIN QUESTION

Gorbachev drew his inspiration for reform not from the horrors of Stalinism but from the "era of stagnation." Gorbachev's initial focus on motivating workers and overcoming structural inefficiencies in the economy showed his awareness of the deepening economic crisis that had overtaken the USSR under Leonid Brezhnev. He intended to bolster the Soviet economy and to revitalize the political sphere by mobilizing both specialists and ordinary citizens. Participation by a mature public, Gorbachev believed, could introduce much-needed constructive feedback and creative input. By turning outside the Party to gather support for an elite reform coalition, Gorbachev demonstrated greater trust in both the intelligentsia and the average citizen than the Soviets had seen since Khrushchev's liberalization. The three prongs of Gorbachev's agenda—glasnost, democratization, and perestroika—all were designed to counter the political impunity of entrenched Party conservatives and to shake up inefficient enterprises. It did not occur to Gorbachev that some people might extend the search for accountability to the more distant past.

Gorbachev seems to have assumed that with the passage of several decades and the relatively benign rule since Stalin's death, interest in the purges had waned. Perhaps generational change heightened Gorbachev's insensitivity to the legacies of Stalin's repressions. His own background, like that of many other Soviet citizens, is complicated: his maternal grandfather actively promoted collectivization while his paternal grandfather spent nine years in labor camps for allegedly hoarding forty pounds of grain. Although Gorbachev is of the age group often referred to as children of the 20th Party Congress, he was not outspoken on the subject of destalinization at the time. In fact, he did not even reveal how the purges had touched his family until 1990. And in 1984 Gorbachev joined conservative Politburo members in approving Molotov's reinstatement in the Party, though he suggested that publicity be limited.[1] In failing to anticipate the intense conflict over the interpretation of Stalinism, Gorbachev displayed the shortsightedness of a pragmatist; his own attention was firmly focused on changing the present, not on dwelling on the past—with the exception of seeking historical precedents for economic reform.

Not only did reformers of the Gorbachev era have a new reference point to justify reform; they also confronted new opponents. The conservative Stalinists who had actively abetted his persecutions had long since retired, so the threat that revelations would upset the power structure had largely passed. But liberalization, as Adam Przeworski has pointed out, is never easy. It takes the perception of "an imminent crisis of some sort" to induce reformers to begin the balancing act involved in "a controlled opening of political space." Reform is a shaky process because "liberalization is to be continually contingent on the compatibility of its outcomes with the interests or values of the authoritarian bloc."[2] Would the Party encounter the same contradictions it did in the Khrushchev era regarding *partiinost'* in criticism? Did the passage of time make it easier to reconcile the Party's preservation of power with its acknowledgment of past abuses? Would destalinization lend itself to liberalization, backlash, or revolution?

## DISINTEREST AND INSENSITIVITY: SPRING 1985–SPRING 1987

Throughout 1985 and 1986 Gorbachev devoted little attention to Soviet history. When he did speak out, he did not contradict traditional interpretations of the past. Gorbachev recalled Stalin's wartime leadership favorably. When a French correspondent questioned him about "Stalinism," he rejected the term as a foreign invention designed to denigrate

---

1. David Remnick, *Lenin's Tomb: The Last Days of the Soviet Empire* (New York: Random House, 1993), pp. 48–49, 518.

2. Adam Przeworski, *Democracy and the Market: Political and Economic Reforms in Eastern Europe and Latin America* (New York: Cambridge University Press, 1991), p. 57.

socialism. Gorbachev credited the Party with having "drawn the proper conclusions from the past," and looked on revision of Soviet history as an unconstructive enterprise. He allegedly told a private gathering of writers in the summer of 1986 that "if we start trying to deal with the past, we'll lose all our energy. . . . We'll sort out the past. We'll put everything in its place. But right now we have to direct our energy forward."[3]

In early 1987, however, Gorbachev responded to a growing discussion of Soviet history in the press by slowly recognizing that a reinterpretation of Soviet history might have a role in perestroika. When he met with representatives of the mass media and propagandists in February to expound on his notion of glasnost, Gorbachev reluctantly turned to the question of Soviet history. After reminding journalists that "criticism should always be *partiinyi*," he unveiled the slogan of filling in "blank pages in history and literature." But he cautioned, "Only let's put things in their proper places. . . . And for the seventieth anniversary of our revolution we don't need to push those who made the Revolution into the shadows. It's vital to bring people up on the example of those who put their lives at the service of the Revolution and socialism."[4] History, then, should serve as a source of positive lessons and indoctrination.

Like Khrushchev, Gorbachev made restoration of the names of honorable Bolsheviks his top priority in revising the past and thereby reinforced the image of the Party as the main victim of the purges. In a remark that must have reassured conservatives, Gorbachev asserted, "One needn't forget names, but it would be even more amoral to forget or keep silent about whole periods of the people's life in which they lived, believed, and worked under the leadership of the Party and in the name of socialism." His overall assessment—"there were mistakes, and serious ones, but the country moved forward"—was positive and downplayed the impact of the repressions.[5]

By July, however, Gorbachev had refined his balanced stance on criticism and Soviet history. Now he claimed that though the Party continued to play a vanguard role, it no longer pretended to possess the absolute truth. And he bluntly declared, "I don't think we can or should ever

3. Quoted in R. W. Davies, *Soviet History in the Gorbachev Revolution* (Bloomington: Indiana University Press, 1989), p. 129.
4. M. S. Gorbachev, "Ubezhdennost'—opora perestroiki," in his *Izbrannye rechi i stat'i*, vol. 4 (Moscow: Politizdat, 1987), p. 373.
5. Ibid., p. 374.

forgive or justify what occurred in 1937–38. Never. For this those who were then in power are responsible."[6] But then he moderated his frank condemnation of the purges by cautioning that they should not be permitted to overshadow present achievements and by presenting a narrow vision of the terror as concentrated in 1937–38 and as having affected only Party and military cadres and the intelligentsia. Gorbachev's early treatment of the Stalin question mirrored Khrushchev's in many respects, but it opened the door to independent, possibly dissonant voices.

## Debates over a Usable Past: Summer 1987–Fall 1988

By the summer of 1987, Gorbachev had come to envision reform as a package of economic, political, and social policies that could not be implemented in isolation from one another. Moreover, reformers had found several advantages in promoting a utilitarian view of the lessons of Stalinism: first, it supported Gorbachev's commitment to a law-governed state; second, it attracted allies among the creative intelligentsia; third, it enhanced Gorbachev's image as the pragmatic moderate, neither catering to sensation nor denying past mistakes. Ideological conservatives such as Egor Ligachev, however, had put Gorbachev on the defensive with warnings that incautious discussion of Stalinism was harming the Party. "Every day is dear to us, even those that were difficult," Gorbachev responded. He reminded the press to be respectful of older generations and to treat Soviet history seriously and without sensationalism.[7] Yet Gorbachev maintained both his basic trust that the Soviet people would evaluate the past responsibly and his belief that a *partiinyi* approach to Soviet history was viable. As the battle over how to remember and commemorate Stalinist repressions raged in the pages of the popular press, however, it appeared that reappraisal of the past might again divide members of the general reform camp. The liberal ideologist Aleksandr Iakovlev and the conservative spokesman Egor Ligachev joined Gorbachev in morally condemning Stalin's repressions, but they ended up diametrically opposed on how to treat Soviet history.

6. M. S. Gorbachev, "Prakticheskimi delami vglubliat' perestroiku," ibid., vol. 5 (1988), p. 217.
    7. Ibid., p. 218–19.

*Liberal Positions*

Encouraged by political pronouncements on glasnost and the need to fill in "blank pages" of Soviet history, liberals in the media published both previously censored and fresh treatments of past human rights violations. Professional historians waged their own battle over the interpretation of the Soviet past, and Stalinism in particular, in the popular press. Letters to the editor make it clear that the public was transfixed by new horrifying stories about the fate of purge victims and by artistic works that dealt with moral problems raised during and as a consequence of Stalinism.

The multilingual newspaper *Moskovskie novosti* (Moscow News) and the journal *Ogonek* (Small Fire) took the lead in revealing new facts about the purges. In early 1987 *Moskovskie novosti* resurrected the "lost fates" of five teenage girls sentenced to long camp terms after their fathers were arrested.[8] In June *Ogonek* featured a long article about the Soviet diplomat Fedor Raskolnikov, who had managed to thwart Stalin's efforts to recall him from abroad to arrest him. Sentenced in absentia as an enemy of the people and unable to return to his homeland, Raskolnikov wrote an open letter to Stalin in which he condemned repressions among the cultural, scientific, and military elite. Raskolnikov's letter showed that even at his post far from home the diplomat understood that Stalin was sanctioning irrational and arbitrary arrests. Although the diplomat had been rehabilitated posthumously in 1963, he had fallen into the memory hole again after conservatives slandered him in 1965. Thus *Ogonek* drew a direct connection between repression under Stalin and censorship under Brezhnev, reinforcing the radical idea that remnants of Stalinism persisted long after the 20th Party Congress.[9]

Insight into generational rifts over the legacies of the purges was also offered by the Georgian director Tengiz Abuladze's film *Repentance*. Shot in the early 1980s, *Repentance* remained on the shelf until Eduard Shevardnadze, who had supported the film's production, arranged a special showing for Gorbachev. In the allegory/fantasy depicting a mythical dictator and his repressions, Abuladze went beyond mere representation of evil to consider the effects of the dictator's deeds on succeeding generations. In

---

8. *Moscow News*, 3 January 1987.
9. Vasilii Polikarpov, "1917–1987: Fedor Raskolnikov," *Ogonek*, no. 26, 1987, pp. 4–7.

the film, the daughter of one of the dictator's victims persists in exhuming the dictator's corpse, because "to bury him is to bury what he did." During the struggle over the tyrant's remains, his grandson comes to question his father about the past. In the end, the father actively seeks to justify and cover up the past, and the disillusioned grandson commits suicide.[10] With its daring theme and harsh moral message, *Repentance* helped to push the issue of Stalinism into the center of public debate.

As during the Khrushchev thaw, the Writers' Union did not undergo rapid liberalization. But editors of individual journals, in particular the newly appointed Grigorii Baklanov of *Znamia* (Standard) and Sergei Zalygin of *Novyi mir,* began to test the limits of glasnost. In 1986 and 1987 they dusted off long-censored works. Anatolii Rybakov's novel *Children of the Arbat,* which addresses the moral dilemmas facing Soviet youth during the 1930s and interprets Stalin's inner thoughts, had been scheduled for publication in *Novyi mir* in 1968 and again in 1978, but both times censors intervened. Excerpts from the novel finally appeared in *Ogonek* in March 1987, and the whole book was published later that year. Though Rybakov offered few new insights into the purges, his descriptions of the diverse ways Stalinism hurt Soviet citizens provoked intense responses.[11] Other resurrected works included Anna Akhmatova's cycle of poems *Requiem,* drawn from her experience of losing loved ones to the purges, and Varlam Shalamov's *Kolyma Tales,* about life in the Arctic labor camps. Other fictional works that appeared in 1987 dealt with topics that had not yet found a place in official discourse, such as the deportation of ethnic minorities during World War II and repression of scientists.[12]

During this period of intellectual ferment, professional historians began to enter into the debates over the past, often in reaction to literary treatments of historical events. A second stimulus for reconsideration of their work was the appointment of the outspoken liberal Iurii Afanas'ev to head the Moscow Historical Archives Institute. In an interview in the popular press in March 1987, Afanas'ev challenged historians to take creative approaches in their search for truth. He not only chided Soviet

10. Remnick, *Lenin's Tomb,* p. 44; Felicity Barringer, "'Repentance,' a Soviet Film Milestone, Strongly Denounces Official Evil," *New York Times,* 16 November 1986.

11. K. Andreev, "Deti Arbata: Pis'ma Anatoliiu Rybakovu," *Ogonek,* no. 27, 1987, pp. 4–5; Irina Rishina, "Zaruki na serdtse," *Literaturnaia gazeta,* 19 August 1987, p. 4.

12. Julia Wishnevsky, "A Survey of Russian Literature Published in the Past Year," *Radio Liberty Research* 387/87 (30 September 1987).

historians for their weak methodology and poor results but excoriated those "specific people who directly 'created' the stagnation." Afanas'ev bluntly challenged historians not "simply to return to the 20th Party Congress" but to "find a new depth of analysis." "We frankly cannot believe the assertion that the mass repression of honest Soviet people in the 1930s was either a 'mistake' or 'shortcoming' 'in observance of socialist legality' (mentioned in the same breath as shortcomings 'in consumer service') or even 'the inevitable costs of class struggle and the revolutionary rearrangement of society.'" Afanas'ev even defended literary works that helped readers understand the flavor of the past.[13]

Responses to Afanas'ev's challenge quickly followed from historians he had wounded. In a style reminiscent of stagnation-era reports, F. M. Vaganov and A. N. Ponomarev declared that despite "difficulties, errors, shortcomings, sharp debates, and disputes," "a Marxist-Leninist historical science emerged, grew stronger, and became a determining force in our country, and produced a mighty detachment of historians capable of tackling more complex and important tasks."[14] The heated exchange of opinions over whether and how historians should take part in efforts to reevaluate the past touched off a prolonged debate. The liberals entered into the fray with two goals: to reveal lost facts about the repressions and to protest the end of the thaw. Their emphasis on the persistence of censorship and cowardice angered conservatives and put pressure on Gorbachev.

## Conservative Approaches

Throughout the summer of 1987 and into 1988, some Party officials, journalists, and citizens responded defensively to revelations about the purges in the press. Drawing on citizens' letters in the best proletarian tradition, the *Pravda* correspondent L. Kurin focused on the idea that under glasnost some people had begun to disparage the achievements of thousands of Soviet citizens. Kurin revealed his own sympathies by quoting at length a letter from Georgii Matveets, whose faith in the system remained unshaken despite the fact that his father had been a victim of the purge in 1937. Matveets delivered a veritable ode to the Soviet people of

13. *Sovetskaia kultura*, 21 March 1987, in *Federal Broadcast Information Service Daily Report on the Soviet Union (FBIS-Sov)*, 30 April 1987, pp. 1–10.

14. *Sovetskaia kultura*, 4 July 1987 in *FBIS-Sov*, 17 July 1987, pp. 22–26.

the 1930s, whose efforts, in his opinion, clearly overshadowed anything unpleasant that might have happened. "All that—the five-year plans, Stakhanov, the success of the kolkhoz peasantry . . . —really happened. And the Soviet people did it not out of fear but out of conscience. . . . The lives of millions of Soviet people cannot be reduced to [Stalin] alone . . . those who are denigrating our history in this way have no sense of respect or love for their country and their people." Kurin concurred with Matveets's definition of patriotism as remembering the good. Without denying the reality of the mass repressions, Kurin managed to discredit those who sought to investigate their depths as somehow suspect, disloyal to socialism, and unfair to ordinary people."[15]

Speeches by two Politburo members in the autumn of 1987 echoed the patriotic themes promoted by *Pravda*. Egor Ligachev voiced a variant of Gorbachev's utilitarian point that "it is very important to sort out the reasons for [the cult of personality] in a responsible way, but the main thing is to create conditions in which such a thing would be impossible." While placing himself rhetorically in the reform camp, Ligachev contended that the Party had already dealt with the cult of personality, and he accused liberals of sensationalism. In language reminiscent of preglasnost times, he argued: "Some people abroad—and in our country too, for that matter—are trying to discredit the entire path of the construction of socialism in the USSR, to present it as an unrelieved chain of mistakes, and to use the facts of unjustified repressions to push into the background the exploit of the people that has created a mighty socialist power." Even more emphatically than Gorbachev, Ligachev urged that positive achievements of the previous generations be passed on to Soviet youth. Finally, Ligachev supported Kurin's rosy view of the Soviet people of the 1930s. "The overwhelming majority of the Communists who were subjected to repressions remained true to Lenin's behests."[16]

Viktor Chebrikov, head of the KGB, joined in with an even more stinging attack on liberals. He charged certain intellectuals with having been led by Western intelligence agents "into positions of carping criticism, demagoguery, and nihilism, of denigrating certain stages of the historical development of our society."[17] Chebrikov defended the reputation of his

---

15. *Pravda*, 23 July 1987, in *FBIS-Sov*, 29 July 1987, pp. 8–11.
16. "Ligachev Reviews Education, Soviet History," *Pravda*, 27 August 1987, in *Current Digest of the Soviet Press (CDSP)*, no. 34, 1987, p. 13.
17. "Chebrikov Decries Abuses of Openness," *Pravda*, 11 September 1987, in *CDSP*, no. 37, 1987, p. 8.

own institution as well, claiming truthfully that thousands of Chekists had been victims of the purges, but falsely ascribing their fate to their resistance to the policy of illegal repressions.

Gorbachev-era conservatives waged a battle not over issues of concrete accountability or institutional remedies but over the popular vision of the past. Conservatives recognized that for a system based on an ideology of historical determinism, control over memory remained a valuable means of ensuring conformity and support. For conservatives the 1930s, the period of the "construction of socialism," embodied the payoffs of the Revolution. A negative image of this period could delegitimate the whole political system. While they worked to persuade the Party to adopt a more self-conscious line on Stalinism, the conservatives couched their debate in the language of patriotism in an effort to recruit social support.

## The Struggle to Uphold a Moderate Party Line

November 1987 marked the seventieth anniversary of the Bolsheviks' seizure of power and Gorbachev was expected to celebrate the occasion with a major public address. This event called for reflection on the passage of seven decades of Soviet power, and on September 28 Gorbachev signaled his intention to deal with the history of repressions by forming a Politburo commission for "additional studies of documents pertaining to repressive measures of the 1930s–1940s and early 1950s." Here Gorbachev accepted a broader temporal definition of the purges than he had done earlier. Unlike Khrushchev's commission, however, the new commission did not provide basic material for the general secretary's address. Indeed, it did not meet until January 1988. But like Khrushchev, Gorbachev faced significant opposition to any revision of official interpretations of Stalinism.

The transcript of the October plenary meeting of the Central Committee demonstrates the leadership's concerns regarding its attempt to assess seventy years of socialist rule. At the end of his presentation, Gorbachev confessed that "not everything I have spoken about will be spelled out in the anniversary report. It includes only the general, aggregate evaluations of complicated periods in our history. . . . Here at a Central Committee plenary meeting, the Politburo deemed it necessary to deal with these matters in greater detail."[18] In short, Gorbachev resorted to extraordinary frankness in this closed session to try to persuade Party officials of the benefits of articulating a thorough but moderate view of Soviet history. But he maintained the distinction between knowledge safe to release to the public and knowledge that should be kept among the most politically mature, the Party elite.

At the plenary session Gorbachev downplayed the costs of reexamining the past ("Nobody demands any rituals of repentance") and decried "attempts to use [revelations] as a pretext to wipe out the fundamental advantages achieved by socialism." In response to Ligachev's claims that to describe Stalin as "criminal" would "mean canceling our entire lives . . . opening the way for people to spit on our history," Gorbachev took his usual carefully balanced stance: "Just as achievements are no reason to go into raptures, so setbacks are no reason for self-flagellation. . . . We need a substantial and objective analysis of our past today . . . [to] understand the sources, roots and causes both of our achievements and of the deformations and stagnation processes in the evolution of socialism that interfere with our work, prevent us from living in full conformity with the lofty ideals of socialism."[19] Gorbachev expressed his accord with those who associated Stalin with victory in World War II, but he did not shrink from speaking of wholesale abuses, and insisted that Stalin was fully aware of them.

In some ways Gorbachev's discussion of coming to terms with the past did not advance beyond notions developed by Khrushchev. He cited some of the same statistics and examples of repressions within the Party that Khrushchev offered in his secret speech. And he attributed Stalin's purges to a combination of personality flaws and methods of struggle inappropriate to a period of peaceful socialist development. But in tracing the development of the command-administrative system back to Stalin, Gorbachev did probe more deeply into the roots of Stalinism. His focus on the command-administrative system reflected his interest in the economic distortions produced by socialism. Though he had at last acknowledged the need to combat ignorance as to the results of Khrushchev-era investigations of the purges, Gorbachev did not draw on the same deep pain felt by Khrushchev and others close to purge victims.

18. "Plenary Meeting of the CPSU CC, October 1987," *Political Archives of the Soviet Union* 1, no. 1 (1990): 63
19. Ibid., pp. 58–59. Ligachev is quoted in Remnick, *Lenin's Tomb*, p. 48.

Gorbachev's anniversary speech on 2 November, though upbeat, did not skirt the issues of collectivization, rapid industrialization, internal Party battles, and repressions. In addressing thorny issues, Gorbachev took a fairly conservative stance: he criticized Leon Trotsky's factional activity; labeled Grigorii Zinoviev and Lev Kamenev oppositionists; and praised Nikolai Bukharin for his role in battling Trotskyism but criticized his opposition to rapid industrialization. Gorbachev also argued that collectivization, though handled badly, was a wise policy. Stalin's repressions, however, he found neither necessary nor inevitable. The broad scope of Gorbachev's historical assessment should not overshadow the fact that it lacked depth and substance in many areas, especially in regard to the mass repressions. Gorbachev cited no statistics or examples, and estimated the number of victims as only "many thousands." Moreover, Gorbachev specifically mentioned only mass arrests and executions; he made no reference to the deported nationalities, the forced resettlement of dekulakized peasants, or the incarceration of former prisoners of war after World War II.

A consistent, limited rationale for admitting to the existence of past repression emerges from Gorbachev's speech. Like Khrushchev, Gorbachev saw some benefits to be gained by strongly worded but substantively limited criticism. Thus he initiated discussion of the 1920s and 1930s by noting, "And if today we scrutinize our history with a critical eye, we do so only because we want a better and fuller conception of the ways that lead to the future. . . . We need truthful assessments [of our history] . . . not to settle political scores or, as they say, to let off steam, but to pay due credit to all that was heroic in the past, and to draw lessons from mistakes and miscalculations.[20] For Gorbachev, then, coming to terms with the past had a purely educational function. He seemed to be afraid to acknowledge that the Party might be looking for scapegoats or responding to popular pressure for truth-telling. He did call repressions "real crimes," but he consistently emphasized the achievements of the Stalin era over its mistakes.

But by the spring of 1988, the Party line on Soviet history set in November had begun to slip. As under Khrushchev, the reformers could not elicit a single view of the past from an establishment that was itself divided on reform. Gorbachev tried to remedy the conflict by meeting with leaders of

20. M. S. Gorbachev, "Oktiabr' i perestroika: Revoliutsiia prodolzhaetsia," in his *Izbrannye rechi i stat'i*, 5:395.

the mass media and creative unions to "synchronize watches." A month later, however, he was again chastising the press for not sticking to his tempo for reform or his stance on historical analysis. The general secretary reminded the media to separate the essence of socialism from its deformations. With irritation he asserted that the whole problem of coming to terms with past repressions could have been resolved long ago if only the Party had followed through with its resolutions in the aftermath of the 20th Party Congress. Here Gorbachev hinted at a renewal of concrete measures to defuse the drive to explore painful aspects of the Soviet past.[21]

Having accepted the inevitability of public reassessment of the purges, the Party leadership responded with a series of practical steps to take control of the process. First, they addressed the sensitive question of how to reevaluate Stalin's "ideological opponents" with a formal investigation into the most prominent show trials of the Stalin period. The Politburo commission set up in late 1987 quickly reviewed major political cases of the 1930s. As a result, on 4 February 1988 the Supreme Court rehabilitated Bukharin and his codefendants, with the exception of the former secret police chief Genrikh Iagoda; and in June it rehabilitated Zinoviev and Kamenev. The commission did not operate openly, but it did publicize the results of its work in the press.[22] And the rehabiliation of old Bolsheviks who had represented "Leninist" alternatives to Stalin caused a stir of excitement among reform-minded Communists.

A second issue addressed by Gorbachev in 1988 was the commemoration of victims of "illegality and repressions." At the end of his speech to the 19th Party Conference Gorbachev revived Khrushchev's proposal for a monument to Stalin's victims. He was "convinced," he said, that "this step will be supported by the whole Soviet people."[23] But he did not mention that an unofficial civic organization had already presented him with a petition with thousands of signatures in support of a monument. Despite a Politburo decree of 4 July initiating preparation for a monument, no immediate steps were taken. On the contrary, as we shall see, the

---

21. M. S. Gorbachev, "Demokratizatsiia—sut' perestroiki, sut' sotsializma" and "Revoliutsionnoi perestroike—ideologiu obnovleniia," ibid., vol. 6 (1989), pp. 18–38, 64.

22. "Commission of the Politburo of the CC CPSU for Additional Studies of Documents Concerning the Repressive Measures of the 30s–40s and Early 50s," *Political Archives of the Soviet Union* 1, no. 2 (1990).

23. Quoted in Davies, *Soviet History*, p. 156.

Ministry of Culture acted only when it appeared unofficial efforts might succeed.

Finally the regime attempted to resolve the legacies of repression through rehabilitations. Decrees in 1988 and early 1989 accelerated the rehabilitation of ordinary citizens. Local KGB and procurators' offices were ordered to review all cases from the early 1930s though the mid-1950s, whether or not a complaint had been registered. The Politburo also requested that local Party organizations accelerate their review of petitions for reinstatement. Then the Politburo decreed that all sentences that had been levied by nonjudicial bodies were to be annulled and the people so sentenced were to be considered rehabilitated; this step allowed the Procuracy to resolve a great many cases quickly. Procedural streamlining and a shift in personnel speeded rehabilitation but did not offer greater material benefits to victims.[24]

Iakovlev publicly touted these rehabilitation policies as a means of "repentance."[25] Other top leaders, however, did not join him in accepting guilt for the system's failings; in fact, "repentance" was a word they shunned. Under Gorbachev there was no official discussion of legal or institutional reform of the police or the Procuracy based on the purge experience, no suggestion that a sense of impunity on their part needed to be overcome. On the contrary, Gorbachev's policy making reflected a wariness of what conservatives called "dangerous nihilism." In an interesting analogy, Gorbachev said, "I do not want to be understood as if I am issuing calls, in the way that was done during the 1966–76 Cultural Revolution in China, to open fire on the headquarters."[26] It seems that the general secretary was quite conscious of the price that reformers might have to pay if liberalization got out of control.

24. "O dopolnitel'nykh merakh po zaversheniiu raboty, sviazannoi s reabilitatsiei lits, neobosnovanno repressirovannykh v 30–40-e gody i nachala 50-kh godov" (11 July 1988); and "O dopolnitel'nykh merakh po vosstanovleniiu spravedlivosti v otnoshenii zhertv repressii, imevshikh mesto v period 30–40-kh i nachala 50-kh godov" (5 January 1989), both in Reabilitatsiia: Politicheskie protsessy 30–50-kh godov, ed. Aleksandr Iakovlev (Moscow: Politizdat, 1991), pp. 16–18.

25. Remnick, Lenin's Tomb, pp. 304–5.

26. Quoted in Stephen Wheatcroft, "Steadying the Energy of History and Probing the Limits of Glasnost': Moscow, July to December 1987," Australian Slavonic and East European Studies 1, no. 2 (1987): 86. This comment was omitted from the transcript of Gorbachev's speech published in the Soviet press.

THE LIBERAL INTELLIGENTSIA SEIZES THE INITIATIVE IN
DESTALINIZATION

As under Khrushchev, the contest between liberal and conservative
politicians became intertwined with the literary world's exploration of
Stalinism. In the late 1980s glasnost opened the door for blunter and more
political critiques, and the persistence of conservative opposition to coming to terms with the purges prompted some liberals to step up their
attacks on the Soviet system. The polarization of views on destalinization
ultimately made Gorbachev's moderate position untenable.

### Defending Lenin: The Shatrov Saga

In January 1988 the journal *Znamia* published a play by the noted
dramatist Mikhail Shatrov. In *Dal'she . . . dal'she . . . dal'she!* (Onward
. . . Onward . . . Onward!) Shatrov presented his vision of the events
surrounding the Bolsheviks' seizure of power in 1917. He gathered major
personages from all camps—White generals, Socialist Revolutionaries,
Bolsheviks, Kadets—and through their actual and imagined speeches created a dialogue in which they commented on the fate of the Revolution.
Because it raised the question whether Stalin's policies were logical con-
tinuations of Lenin's, Shatrov's play became the focus of a new round of
debates on Soviet history. Like Grossman before him, Shatrov delved into
the nature of socialism: if the terror was inevitable, then did the achievements of the Revolution really outweigh the costs? But unlike Grossman,
Shatrov clearly admired Lenin; and though he had the character of Lenin
accept moral responsibility for Stalin, Shatrov upheld the proposition that
Stalin and the terror were not the inevitable outcome of the Revolution.

Conservatives immediately blasted the play for its un-Marxist focus on
individuals rather than classes.[27] The argument that historical development does not depend on individuals, as Shatrov later observed, allowed
them to rescue Stalin from liberals' attacks. In the true Stalinist tradition,
reactionaries put all the blame for the purges on the hostile environment
created by real and imagined enemies of socialism.[28] Meanwhile, a glow-

27. See V. Glagolev, "Khudozhestvennaia istoriia i istoricheskie sud'by," *Pravda,* 10
January 1988, in *"Dal'she . . . dal'she . . . dal'she!" Diskussiia vokrug odnoi p'esy,* comp.
Gennadii Li (Moscow: Knizhnaia Palata, 1989), pp. 85–86.
28. Gennadii Li, "Khronika diskussii vokrug odnoi p'esy v kontekste perestroiki" (interview with Mikhail Shatrov), ibid., p. 72.

ing review in *Moskovskie novosti* praised the play precisely because Shatrov staged a trial not just of Stalin or of Lenin but of all the major players in the Revolution for "the steps backward taken after Lenin's death which led to the 1937 tragedy." By having Lenin accept the blame for the purges, the reviewer argued, Shatrov restored a sense of morality that Lenin embraced but Stalin did not. He especially commended the play's ending, in which the other characters faded away, leaving Lenin alone except for Stalin, who stubbornly remained even though his presence was not wanted. Stalin, he concluded, will 'remain onstage' as long as each of us has not fully clarified our attitude toward him. From the point of view of a revolutionary and a Leninist."[29] This final scene received a startlingly different interpretation in *Pravda;* there three historians charged that Shatrov was trying to make Stalin out to be "not an antipode but another hypostasis of Lenin," and "this is particularly evident in the finale of the play, in which . . . Stalin converges with Lenin." These critics accused Shatrov of drawing a wholly negative portrait of the period of socialist development and warned ominously that, given the current hunger for frank writing about history, Shatrov's arbitrary treatment of the Revolution might be accepted as true by people who lacked the proper Marxist training.[30]

The distortions and name-calling directed at *Dal'she* and at Shatrov personally reminded liberals of earlier campaigns against "anti-Soviet literature." One reader compared the current *Pravda* with *Pravda* during the Stalin era, when it threatened Bukharin, Shostakovich, and Akhmatova.[31] But this time the campaign emanated only from one camp within the Party and the intellectual establishment. Shatrov's play raised the hackles of professional Party historians and orthodox ideologists, who wanted to avoid the question of responsibility for the public hunger for historical knowledge and the lack of satisfactory explanations of the relation of Stalinism to socialism. Shatrov's play also evoked hostility because in following Gorbachev's intent in promoting glasnost to the letter, it showed where the policy must lead. *Dal'she* was fresh and exciting in style, sincerely Leninist in content, aimed at drawing lessons for the pre-

29. Dmitrii Kazutin, "Istorii podsudny vse: Interv'iu s samim soboi," *Moskovskie novosti,* 10 January 1988, ibid., pp. 86–91.

30. G. Gerasimenko, O. Obichkin, and B. Popov, "Neposudna tol'ko pravda," *Pravda,* 15 February 1988, ibid., pp. 175–80.

31. A. Aleksandrov, ibid., p. 217.

sent, and based on trust in the people's ability to choose wisely among conflicting truths. Yet Shatrov had outstripped Gorbachev by recognizing the terror as a major issue that still needed to be addressed in both real life and socialist theory. As a profoundly pro-perestroika vehicle, *Dal'she* helped clarify and crystallize the conflict between conservatives and liberals within the establishment; ultimately, the controversy sparked by the play would force Gorbachev to take sides, either to support a more radical version of glasnost or to retreat.

### Defending Stalin: The Nina Andreeva Letter

On 13 March 1988 conservatives dropped a bombshell into the debate over reassessing the past with the publication in *Sovetskaia Rossiia* of a letter from a Leningrad schoolteacher who ostensibly was worried about the effect of glasnost on the ideological orientation of her students. At a meeting with a hero of World War II, Nina Andreeva wrote, one student asked about political repressions in the army, and seemed disappointed when the veteran said he knew of none. She argued, "Having become a constant theme, repressions are abnormally exaggerated in the education of some youth, and block objective assessment of the past." Criticism of the past produces nihilism and ideological confusion in some youngsters. "More than once," Andreeva reported, "I've heard the assertion that it's time to bring the Communists to account for the alleged 'dehumanization' of the life of the country after 1917."

Andreeva criticized Shatrov for "distorting the history of socialism in our country" and bemoaned the failure of Party leaders' efforts to turn the public's attention to the achievements of socialism. Like Kurin, Andreeva contended that an attack on Stalin was really an attack on the whole epoch. She defended Stalin as energetic, erudite, resolute, and humble, and attributed antistalinism to the "spiritual heirs of Trotsky or Iagoda, and those hurt by socialism—the offspring of NEPmen . . . and kulaks." Andreeva established her credentials for judging the era by explaining that neither she nor her family had any ties to Stalin or his entourage; in fact, one of her relatives was purged and then rehabilitated after the 20th Party Congress.[32]

Throughout her diatribe, Andreeva presented herself as a loyal Party

32. Nina Andreeva, "Ne mogu postupat'sia printsipami," *Sovetskaia Rossiia*, 13 March 1988.

member, concerned that the Party might be endangering its leading role through incautious reform. Indeed, she hinted at a threat that reformers preferred to ignore—the talk of settling accounts with Communists by force. In keeping with *partiinost'*, Andreeva endorsed the Central Committee's 1956 decree on the cult of personality and Gorbachev's speech on the seventieth anniversary of the Revolution as definitive judgments of Soviet history. In this and other respects, Andreeva tried to gloss over divisions within the Party and to create the impression that her conservative interpretations of perestroika, socialism, and Soviet history were definitive. Her tone and the letter's prominent publication in a Party newspaper gave the impression that it was an authoritative document—the sort of broadside the Party used to launch to quash debate. Newspapers across the nation reprinted and distributed the essay, and many Party organizations discussed it. When more than two weeks of silence followed from the liberal media, reform-minded segments of the population came close to panic.[33]

Only on 5 April did official reformers respond to Andreeva's manifesto with an angry, hard-hitting unsigned editorial in *Pravda*. The article, written by Aleksandr Iakovlev, bluntly assessed Andreeva's communication as antiperestroika and unsocialist. It rejected her claim that democratization and glasnost had gone too far and scorned her fatalistic view of history as reminiscent of Stalin's comment that "when you chop wood, chips must fly." By whitewashing the past, Andreeva justified political distortions and crimes against socialism. The Party had bravely chosen to investigate past repressions and to continue the process of restoring justice. The editorial admitted that Stalin was an extremely contradictory person, but it reminded the public that the guilt of Stalin and his entourage was beyond doubt, and that his cult "was alien to the nature of socialism and was made possible only by a retreat from its basic principles." Iakovlev then defended Gorbachev's reform program, alleging that conservatives supported Stalin because they wished to defend the right to arbitrariness. As for nihilism, its roots lay in the past, not in present reforms. The article called for a new definition of patriotism—one that did not blame internal enemies for the nation's problems but accepted responsibility and embraced perestroika.[34]

33. William Taubman and Jane Taubman, *Moscow Spring* (New York: Summit, 1989), pp. 146–60.
34. "Printsipy perestroiki: Revoliutsionnost' myshleniia i deistvii," *Pravda*, 5 April 1988.

## The End of Moderation

After the Nina Andreeva drama, shamefaced liberals returned to glasnost with greater determination. When liberal intellectuals pressed Gorbachev to accelerate reform in all areas, to make reform irreversible, he urged them yet again to be patient and to show respect for Party cadres.[35] But the Party's will to control the press seemed to have ebbed. In October 1988, Sergei Zalygin attracted one of the last salvos against antistalinism when his announcement of *Novyi mir's* forthcoming publication of Solzhenitsyn's *Gulag Archipelago* was censored on orders from above. But in 1989 he succeeded in publishing selected chapters. Other long-suppressed works also appeared during that year, including George Orwell's *1984* and Grossman's *Forever Flowing*. And in June 1989 *Novyi mir* published a long piece critical of Lenin by the publicist Vitalii Selunin. This article, aptly titled "Roots," presented an entirely institutional critique of socialism as based on the exploitation of the individual.[36]

The extent of change in writers' attitudes toward censorship and *partiinost'* can also be seen in Rybakov's sequel to *Children of the Arbat*. *Thirty-five and Other Years,* published in 1989, was notably more political in tone and more explicit in its treatment of the roots of Stalinism. Here Rybakov examined the issue of ordinary citizens' complicity in the creation of the Stalin cult: "Everywhere there are trials, mass executions. . . . And the people? Are the people silent? . . . The people are not silent . . . they demand reprisals. Throughout the whole country, from Vladivostok to Odessa, there are meetings: uncover, destroy, shoot!" Rybakov captured the strangeness of ordinary life in the midst of extraordinary events; in Moscow, he observed, "life continued as if there were no exiles, neither prisons nor camps, as if there were no prisoners."[37] Conservatives were claiming that ongoing normal activities somehow negated the possibility of mass repressions. Rybakov demonstrated that, on the contrary, everyday life had expanded to include new rituals, such as rote condemnation of newly discovered enemies of the people.

In November 1989, despite his plea that reformers concentrate on

35. M. S. Gorbachev, "Na novom etape perestroiki," in his *Izbrannye rechi i stat'i,* 6:568–76.
36. Vasilii Selunin, "Istoki," *Novyi mir,* no. 5 (1988).
37. Anatolii Rybakov, *Tridtsat' piatyi i drugie gody* (Moscow: Sovetskii Pisatel', 1989), pp. 10, 19.

deeds instead of debates, Gorbachev devoted a major article to the ever-intensifying public criticism of Soviet rule. Tacitly admitting that glasnost had escaped its intended bounds, Gorbachev conceded that "the vitality of the socialist idea itself" was being challenged. He defended the Revolution but admitted the validity of the question "Why did Stalin succeed in imposing his program and his methods on the Party and all of society?" He answered that Stalin played on the vanguard's impatience with the masses and its desire to achieve the Revolution's goals quickly, which led to limitation of creative discussion and to an authoritarian bureaucratic administrative system. The Party lost sight of humaneness in its pursuit of political expediency.[38]

As for the consequences of Stalinism, Gorbachev finally admitted the importance of this legacy. But deep reform, he argued, should not be understood to imply that the root of the USSR's problems lay in the socialist choice itself. Gorbachev blamed the 20th Party Congress for leaving the bureaucratic system itself generally unchanged: "It was able to survive, helped by the illusion that it was enough to remove the excesses of the Stalin regime for the liberated energy of socialism to bring our society to the supreme phase of communism in the very near future."[39] Gorbachev's reforms, on the contrary, relied on "the human factor" to dismantle the command administrative system.

By 1989, when Gorbachev yielded to the liberal establishment the right to question both the Leninist roots of the old system and the depth of change necessary to repudiate repression, liberals had already seized the initiative. Writers and Party members were pursuing their own beliefs, embracing the arrival of pluralism and the decay of *partiinost'*, and emphasizing disagreements instead of assisting Gorbachev in his efforts to develop a new, conciliatory Party line.

Nikita Khrushchev and the Party elite of his generation could not completely sever their bonds to Stalin. Khrushchev's speeches and memoirs show that though he detested Stalin's purges of the Party, he had trouble sorting out his own feelings of inferiority to and admiration of Stalin. Gorbachev, by contrast, was not encumbered by personal ties to Stalin or tainted by complicity in the purges. Thus Khrushchev sometimes

38. M. S. Gorbachev, "The Socialist Idea and Revolutionary Perestroika," *Pravda*, 26 November 1989, in *FBIS-Sov*, 27 November 1989, pp. 71, 73.
39. Ibid., p. 74.

defended Stalin personally but Gorbachev did not. Yet Khrushchev's emotional links to Stalin's victims and his own feelings of having been terrorized allowed him to anticipate the highly charged nature of rejecting repression. In contrast, despite a family history that included survivors of the purges, Gorbachev did not seem to identify with the victims of Stalinism.

Despite their differences, the leaders shared a commitment to rooting out the arbitrary use of force, loosening restrictions on speech, expanding political participation, and restoring people's enthusiasm for socialism. Gorbachev and Khrushchev began with classic liberalization strategies; believing that they could control reform, they opened up the political arena to allow some criticism. Khrushchev and Gorbachev were prepared to recognize past political errors to reinforce their calls for reform, but only because they believed they could preserve the Party's reputation for its accomplishments while limiting its responsibility for its crimes. In essence, they chose to romanticize the 1930s as a period of extraordinary industrial growth and tremendous social mobility, while placing most of the blame for the purges on Stalin and a few of his associates.

Like liberalizers everywhere, Khrushchev and Gorbachev polarized the political elite with their decisions to promote reform. Their respective decisions to sanction public condemnation of previous repressive policies sharply heightened tensions within the Communist Party. Reformers within the Party saw destalinization as an opportunity for the Party simultaneously to distance itself from Stalin's excesses and to display its confidence in society's assimilation of socialism. The liberal intelligentsia seized on reform and destalinization as processes that reinforced each other. Repudiation of repression became the cornerstone of and inspiration for independent, society-initiated liberal programs. As Dina Spechler noted, "In condemning Stalin and Stalinism, the *Novyi mir* writers were attempting to build an alliance for change that would involve the whole society . . . in effect challenging the population to assume a political role, urging it to make its voice heard on behalf of more thorough de-stalinization."[40] Increased participation, according to the liberals, would address the shortcomings of the socialist system—the need for critical feedback and the introduction of some checks on the leadership. In developing an institutional critique, however, more radical thinkers began to challenge the

40. Dina R. Spechler, *Permitted Dissent in the USSR: "Novy mir" and the Soviet Regime* (New York: Praeger, 1982), p. 148.

bases of socialism as Lenin had constructed them. If the Lenin period were disparaged, however, the Soviet government would find little in the past that justified its continued existence.

Conservatives, therefore, resisted any revelations of serious errors, arguing that they would discredit the Party in the eyes of those citizens who had faithfully served it. Citizens who trusted the Party would feel distress at having been abused and deceived, and those who had been injured by it would feel justified in attacking it. The conservative perspective on polarization of the Party over coming to terms with the past is well articulated by Ligachev: "At first this striving to restore historical justice was salutary: it emancipated people's minds, liberated them from a feeling of fear, and generated initiative. . . . But later, the stress shifted and some writers started talking about past lawlessness caustically, gloatingly; with castigation rather than healing. . . . In so doing, they were leading the readers to a single conclusion: the social system was guilty of everything, and therefore had to be changed."[41] Modern conservatives no longer urged that negative aspects of the past be forgotten altogether. Instead, a series of revisionist explanations diminished the impact of the purges. Some conservatives accepted the Stalin regime's claim that the existence of real internal enemies justified harsh use of force. Others emphasized the patriotic actions of millions of citizens in their daily lives, and pushed the consciousness and impact of repression to the periphery.

Khrushchev frequently succumbed to pressure to crack down on perceived threats, and his later inconsistent statements about Stalin both reflected and contributed to the fragility of liberalization. Khrushchev failed to create institutional guarantees to protect reformers; the system he created thus seemed liberalized on the surface but retained all the features of a totalitarian regime. Zhores Medvedev quotes an old Bolshevik friend as saying: "Many people think that we had a democracy under Khrushchev. That is nonsense. There was no democracy. There was *occasional* liberalism, but in the conditions in which we live, that does not mean very much. It's a humane form of arbitrariness."[42] Khrushchev's stabs at reform allowed conservatives to condemn him for "voluntarism." Indeed, his leadership was not based on solid norms; Khrushchev had

41. Yegor Ligachev, *Inside Gorbachev's Kremlin*, trans. Catherine A. Fitzpatrick, Michele A. Berdy, and Dorochna Dyrcz-Freeman (New York: Pantheon, 1993), p. 285.

42. Zhores Medvedev, *Ten Years after Ivan Denisovich*, trans. Hilary Sternberg (London: Macmillan, 1973), p. 196.

rejected orthodox Stalinism but could not consolidate a new regime without embracing a new system of beliefs.

Gorbachev embraced perestroika, glasnost, and democratization as a package without initially being aware that by committing himself to glasnost he had in effect endorsed destalinization. His concern with the primacy of economic reform at first blinded him to the need to take a stand on the purges. Thus, rather than seizing the initiative and getting credit from liberals for introducing the subject of destalinization, he reacted to debates that were already under way. Despite his admission that the Party had no monopoly on truth, Gorbachev did formulate and propagate a balanced Party line on Stalinism. But under glasnost, Gorbachev found his moderate, utilitarian approach to Soviet history under attack from both sides. When Nina Andreeva's letter ultimately forced Gorbachev to resolve the ambiguity in his definition of glasnost as free speech plus *partiinost'*, he remained firm in his commitment to pluralism in expression of ideas, even though it required him to sacrifice censorship of nonsocialist views and hence to prolong the public battle over how to treat Stalin's excesses.

Rifts over destalinization reveal the difficulties of liberalization in general and the specific weaknesses of Communist rule. During the Gorbachev era, both liberals and conservatives developed sophisticated and divergent rationales to reconcile the continuity of the regime with the admission of its criminal actions in the past. For a regime that based its legitimacy on its history, challenges to the virtues of Leninism and to the achievements of the push to construct socialism threatened to undermine its very basis. The passage of time did not make inverse legitimacy a better basis for reform communism. Nor was the Party more prepared to relinquish its messianic self-image. In the eyes of the leadership, reform still meant an improved leadership, not a new political system. Explorations of socialism for the seeds of repression were seen as malicious attacks, not as sincere efforts to improve the lives of citizens.

# 4 ANTISTALINISM
# AND THE DISSIDENTS

Soviet leaders were hardly alone in their desire to see an end to the ferocious, arbitrary mass purges. But only the top political leaders had the power to act and the liberty to criticize Stalin. Over time, however, liberal writers and artists used the thaw to test the boundaries of official tolerance of expressions of antistalinism. The cautiously worded articles and the scattering of literary works about the purges permitted by the authorities failed to provide an outlet for victims' anger and grief or for increasingly sophisticated critiques of Stalinism. Discussion of Stalin's "errors" had led some intellectuals to reflect on the roots and consequences of Stalinism, and to uncover what they interpreted as systemic flaws in Soviet-style rule. When Brezhnev led the retreat from liberalization, antistalinists had either to return to silence or to devise unofficial channels for dissent.

Organized dissent, what came to be known in the 1970s as the human rights movement, did not arise full-fledged from Stalin's ashes. Protest requires a complex transformation in political consciousness. Not only must one feel that the system has lost some legitimacy, but one must embrace the idea of asserting one's rights, which implies a demand for change. Then, to recruit and organize others, one must develop a sense of personal efficacy that can be translated into a rationale for collective action. After a problem has been identified and a solution envisioned, a protest movement can arise if individuals are brave enough to flaunt the law or tradition and strong enough to act collectively.[1]

How did post-Stalin society measure up according to these criteria for protest? Institutional reforms from above, especially the restoration of due process in cases involving political crimes, at least partially satisfied the desire for physical security and predictability, but people directly harmed by the terror remained fearful and isolated. Instead of receiving recognition, remuneration, and medical and psychological support, labor camp veterans were instructed not to speak about their experiences, and few received public acknowledgment of rehabilitation or full restoration of their positions. Some survivors even avoided associating with other ex-prisoners for fear of being accused of forming new criminal conspiracies.

Those who lost family members in the purges received no apologies, no reparations, and little information about the fate of their relatives. Many of these people also suffered in silence, hoping to avoid the stigma of being related to enemies of the people. Besides, in private each could cherish the belief that a genuine mistake had been made in the case of his or her own loved one without questioning whether the government could have made dozens or even hundreds of such "mistakes."[2] (Millions were beyond imagining.) Thus liberalization did not empower the survivors, did not even create outlets for exchange of information, mutual support, or collective expression of anger.

As for Soviet citizens at large, two decades of arbitrary arrests, massive penetration of social institutions by informers, and strict censorship left them in what one dissident called a "half-awake state of shock" after Stalin's death.[3] Claims that Soviet citizens under Stalin were victims of "hypnosis" or "mass hysteria" seem exaggerated, but it can be argued that people had grown so unaccustomed to thinking critically and independently about politics and were so totally cut off from reliable information about the purges that many Soviets had not grasped or formulated

1. Frances Fox Piven and Richard A. Cloward, *Poor People's Movements* (New York: Pantheon, 1977), pp. 3–4.

2. Evgenia Ginzburg and Lidia Chukovskaia describe such thinking during the 1930s. See Ginzburg, *Journey into the Whirlwind*, trans. Paul Stevenson and Max Hayward (New York: Harcourt Brace Jovanovich, 1967); and Chukovskaya, *The Deserted House*, trans. Aline B. Werth (Belmont, Mass.: Norland, 1967).

3. Ludmilla Alexeyeva, *Soviet Dissent: Contemporary Movements for National, Religious, and Human Rights*, trans. Carol Pearce and John Glad (Middletown, Conn.: Wesleyan University Press, 1985), p. 3.

opinions on Stalin's repressions. The arbitrariness of the purges undoubtedly made some people skeptical of the Party's pronouncements, but the atomization of society left many Soviets unwilling to speak of political matters, let alone criticize the regime.

Only after Khrushchev's secret speech did many people outside the camps begin to conceive of the scope and horror of the injustices perpetrated under Stalin's direction, and even then the information available was sketchy. Khrushchev's revelations spurred victims and accomplices (witting and unwitting), as well as the truly ignorant, to explore intellectually the phenomenon of Stalinism. How, they asked themselves, could the cult of personality arise in a Leninist party? Who should be held responsible for the arbitrary repressions? Was ignorance an excuse for passivity?[4] Official reformers gave only partially satisfactory answers and allowed only rare opportunities for expression of such misgivings. Ritual condemnations of Stalin alone could not answer the tentative questions from below about the roots of the terror; and *Novyi mir* and other liberal journals could publish only a small, discrete portion of the camp memoirs that flooded publishing houses after 1956. Thus citizens' curiosity about the terror and their desire to exchange experiences were frustrated by official policy.

As for assertion of individual rights and demands for change, even in the climate of the thaw such activity was problematic. Censorship blocked the publication of many forms of antistalinist criticism. Indeed, the official attitude toward criticism presented a unique difficulty. After Khrushchev's liberalized publications policy widened the sphere of permissible political debate in the USSR, Western scholars sought to distinguish among the types of criticism tolerated and rejected by the Party-state. Definitions of "constructive criticism" vs. "opposition," "dissent" vs. "protest," and "sectoral," "factional," and "subversive" dissent, however, all ultimately break down because of the Party's own basic incapacity to maintain consistent distinctions between loyal and disloyal opposition.[5]

4. For an eloquent account of personal awakening to the scope of the purges, see Raisa Orlova, *Memoirs,* trans. Samuel Cioran (New York: Random House, 1983), esp. chaps. 10–12; for an interesting debate over ignorance and complicity, see Priscilla Johnson with Leopold Labedz, *Khrushchev and the Arts: The Politics of Soviet Culture, 1962–64* (Cambridge: MIT Press, 1965), pp. 129–30.

5. Dina R. Spechler, *Permitted Dissent in the USSR: "Novy Mir" and the Soviet Regime* (New York: Praeger, 1982), p. xx; Howard L. Biddulph, "Protest Strategies of the Soviet

As Robert Dahl notes, the Party created a self-fulfilling prophecy by fearing and persecuting any sort of opposition, thus alienating potentially loyal critics, increasing the ranks of the "true opposition," and in the process affirming its suspicions that all opposition was dangerous.[6] Nevertheless, Party leaders distinguished between criticism they had solicited and criticism expressed spontaneously by outsiders. These distinctions did not go unnoticed by Soviet intellectuals. Thus Solzhenitsyn submitted his manuscript on the camps, which became *One Day in the Life of Ivan Denisovich*, to *Novyi mir* only after hearing Tvardovskii's speech at the 22d Party Congress, when he invited writers to submit straightforward, honest accounts of repressions.[7]

Any manuscript went through several layers of screening before it could be published—first by the editors of the journal or publishing house and then by the state censors. Once the censors vetoed a manuscript, its author had no legal means of reaching an audience. Under Khrushchev the Party came to tolerate, if not encourage, constructive criticism of the old regime in the official press, but it did not extend its blessing to private reproduction and circulation of manuscripts. Samizdat or "self-publishing" sidestepped the censors and, despite its meager output, was viewed by the Party as challenging the whole Communist monopoly on mass communication. Samizdat violated all the taboos surrounding permitted speech: it emanated spontaneously from below, it evaded all official controls, and worst of all, its production and circulation involved the formation of nonstate networks. Anyone caught distributing samizdat could expect a prison term.

The Party constantly spread the idea that reversal of the cult of personality was a matter for professional politicians. Khrushchev's secret speech and the subsequent release of political prisoners reinforced the notion that the Party could and would carry out destalinization itself. Until Khrushchev's ouster, few people directly questioned the regime's ability

---

Intellectual Opposition," in *Dissent in the USSR: Politics, Ideology, and People,* ed. Rudolf L. Tokes (Baltimore: Johns Hopkins University Press, 1975), pp. 96–97; Frederick C. Barghoorn, "Factional, Sectoral, and Subversive Opposition in Soviet Politics," in *Regimes and Oppositions,* ed. Robert Dahl (New Haven: Yale University Press, 1973), p. 39.

6. Dahl, Introduction to *Regimes and Oppositions,* p. 13.

7. Aleksandr I. Solzhenitsyn, *The Oak and the Calf: Sketches of Literary Life in the Soviet Union,* trans. Harry Willetts (New York: Harper & Row, 1975); for Tvardovskii's speech, see *XXII s"ezd Kommunisticheskoi Partii Sovetskogo Soiuza, 17–31 Oktiabriia 1961 goda: Stenograficheskii otchet* (Moscow: Gospolizdat, 1962), 2:529–30.

and intention to repudiate arbitrary rule, reform the legal system, and relax controls on free speech. Despite fluctuations in the literary and political climate, public events such as Khrushchev's denunciation of Stalin at the 22d Party Congress and the publication of *One Day in the Life of Ivan Denisovich* sustained the impression that destalinization had built up an unstoppable, if slow, momentum.

The final step in mental preparation for protest—the development of a sense of efficacy—depends on identifying some means for successfully influencing the political system. Though the totalitarian regime increased its attention to society during liberalization, it permitted only individualized, nonpolitical, private forms of participation. Totalitarian penetration of society can be seen in the Party's continued hostility to all manner of alternative associations, from factions in the CPSU to independent clubs of any sort. Khrushchev's limited liberalization of policy toward free speech definitely did not signal a similar relaxation of the Party's control over association. In attacking liberal intellectuals, conservatives merely had to cite the formation of "circles" around certain journals to raise alarms.

Overall, the history of independent association in the Soviet Union up until 1987 is brief and tragic. Lenin imprisoned many of his political opponents and outlawed factions in the Bolshevik Party, and Stalin extirpated any remaining traces of independent organization. He persecuted even inactive members of prerevolutionary parties. By the late 1930s the only "opposition groups" the NKVD could find were occasional tiny discussion clubs, usually comprising adolescents who leaned toward radical interpretations of Marx.[8] And, although political prisoners sometimes observed that at least in labor camps one could speak freely, even prisoners had to be careful to avoid informers. After Stalin's death the Party leadership retained its loathing of independent associations and continued to root out and destroy new tiny underground circles.[9]

As for "private" forms of asserting one's rights, petitions were the most common choice. The Russian tradition of sending letters and petitions to high authorities dates back to tsarist times and continued throughout the

---

8. See S. Pechuro and V. Bulgakov, "Delo Dzhalal-Abadskikh shkol'nikov: K istorii molodezhnykh antistalinskikh organizatsii," in *Zven"ia*, ed. N. G. Okhotin and A. B. Roginskii (Moscow: Progress, 1991); and Anatolii Zhigulin, *Chernye kamni*, in *Zarok: Povest', rasskazy, vospominaniia* (Moscow: Molodaia Gvardiia, 1989).

9. Alexeyeva, *Soviet Dissent*, p. 10.

Soviet period. Appeals for rehabilitation were individualized in form and substance—these were private requests for justice and mercy, not open critiques of state policy.[10] Under Khrushchev the state responded favorably to many appeals. In fact, Khrushchev used personal pleas for release and rehabilitation to impress on his colleagues the need for mass reviews and amnesties. By the mid-1960s, the Central Committee was receiving several petitions a month, usually signed by a half-dozen old Bolsheviks, asking for the commemoration of revolutionaries who had died in the purges.[11] Though the Society of Old Bolsheviks, banned in the 1930s, apparently never was revived, *joint* petitions by the elite surviving revolutionaries for *public* recognition of old Bolsheviks sometimes met with success. These activities came as close to lobbying as was possible under Khrushchev.

Another individualized reaction to destalinization which contained the seeds of opposition was the writing of fiction and memoirs about the purges. Just as Khrushchev relied on literary works to expound his vision of the Party line on Stalinism, many others aspired to use the same means to preserve and share their experiences of persecution and to propagate their own views of Stalin. The experience of the terror inspired not only cautious professional writers but thousands of amateurs. These new writers penned autobiographies as well as fiction and poetry. The effort to testify to one's own sufferings may well have provided some therapeutic benefits. Psychologists who work with torture victims note that in recounting their stories victims often realize that they should not feel guilty for what happened to them, that they were powerless to affect their treatment. In finding a sympathetic audience, survivors also feel a restoration of power and efficacy because they overcome the oblivion to which the state condemned them.[12]

10. The philosopher Pavel Shabalkin's petition to Khrushchev to prosecute the colleagues who slandered and denounced him unjustly is a rare, and unsuccessful, example of an appeal for broader justice. See his "I Accuse," in *An End to Silence: Uncensored Opinion in the Soviet Union*, ed. Steven F. Cohen (New York: Norton, 1982), pp. 124–28.

11. Many such petitions are preserved in Tsentr Khraneniia Sovremennoi Dokumentatsii, Moscow, fond 5, opis' 55.

12. Ana Julia Cienfuegos and Cristina Monelli, "The Testimony of Political Repression as a Therapeutic Instrument," *American Journal of Orthopsychiatry* 53, no. 1 (1983): 43–51; Shaun R. Whittaker, "Counseling Torture Victims," *Counseling Psychologist* 16 (April 1988): 272–78.

## Awakening to Action

Because the Khrushchev regime limited the amount of camp materials and the scope of criticism permissible in the Soviet press, official publications did not begin either to satisfy readers' interest or to make a dent in the outpouring of manuscripts. Writers need audiences. With official channels constricted, writers sought informal means of distributing their works. Samizdat versions of Evgenia Ginzburg's camp memoirs (published in the West as *Journey into the Whirlwind* and *Within the Whirlwind*) circulated widely in typescript. Many manuscripts went directly into samizdat after publishers rejected them as too daring. This was the beginning of dissent.[13]

From the mid-1950s to the mid-1960s, increasing numbers of citizens acquired the privacy to engage in criticism because Khrushchev's housing program reduced the number of communal apartments.[14] Urban liberals, including former prisoners, writers, artists, and university students, took advantage of increased private space to form *kompanii*—social groups of twenty to fifty people. One participant explains that the *kompanii* "performed the functions of publishing houses, speaker bureaus, salons, billboards, confession booths, concert halls, libraries, museums, counseling groups, sewing circles, knitting clubs, chambers of commerce, bars, clubs, restaurants, coffeehouses, dating bureaus, and seminars in literature, history, philosophy, linguistics, economics, genetics, physics, music and art."[15] These multipurpose gatherings brought people together in a forum other than the family in which they could freely exchange ideas. These loose circles in no way resembled formal organizations; given the regime's unwavering hostility toward independent collective activity, they engaged in private discussions, not public activism. Yet one can find in reactions to destalinization from above the seeds of an intellectual reawakening, a growing assertion of competence in the political sphere, and new forms of social organization. Early personal contacts and experience in sharing and disseminating antistalinist manuscripts formed the framework for the dissident movement.

13. Solzhenitsyn, *Oak and Calf.*
14. Leszek Kolakowski, "Amidst Moving Ruins," *Daedalus,* Spring 1992, p. 46.
15. Ludmilla Alexeyeva and Paul Goldberg, *The Thaw Generation: Coming of Age in the Post-Stalin Era* (Boston: Little, Brown, 1990), p. 83.

## REACTION TO REACTION: THE CHOICE TO DISSENT

Brezhnev's accession to power initiated a new political age in respect not only to official policies but also to protest and social organization. The defeat of a reformer and subsequent reversal of liberalization provided grounds both for increased protest and for withdrawal from the public realm. Growing official intolerance of opposition caused many people to retreat into self-censorship. The end of the thaw confirmed the cynicism of those already frustrated by Khrushchev's seemingly inconstant commitment to antistalinism or disillusioned with the Communist Party's rule in general. It disheartened and radicalized others who, though critical of the regime, had hoped the Party could reform itself. The Marxist Roy Medvedev, for instance, founded his samizdat journal to publicize and protest the circumstances of Khrushchev's fall. Thus, while Brezhnev's retreat from reform curtailed official and semiofficial expressions of liberalism, it politicized critics of the regime, forcing them to make the terrible choice between dangerous unsanctioned means of expression and a return to coerced silence. Those who chose dissent began to develop sophisticated radical critiques of Soviet rule based on their understanding of the horrors of Stalinism. And antistalinists and neostalinists continued to battle over substantive issues, including interpretation of Soviet history and the right and means to contest such issues.

Brezhnev's reversal of liberalization occurred slowly in most fields except culture, where conservatives moved quickly to consolidate their positions and to curb permitted dissent. In October 1965, just a year after Khrushchev fell from power, writers were instructed not to submit any more negative treatments of the 1930s or prison camp stories.[16] This retreat from criticism of Stalin did not surprise skeptics, but for other liberals each step backward renewed the inner turmoil they had experienced since the unmasking of Stalin. Solzhenitsyn aptly captured the gap between those already disabused of illusions about Soviet rule and those who hesitated to go beyond sanctioned reform by contrasting his own political development with that of his friend and supporter Tvardovskii: "My mind had been cleared by my first years of imprisonment. For [Tvardovskii] the same process had begun with Khrushchev's speech at the Twentieth Congress. But for him as for the Party at large, it was soon

16. Spechler, *Permitted Dissent*, p. 218.

slowed down, tangled in contradictions, and even put into reverse."[17] But when the official press refused to publish Tvardovskii's poem "By Right of Memory," Tvardovskii—who as an "in-system reformer" had always eschewed samizdat—allowed it to circulate privately in early 1969.[18] Publication of this poem in an émigré journal, albeit without Tvardovskii's permission, hastened the end of his career.

The contents of both literary and nonfiction samizdat of the mid-1960s demonstrate the force of pent-up antistalinism. Not only did articles about Stalinism dominate Medvedev's political magazine, but an entire journal—called *Crime and Punishment*—devoted itself to exposing the names and fates of Stalin's informants and executioners.[19] Not all underground authors came to dissidence from prison camps or from the loss of a family member to the purges, but many had experienced one or both.

Even Party officials recognized that the injustices of the Stalin era provided potent motivation for protest. In a revealing conversation, Iurii Andropov, then head of the KGB, allegedly told Viktor Krasin, who had recanted his political activism under KGB pressure: "No one will permit Stalinism to come back. We are very firm about this in the Politburo . . . I know your father and the father of Piotr Iakir [Krasin's codefendant] were killed during the great purges. I myself was almost arrested at the time . . . I waited for my own arrest every day. But I was very lucky. That's why I understand the origins of your feelings toward the Soviet Union."[20] Recognition of the impact of the purges on individuals, however, did not equal tolerance. The Brezhnev administration had decided to take any means necessary to halt what it saw as destructive, unpatriotic criticism of Stalin. With the arrest of the professional writers Andrei Siniavskii and Iulii Daniel in September 1965, Brezhnev initiated a two-decade, often public struggle against "anti-Soviet elements."

Under pseudonyms, Siniavskii and Daniel had arranged for overseas publication of their frank stories about Soviet life—so-called *tamizdat* (published there [*tam*]), as distinguished from samizdat (published by oneself [*sam*]). Using the soon notorious articles 190 and 70 of the USSR

17. Solzhenitsyn, *Oak and Calf,* p. 132.

18. Spechler, *Permitted Dissent,* pp. 213–18, 225.

19. Excerpts from *Crime and Punishment* can be found in Peter Reddaway, ed., *Uncensored Russia: Protest and Dissent in the USSR* (New York: McGraw-Hill, 1972); an entire issue is reproduced in *Sobranie dokumentov samizdata* (Munich, 1972), as 1025.

20. Quoted in Mark Hopkins, *Russia's Underground Press: The Chronicle of Current Events* (New York: Praeger, 1983), p. 79.

and RSFSR criminal codes, which prohibit "deliberately false statements derogatory to the Soviet state and social system" and "slanderous fabrications" respectively, the court convicted the two writers of anti-Soviet propaganda on the basis of the words they put into their characters' mouths.[21] The trial of the samizdat publishers Iurii Galanskov and Aleksandr Ginzburg followed on the heels of the Siniavskii-Daniel convictions. These trials, with their facade of civilization and respectability, made it clear that though Brezhnev would not use extreme Stalinist methods, even indirect uncensored speech would lead to prosecution and imprisonment in a labor camp or a psychiatric ward.

The Galanskov-Ginzburg case triggered a cycle of civic protest and suppression. Small public demonstrations in December 1965 and January 1967 immediately after the two were arrested led to more arrests and more protests—in print, not in public squares. In this manner antistalinism and contemporaneous defense of human rights became inextricably intertwined as expressions of old grievances resulted in new repressions and fresh grievances.

Public protest intensified in the late 1960s, when a reversal of destalinization turned into a rehabilitation of Stalin. Having banned fresh criticism of Stalin, the Brezhnev regime began to revive the cult of personality in the press and prepared for a lavish commemoration of Stalin's ninetieth birthday in 1969. Ultimately the regime shelved its plans to celebrate Stalin's birth, but it placed a marble bust on his grave near the Kremlin wall. At this juncture, protest against neostalinism finally took the form of direct policy critiques. One approach drew explicitly on Soviet law to support radical demands. In an unpublished letter to the Party journal *Kommunist*, Petr Iakir cited the RSFSR criminal code to charge Stalin "as the greatest criminal our country has ever known."[22] And while petitioners still turned to official bodies, they used samizdat to try to influence public opinion as well. The writer Aleksei Kosterin, for instance, directed his complaints about the Party's reversal of liberalization to the Central Committee, *Pravda,* and his regional party organization, but he also passed copies to samizdat circles.[23] Legalistic and policy aspects of pro-

21. Both articles appear in full ibid., p. 14. For a complete account of the Siniavskii-Daniel trial, see L. S. Eremina, ed., *Tsena metafory: Ili prestuplenie i nakazanie Siniavskogo i Danielia,* comp. E. M. Velikanova (Moscow: Kniga, 1989).

22. Pyotr Yakir, "A Posthumous Indictment of Stalin," in Cohen, *End to Silence,* pp. 56–61.

23. Reproduced in Cornelia Gerstenmaier, *The Voices of the Silent,* trans. Susan Hecker (New York: Hart, 1972), pp. 410–14.

An admirer of Stalin lays flowers at his grave on the anniversary of the leader's death. Moscow, 5 March 1991. *Photo by Kathleen E. Smith*

test, as well as underground dissemination, marked significant departures from earlier timid petitions pleading for reform.

The content of post-Khrushchev protests also demonstrated new levels of sophistication in analyses of Stalinism. For instance, Lidia Chukovskaia's letter to *Izvestiia* on the fifteenth anniversary of Stalin's death made an eloquent plea for social justice for the victims of repression and for "unravel[ing] the knot of cause and effect." She also directly linked the contemporary treatment of dissidents to the purges: "Even if our memories should fail us, the current trials over the word and the dry crackle of contemporary newspaper articles would still convey to us the familiar stench of past ashes."[24] Medvedev probed even more deeply into the sources of support for neostalinism in his samizdat essay "The Danger of a Revival of Stalinism."[25] Both writers openly connected Stalinism with Brezhnevism, while linking antistalinism to free speech, human rights, the rule of law, and even modernization.

Two final factors must be mentioned regarding the development of the human rights movement: the Warsaw Treaty Organization's invasion of Czechoslovakia and the creation of the human rights periodical *Khronika tekushchikh sobytii* (Chronicle of Current Events). The "Prague spring" inspired Soviet liberals, who hoped that they too might someday find reform Communists with whom they could work to liberalize the political system. But Brezhnev's use of military force to crush reform Communists and their civic allies in Prague demonstrated not just the regime's political intolerance but also its willingness to employ force against civilians. Many observers date the human rights movement from 25 August 1968, when seven dissidents demonstrated in Red Square against Soviet intervention in Czechoslovakia, perhaps because this gesture was in defense of the basic rights of others and was aimed at Soviet and world public opinion. In and of itself, criticism of Soviet foreign policy represented an escalation in confrontation, a greater encroachment on the Party's turf.

Events in Czechoslovakia also added momentum to the trend toward radical analysis of the political system. The growing association of Stalinism and Brezhnevism in the late 1960s is epitomized by a poem by a nineteen-year-old Moscow student, Valeria Novodvorskaia:

---

24. Lidia Chukovskaya letter to *Izvestiia*, ibid., pp. 433–40.
25. Roy Medvedev, "The Danger of a Revival of Stalinism," in Cohen, *End to Silence*, pp. 153–57.

I thank you, Party, for lies and deceit,
For cleverly organized smear campaigns,
For crackling gunshots on Wenceslas Square,
For all the lies that continue to come,

For ultramodern housing complexes
Supported by the crimes of the past.

　　　．　．　．

For the bitterness and confusion,
For that crippling, criminal silence. . . .[26]

Novodvorskaia broke the "crippling, criminal silence" enforced by the Party by dropping copies of her poem from a theater balcony on Soviet Constitution Day in 1969. She was detained immediately and imprisoned, like many dissidents, in a psychiatric hospital.

Novodvorskaia's poem and information about the fates of the Red Square demonstrators would have had almost no effect without the newly established underground *Khronika*. Petitions addressed simply to Soviet authorities met with silence and various forms of retaliation against the signers, so dissidents opted to publicize their appeals and broaden their audiences by creating a journal. One copy went immediately to the foreign press, which broadcast excerpts back to the USSR by radio.[27]

From its inception, *Khronika* was a unique vehicle for dissent. Its editors strove to be objective, dispassionate, and scrupulously accurate, in part because articles 190 and 70 technically applied only to dissemination of false statements. *Khronika* reproduced petitions, protests, trial transcripts, and other documents of the human rights movement, nationalist movements, and religious organizations. It collected information from the Russian provinces and other Soviet republics and fed the data to its far-flung readers and to the foreign press. Constant pressure by the KGB spurred *Khronika* to invent a compartmentalized system of information gathering: a person with a news item had to pass it to his or her distributor of the paper, rather than attempt to contact the editors directly. This system hampered the formation of organizations but limited the damage done by individual arrests. Persecution caused frequent turnovers in editors, limited the journal's growth, and occasionally led to temporary sus-

26. Gerstenmaier, *Voices of the Silent*, pp. 425–26.

27. Natalia Gorbanevskaia finished the first issue of *Khronika* on 1 May 1968. It contained a copy of the UN Declaration on Human Rights as well as seven news stories. See Hopkins, *Russia's Underground Press*, p. 1.

pension of publication. Nevertheless, in the 1970s the chief functions of the dissident movement became collection and dissemination of information regarding human rights violations.

The totalitarian regime's intolerance of most forms of criticism and all forms of independent organization left an indelible imprint on the dissident movement. Even during the thaw people who wished to explore the roots of Stalinism were barred from the public arena. But the relaxation of repression did allow liberals to engage in consciousness-raising experiences such as the exchange of samizdat and the formation of *kompanii*. When the reversal of liberalization ended the myth that the Party would consistently move toward a more open political system, a brave few chose to protest through unconventional channels. Though Brezhnev never reverted to mass arbitrary purges, he did enforce censorship and the ban on association.

Constant surveillance and harassment led to a uniquely compartmentalized "movement." Though dissidents reached thousands through samizdat and foreign radio, they could not break the Party's monopoly on organization. Dissent did not take the form of traditional political opposition. As one former dissident observed a month after the Soviet regime collapsed: "We never advocated revolution bloodless or otherwise, and never tried to create a political organization. . . . Perhaps our strategy of moral resistance contributed in some way to the 'velvet' nature of the anti-Communist revolutions. Yet if that is so, our refusal to organize an opposition political force must also bear some responsibility for the messy transition the country now faces."[28] The human rights movement did not constitute a resurrection of civil society of the sort that has occurred elsewhere. Instead, a loose network of individual dissidents formed in response to the end of the thaw and struggled to survive in the face of persecution.

The form of popular mobilization was not the only aspect of dissent affected by the regime's insistence on total control. From the very first illegal protest by representatives of deported nationalities in 1956, the dissident movement was inextricably linked to antistalinism.[29] The purges provided the strongest rationale for questioning the legitimacy of

28. Vladimir Bukovsky, "Tumbling Back to the Future," *New York Times Magazine*, 12 January 1992, p. 34.
29. Alexeyeva, *Soviet Dissent*, p. 7.

the Communist Party's rule. The revival of memory holes under Brezhnev led some dissidents to explore the continuities in rule between Stalin and Brezhnev and to develop a critique of the regime that focused on institutions rather than personalities. Dissidents recognized that the regime deliberately manipulated history to legitimate itself, and that it would not long tolerate pluralism.

Questioning of the regime's legitimacy and assertion of demands for change did not suffice to turn individual grievances into effective political influence. Along with frustration, however, came a better understanding of the roots and consequences of arbitrary rule. The publication of Solzhenitsyn's *Gulag Archipelago* in the West in 1973 revealed new information on the purges; and the author's expulsion from the USSR underlined the Communist Party's retreat from self-criticism and sparked new calls for openness about the purges.[30] Stalinism remained a subject for dissidents throughout the Brezhnev era, though its centrality declined in the face of new persecutions. The human rights movement supported glasnost in history, but ongoing repression left dissidents with little time to devote to history for its own sake.[31] Questions about coming to terms with earlier repressions were buried by the Soviet government, but they were not resolved. Suppression of discussion of the past led not only to frustration but to a more radical and informed constituency interested in a settlement of accounts with the old regime.

30. See Larisa Bogoraz, "Open Letter to the President of the KGB Iu.V. Andropov," 9 May 1975, AS no. 2159 in *Materialy samizdata*, no. 26–27, 1975.
31. Robert M. Slusser, "History and the Democratic Opposition," in Tokes, *Dissent in the USSR*, pp. 329–30.

# 5 FROM PETITIONERS TO PROTESTERS: THE BIRTH OF THE MEMORIAL SOCIETY

In the late 1980s rejection of Stalin's repressions served as a catalyst for mass organization. Though fifty years had passed since the height of the purges, commemoration of Stalin's victims sparked fierce debate and spurred both politically radical and moderate citizens to venture into the newly emerging public sphere. The formation of the Memorial Society illuminates the evolving desire of many citizens from diverse walks of life to remember and reinterpret the experience of state-sponsored repression. Most important, the origins of the movement demonstrate how nonstate actors originally attempted to advance their objectives within the framework of glasnost and perestroika, and how, ironically, the state's reactions provoked a more radical critique of Soviet rule.

Gorbachev extended glasnost not only to the official media and creative intelligentsia but to the public at large: let everyone participate in reform. Party ideologists touted a new doctrine of "socialist pluralism," which seemed to mean tolerance of constructive criticism aimed at achieving the leadership's goals. Socialist pluralism differed from permitted dissent in allowing self-constituted social groups to express their special interests. Gorbachev thus took the first step toward recognizing the merit of a public forum for popular participation in politics. Socialist pluralism, however, bore little resemblance to a "public sphere" as the term is understood in the West, as "a set of arrangements allowing people freely and openly to address one another concerning public matters, to judge, support or criticize the policies of authorities and to organize themselves into groups in order to shape public opinion and promote alternative policies."[1] Gorbachev did not intend to put the people in a position to judge or protest his policies. As for the freedom to form political organizations, legislation defining the rights of independent associations was passed only in 1991. When Latin American dictatorships were undergoing liberalization, the opening up of the public sphere permitted the resurrection of civil society. But in the USSR there were no dormant parties or trade unions to be revived. Social groups and shared interests had to be generated from scratch. Moreover, there was no commonly held vision of ideal state-society relations. What did reformed communism look like? How much criticism was too much for a "liberal" CPSU to tolerate? Could liberalization ever be irreversible? Would-be activists operated in an environment of profound uncertainty.

Who was ready to participate in politics under the novel but contingent liberalization promoted by Gorbachev? Industrialization, urbanization, and education created—even in the USSR—an informed and articulate public. Urban professionals, therefore, might take the lead in pursuing civil society to represent their material and status interests.[2] A second potential constituency for mobilization might be the younger generation, who, because they had not been directly exposed to mass repressions, would be less afraid to challenge the state's restrictions on speech and association.[3] Young Soviet citizens of the 1980s had not experienced the disappointment of those who suffered from the reversal of the thaw. But why would either of these groups be interested in Stalin's repressions? To answer this question we must return to Guillermo O'Donnell's theory of a "rebound" in mobilization after periods of repression, and look at the actual emergence of Memorial and its place in the new associational scene.[4]

1. Gianfranco Poggi, *The State: Its Nature, Development, and Prospects* (Stanford: Stanford University Press, 1990), p. 151.

2. Moshe Lewin, *The Gorbachev Phenomenon* (Berkeley: University of California Press, 1988).

3. Krzysztof Nowak, "Covert Repressiveness and the Stability of a Political System: Poland at the End of the Seventies," *Social Research* 55 (Spring/Summer 1988): 203.

4. Guillermo O'Donnell, "On the Fruitful Convergence of Hirschman's *Exit, Voice, and Loyalty* and *Shifting Involvements:* Reflections on the Argentine Experience," in *Development, Democracy, and the Art of Trespassing*, ed., Alejandro Foxley (Baltimore: Johns Hopkins University Press, 1986), p. 261.

O'Donnell attributed intense interest in public life after periods of forced inactivity to the rediscovered pleasures of open exchange of opinions with sympathetic peers. The sharing of grievances may act as a healing process for people who feel wounded by the system. Participation offers the individual a new identity, new comrades, and, when it takes the form of dialogue with the authorities, a new feeling of empowerment. Soviet citizens had decades of suppressed grievances, but the intensity and duration of the state's hostility toward independent groups had conditioned people to avoid politics. Thus any rebound of activism might well involve old grievances and symbolic concerns rather than material demands or direct challenges to the current administration. But an issue had to have strong emotional and political resonance to overcome decades of inactivity and to stand out among the long list of complaints of the average citizen. Acknowledgment of victims of repression had ethical and political aspects, personal and public sides, and possible cross-generational appeal, since repudiation of past human rights abuses could be linked to a new, more principled way of life.

## The Emergence of "Informals," 1986–1987

The first independent organizations to surface during the Gorbachev era were the so-called *neformaly,* or "informals." In 1986 hundreds of clubs appeared, formed for the most part by young people who spontaneously came together on the basis of shared interests ranging from heavy metal rock music to avant-garde art, from soccer to socialist theory. Most informals consisted of a dozen or so people and had no formal membership or structure. The label "informal" referred not to the internal nature of the groups but to their status as nonstate organizations. Although Gorbachev sanctioned independent associations in principle, they had no legal standing, so they could not officially open bank accounts, sign contracts, or rent meeting space unless local authorities agreed to grant them registration under an old law of the 1930s. The treatment of amateur groups, therefore, depended on the attitudes of local Party-state officials.

The Party's reputation for intolerance of any encroachment on its domain led political activists to work cautiously. Few groups that emerged in 1986–87 had any overtly political agenda; the exceptions were "grievance committees," which focused on single issues such as the environment, and "discussion clubs," which ostensibly brought together supporters of perestroika to analyze the possibilities for economic, social, and political reform. Discussion clubs served several valuable functions in the absence of a free press or civil society. They encouraged intellectual debate and the refinement of political ideas and they provided stepping-stones for further organization by serving as forums where like-minded people could meet. Like the *kompanii* of the Khrushchev era, discussion clubs engaged in consciousness raising, but the new groups considered themselves to be genuine organizations.

Two serious discussion clubs sprang up in Moscow in early 1987. Former political prisoners whose offense had been participation in an underground socialist group, together with newly politicized young people, made up the core of the Klub Sotsial'nykh Initsiativ (Club for Social Initiatives), or KSI; liberal academics and prominent intellectuals formed the Klub Perestroika under the auspices of the Central Econometrics Institute.[5] Both groups exploited the promise of perestroika to experiment with politicized association. Despite their different constituencies, these groups combined forces under the Klub Perestroika in the spring of 1987. They then drew more members—including radical opponents of the Soviet system—and briefly formed what one observer has called "a socialist opposition."[6]

The "radicals" in this coalition were recently returned political prisoners who had already formed explicitly anti-Soviet associations under the leadership of Valeria Novodvorskaia and Igor' Tsar'kov. In 1987 Novodvorskaia's seminar "Democracy and Humanism" developed a program calling for the amnesty of political prisoners, including religious believers and participants in national movements; removal of articles covering political crimes from the Soviet constitution; and full democratization.[7] Though factions eventually split the club, the temporary union

5. Vyacheslav Igrunov, "Public Movements: From Protest to Political Self-Consciousness," in *After Perestroika: Democracy in the Soviet Union*, ed. Brad Roberts and Nina Belyaeva (Washington, D.C.: CSIS, 1991), pp. 16–17.

6. Mikhail Maliutin, "Neformaly v perestroike: Opyt i perspektivy," in *Inogo ne dano*, ed. Iurii Afanas'ev (Moscow: Progress, 1988), p. 220.

7. Igrunov, "Public Movements," p. 18; Michael McFaul, "The Last Hurrah for the CPSU" (an interview with Iurii Skubko), *Radio Liberty Report on the USSR* 2 (27 July 1990): 11; "On the Necessity of Constitutional Reforms," *Samizdat Bulletin*, no. 177 (Spring 1988), pp. 1–3.

Three of the former dissidents who founded Memorial (from left to right): Pavel Kudiukin, Arsenii Roginskii, Viacheslav Igrunov, Moscow, 1989. *Courtesy Interregional Memorial Society Archives, Moscow.*

of in-system reformers, dissident socialists, and genuine revolutionaries made the Klub Perestroika a springboard for the formation of politicized, action-oriented organizations, including Memorial.[8]

The liberal press had already begun its campaign to fill in blank spots in history when the discussion clubs took up the issue of destalinization. At a KSI meeting in June 1987 Iurii Samodurov, a thirty-five-year-old geologist whose grandmother survived Stalin-era labor camps, proposed that the club resurrect Khrushchev's idea of a monument to the victims of the terror. The current leadership, Samodurov hoped, would respond favorably to such a petition. Together with the KSI members Pavel Kudiukin, Viktor Kuzin, and Iurii Skubko, Samodurov began to outline his project for rallying public support for a monument. Pushed by the former Odessa

8. Maliutin, "Neformaly"; Igrunov, "Public Movements."

dissident Viacheslav Igrunov, Samodurov extended the scope of his idea for a monument to include *all* victims of Soviet repressions, not just those who had been officially rehabilitated. Igrunov also persuaded Samodurov to address the petition not to Party leaders but to the nation's ostensibly elected organ, the Supreme Soviet.[9]

At this stage, Samodurov and his associates were not pursuing material, status, organizational, or political advantages. They acted out of idealism and a moral concern to honor those who had suffered past injustices. Though the project had a concrete end in view—a monument—mobilization around the commemoration of victims was more expressive than instrumental. For the regime a positive response to expressive mobilization would also have entailed more ideological than material costs. And Samodurov sought to minimize criticism of the present government. A petition to the authorities was peaceful and respectful, and it demonstrated faith in the new leadership's commitment to glasnost. Admittedly, some organizers sought to generate public support by playing on resentment toward the executioners, who not only went unpunished but were rewarded with good pensions.[10] But by commemorating only victims and saying nothing about perpetrators, the monument would only indirectly raise the potentially damaging issue of accountability. The project's most controversial aspect was the broad definition of repressions as having extended before and after the cult of personality.

Samodurov presented his program for a citizens' group to raise funds for a monument and to oversee its construction at a conference on the role of civic initiative in perestroika jointly sponsored by the Moscow City Party Committee and the KSI in August 1987, which brought together several hundred participants in various aspects of the informals movement. The proposal attracted both radical dissidents and moderate scholars. Its practical and moral aspects appealed to moderates, and radicals saw it as a means to hold Gorbachev to his promise of filling in blank spots in Soviet history. As for the authorities, one participant recalled, Samodurov's speech "caused no small panic among the Party apparatchiks, who, so to speak, controlled this meeting. Here was this anti-Soviet organization that had spoken out against the repressions of Leninist

---

9. Interview with Viacheslav Igrunov, head of the Moscow Bureau for Information Exchange and member of the Working Collegium of the Interregional Memorial Society, Moscow, 14 April 1991.

10. See the article by the Leningrad activist Elena Zelinskaia, "Pepel klaasa stuchit v moe serdtse!" AS no. 6132, *Materialy samizdata*, 22 January 1988.

times, not just Stalinist times. Stalinist repressions were then almost—not quite but almost—permitted [as a topic of discussion]."[11]

Though the "radical" results of the conference never made it into the Soviet press, a group called To Keep Alive the Memory of Victims of Repression (later renamed Memorial) quickly coalesced in the months after the August conference. It united approximately a dozen young professionals and scholars.[12] The absence of survivors of the purges in the early stages of the movement may be ascribed to the fact that, without the benefit of publicity, all of the informals were developing simultaneously from the same small pools of rebellious youth, educated young professionals, and former dissidents, and only the dissidents included any older people.

Memorial was not the only informal to take an interest in antistalinism. The radical democrats who participated in the "Democracy and Humanism" seminar cited current and earlier repressions as reasons to oppose Communist rule, including the Gorbachev regime. But radicals mobilized with a specific instrumental aim—to destroy the totalitarian regime. In May 1988, the radicals merged several tiny groups into a self-proclaimed political party called Demokraticheskii Soiuz (Democratic Union), or DS. DS held numerous unsanctioned demonstrations, many of which explicitly commemorated Soviet repressions.[13] But for DS rejection of repressions was only one means of attracting adherents to its larger goal of destroying the Party-state system.

## TESTING THE WATERS: CONCILIATION OR CONFRONTATION?

The informal associations that arose from 1986 to 1988 were bound to test the regime's commitment to liberalization and its tolerance for diverse

11. Interview by the author and Michael McFaul with Iurii Skubko, founding member of Memorial and Demokraticheskii Soiuz, Moscow, 2 March 1991.

12. A document dated 7 October 1987 lists members as Iurii Samodurov (candidate in geological sciences), Lev Ponomarev (doctor of physics and math), Pavel Kudiukin (historian), Iurii Skubko (economist), Viktor Kuzin (lawyer), Dmitrii Leonov (economist), Mikhail Kovalenko (lawyer), Aleksei Zverev (translator), Gennadii Demin (theatrical director), Dmitrii Iurasov (amateur historian), and Evgenii Krasnikov (profession not given). Other early members include Aleksandr Vaisberg (historian-archivist), Vladimir Lysenko (teacher of scientific communism), Nina Braginskaia (philologist), and Elena Zhemkova (graduate student). Author's collection.

13. Ekspress-Khronika, no. 21, 27 December 1987, p. 1.

agendas and independent policy initiatives. The Party leadership had initiated an experiment in easing its monopoly on debate and organization, but it had not relinquished its self-ascribed role as final arbiter in all political matters. If the Party came to view conflict as a normal part of politics, it might open institutional channels to facilitate participation. If the Party found conflict destabilizing and destructive, it could reverse liberalization by co-opting or suppressing civic groups. Activists also had an option: they could try to work within the system to become accepted representatives of certain discrete interests or try to polarize society and destroy the regime.

The potential for antagonistic state-society relations can be seen in the clashes between the radical DS and Moscow officials. DS took an unyielding, hostile position toward Soviet rule; and though it eschewed violence, DS tried to undermine the regime by propaganda and protest. To publicize the contradictions between the regime's talk of glasnost and democratization and its restrictive policies, for instance, DS challenged the ban on unauthorized demonstrations. Rather than ask permission to hold a public rally, DS would simply notify the city authorities that it would be holding one; and the militia would consistently, forcefully, and rapidly break it up.

DS further challenged the authorities by declaring itself a political party in opposition to the CPSU. After the first day of DS's founding conference, authorities detained delegates from other cities and shipped them back home; on the second day they seized the suburban dacha where participants attempted to meet, so that the remaining delegates had to finish their work on the platform of the local train station.[14] In general, radicals suffered sorely for their stance: KSI lost its meeting place when it raised an uproar over a violent attack on hippies by the militia; after an antistalinist demonstration in March 1988, Perestroika-88, the radical offshoot of Klub Perestroika, was driven out of the basement it had rented as a meeting place. Like the human rights movement under Brezhnev, DS became swept up in a cycle of repression and protest, and its radical goals attracted only a few brave souls. DS gained considerable notoriety for its open anti-Gorbachev stance, but it could not muster the resources or space to pursue its objectives seriously.

14. Igrunov, "Public Movements"; interview by the author and Michael McFaul with Viktor Kuzin, founding member of Memorial and Demokraticheskii Soiuz, Moscow, 22 May 1991.

Memorial, in contrast, hoped to exploit liberalization to achieve moderate, concrete goals, especially to create a forum for survivors to express their grief and anger publicly. Thus Memorial activists tried a variety of approaches in 1987 to win over both the public and the authorities. Rather than hold an illegal rally, in November Memorial sent members in pairs onto the Moscow streets to inform citizens about the group's existence and to ask them to sign a petition asking the Supreme Soviet for permission to construct a monument to be dedicated to the victims of Stalinism and a research center devoted to the history of the repressions.[15] Memorial had already informed the Moscow city authorities that it intended to do so, "in accord with the Party line on restoration of historical truth regarding all stages of the development of our society and government." The group listed the times and locations at which members would appear and expressed the hope that the city council would support its initiative.[16] But the militia and plainclothes KGB agents broke up each of Memorial's five forays into the streets, detained its activists, and confiscated its materials.

Conflict with the militia ostensibly focused on two main points: whether two people equaled a demonstration and hence fell under the city's rules on public gatherings in Moscow; and the militia's claim that "the people don't need Memorial"—to which Memorial responded that they were trying to find out what people wanted by sampling public opinion. The police interrogated the activists, threatened them with repercussions at work, and on occasion turned them over to the courts for "malicious failure to obey legal orders of representatives of the authorities."[17]

When the court levied fines on the "demonstrators," it informed their employers; thus the Institute of Africa, where Iurii Skubko worked as a researcher, received a letter from a judge lamenting Skubko's "lack of political consciousness" and requesting that the institute "improve the

---

15. "Khronika 'Memoriala,'" *Tochka zreniia,* no. 4, 1987, pp. 1–4; and "Obrashchenie v Verkhovnyi Sovet SSSR," author's collection.

16. Dmitrii Leonov, Lev Ponomarev, and Iurii Samodurov to V. T. Saikin, president of Moscow City Executive Committee, 13 November 1987, ibid.

17. Petition to the Moscow city procurator from V. A. Kuzin, D. N. Leonov, L. A. Ponomarev, Iu. V. Samodurov, Iu. S. Skubko, and A. D. Vaisberg, members of the initiative group To Keep Alive the Memory of Victims of Repression, 16 November 1987, ibid.

political-educational work in [Skubko's] work collective."[18] By holding the work collective responsible for the individual employee's private actions, the authorities had exerted tremendous pressure on dissidents without recourse to legal sanctions. Skubko, however, was not a Party member, so he could not be forced to attend the Party meeting convened to reprimand him. In his letter declining to appear, he explained that his fine had been suspended pending the outcome of Memorial's appeal. Memorial lost its appeal, but—apparently because of the new political atmosphere—Skubko's institute took no further steps to punish him.[19] Other institutions were less forgiving, and Memorial, like DS, was swept up in the struggle to survive as an organization.

Frustrated by constant interference in their efforts to operate openly and independently, in December 1987 Memorial activists tried more conciliatory measures. In an exceedingly polite and restrained letter, Memorial expressed the "hope that partnership and cooperation of informal initiative groups and legislative and Party organs in the realization of important social projects will become an important factor in the development and acceleration of perestroika." Memorial explained what it could do to this end and what official organs could do to support its efforts: guarantee the group's registration, give it documents stating that it was not illegal to gather signatures in the streets, allow the press to print information about Memorial, and intervene to halt the "illegal activities of the KGB and militia" against members circulating petitions.[20]

This letter led to a meeting between the group's members and officials of the Propaganda Department of the Moscow Party organization. These Party officials, though purporting to support a monument to Stalin's victims, resolutely opposed the Memorial initiative. "Until the tasks of economic reform are completed," they said, "it is premature to solicit workers' participation in resolving other problems. . . . This question [of commemorating Stalin's victims] requires serious educational work and serious agitation. And we have other tasks now. You are arousing people's interest in the idea of a monument, which is premature at present." As for

18. People's Judge G. N. Satskov, People's Court of the Kievskii region, to secretary of the Party committee of the Institute of Africa of the Academy of Sciences of the USSR, n.d., ibid.

19. Interview with Iurii Skubko, 2 March 1991.

20. Members of Memorial to Iu. V. Liubtsev, deputy head of Department of Propaganda, Brezhnevskii raikom, CPSU, 3 December 1987, author's collection.

relaxation of the Party's monopoly on political agitation, they added, liberalization meant only that some initiative would be "transferred to the trade unions and the Komsomol." Agitation might be conducted in the workplace, but not in the street.

On a practical level, the officials noted that the Ministry of Culture had already planned the construction of monuments in Moscow through the year 2010, and suggested that the group's members could volunteer their labor for the already approved statues of important victims, such as General Mikhail Tukhachevskii. Or interested citizens could gather historical information on the purges in public libraries (as distinguished from Party-state archives, which contained unpublished documents). When Memorial activists defended their initiative, the Party officials said, "We'll find ways to block you . . . to stop your activity."[21] Thus, despite Memorial's conciliatory approach, the Party refused even minimal cooperation and insisted on control over the political agenda.

Beyond a reflexive reaction against unofficial political activity, the Party representatives' stance against independent mobilization reflected the old fear that to lift the taboo on discussions of Soviet history was to open Pandora's box. Indeed, the call for commemoration of the regime's past victims threatened the Party's reform program, but not by diverting attention from critical economic matters. As under Khrushchev, reassessment of previous repressive policies unleashed dissatisfaction with the continued absence of meaningful guarantees of individual rights. The Party's suggestions for appropriate forms and forums for citizens to participate in perestroika also exposed the gulf between the regime's and even moderate activists' conceptions of a public sphere.

## MEMORIAL'S STRUGGLE FOR MASS ORGANIZATION, 1988–1989

After both confrontation and conciliation had failed to win publicity and support for Memorial, activists began to rethink their goals and strategies. In early 1988 Lev Ponomarev and Iurii Samodurov floated the

21. "Konspekt besedy v MGK KPSS s predstaviteliami initsiativnoi gruppy 'Za uvekovechenie pamiati o zhertvakh repressii,' 11 December 1987, (summary of a two-hour discussion with V. A. Landratov and A. I. Arkalov, respectively head and deputy head of Department of Propaganda, Moscow *gorkom,* based on notes taken by Iu. V. Samodurov and D. N. Leonov), ibid.

idea of turning Memorial into a broad popular movement that would pursue other means to commemorate victims, such as collection and publication of oral histories about the terror, creation of a computer data base of names, and revision of history textbooks on the Stalin era.[22] A movement might educate the public about the causes and means of preventing future repression and help survivors with their pressing material needs. The Memorial activists were edging toward a more powerful form of collective action, but their goals were still relatively tame; they were focusing on consciousness raising, not demanding justice.[23]

In the West, the model of a formally structured organization with mass membership has appealed to activists of all persuasions, as it seems to guarantee strength from combined resources, the ability to wield resources strategically in political battles, and continuous mobilization.[24] The totalitarian state gave Memorial several additional practical reasons to want to become a formal mass organization. First, its leaders recognized that their only solid resource was the number of supporters they might recruit; and the outpouring of letters in the press from people who had suffered under Stalin or who were curious about the purges indicated a large pool of potential adherents for an antistalinist organization. Second, a formal organization might recruit respectable members of the liberal establishment who could "protect" Memorial. Publications provided evidence of famous writers and scholars who shared Memorial's views of Stalin. Third, members of Memorial, drawing a lesson from the Khrushchev era, feared that if the authorities took up the idea of commemorating victims, the whole thing might still come to nothing, or the project might be reduced to a statue of a "brave prisoner" in the socialist realist style. A permanent organization could exert influence throughout the process of selecting a design and building a memorial.

Once Memorial's members decided to try to become a mass movement, they faced the problem of moving from petitions to protests. Constructing collective action would require them to diagnose the problem, propose a solution, recruit supporters, and gather resources. Memorial also had somehow to get the state to expand the small, fragile window of oppor-

22. Iurii Samodurov to Memorial members, 26 March 1988, ibid.

23. Laura Woliver, *From Outrage to Action* (Urbana: University of Illinois Press, 1993), pp. 158–60.

24. Frances Fox Piven and Richard A. Cloward, *Poor People's Movements* (New York: Pantheon, 1977), p. x.

tunity for political participation that Gorbachev had opened. To succeed in forming a movement, Memorial had to find a form of action that was both public and political, but not so political as to be subject to intense repression. Overcoming this problem would require an unprecedented commitment to liberalization on the part of reformers and novel tactics on the part of Memorial.

Consensus among Memorial's founders on the form of the movement did not carry over to the question of what tactics would foster an independent yet influential movement. Because they disagreed over the benefits of trying to work alongside establishment reformers, the group's members continued to experiment with both radical and moderate tactics. Thus Samodurov, together with the mathematician Lev Ponomarev, resumed his search for authoritative support for Memorial, but among the liberal intelligentsia rather than among Party-state officials. Winning the open support of the intelligentsia was not an easy process, as no one wanted to be the first to sign.[25] More radically inclined members persisted in soliciting signatures from ordinary citizens, but, with the permission of theater managers, worked in the relative safety and warmth of theater lobbies. The radicals, moreover, did not limit their activity to Memorial. Iurii Skubko and Viktor Kuzin, for instance, participated in the March 1988 antistalinist demonstration that was violently suppressed by the police, and that served as a catalyst for the formation of DS. The radicals realized that while *mitingovaia politika* (the policy of street confrontations) served DS's goal of showing the regime's hypocrisy toward real democrats, such tactics affected only small groups of spectators and impressed even fewer. Through Memorial the radicals and moderates sought to find a middle ground where they could avoid debilitating repression yet not become puppets of the authorities.

In early 1988 Memorial's two-front tactics began to reap dividends. On January 20 Memorial received its first mention in the official Soviet press. In a brief article in *Literaturnaia gazeta,* Iurii Shchekochikin painted a respectful picture of sincere young activists gathering signatures in the lobby of the Ermolova Theater in central Moscow. Though he provided few details about Memorial's agenda, Shchekochikin stressed the ethical nature of this genuine social initiative and cited the support given the group by such prominent figures as the historian Iurii Afanas'ev and the

25. Interview with Viacheslav Igrunov, 14 April 1991.

dramatist Mikhail Shatrov.[26] The publicity gained by appearances in theater lobbies and the *Literaturnaia gazeta* piece drew new people—including former victims of repression—into the group, enlarging its membership from two dozen to approximately seventy-five in Moscow. Still, this was a difficult period for the group because it could not act openly but had already taken the decision to become a mass movement.[27]

Having broken through the barrier of media silence and won new allies, Memorial sought to exploit the Party's steps toward reform. In the months before the June 1988 Party Conference fresh debates arose in the press and the Party over the shape of reform. Memorial took advantage of the Party's desire to mobilize public support for perestroika and of its own growing reputation to get permission from Moscow authorities to hold two public meetings—the first in May in a park far from the city center, the second in June in Moscow proper. Both meetings attracted several hundred participants and provided a platform for Andrei Sakharov and other dissidents, liberals, and young activists to expound upon the importance of antistalinism and civic initiatives. At the second meeting Memorial ceremonially handed over its petitions, now bearing thousands of signatures, to Iurii Afanas'ev and Elem Klimov, president of the Filmmaker's Union, for them to present at the Party Conference. In his closing remarks on the last day of the Conference, Gorbachev did support the idea of a monument, but he did not mention Memorial. To one observer "Gorbachev's words had a tacked-on feel to them; they sounded like an afterthought."[28]

Inasmuch as Gorbachev's instructions to look into the matter of a monument went to the same Moscow officials who had earlier discouraged Memorial, the group's leaders worried that the project would be distorted beyond recognition. It was time to mobilize the resources that had brought Memorial to the attention of the authorities—publicity in the mainstream press, prominent patrons, and public sympathy for the victims of Stalinism. With the help of *Literaturnaia gazeta,* in the summer of 1988 Memorial launched a drive to collect nominations from the public for a council of luminaries who would control the fund-raising and design

---

26. Iurii Shchekochikhin, "Vspomnit' i ne zabyvat'," *Lituraturnaia gazeta,* 20 January 1988.

27. Interview with Iurii Skubko, 2 March 1991.

28. David Remnick, *Lenin's Tomb: The Last Days of the Soviet Empire* (New York: Random House, 1993), p. 119.

competition for the memorial complex. The newspaper also opened a bank account to which people could send donations for the monument.

These efforts gained Memorial several powerful institutional sponsors—the Artists', Filmmakers', Theater Workers', Architects', and Designers' unions and the journal *Ogonek,* as well as *Literaturnaia gazeta.* The Obshchestvennyi Sovet (Social Council) produced by the public poll included Andrei Sakharov and Boris Yeltsin; the writers Ales' Adamovich, Anatolii Rybakov, Mikhail Shatrov, Evgenii Evtushenko, Bulat Okudzhava, and Lev Razgon; the philosopher Iurii Kariakin; and the historians Iurii Afanas'ev and Roy Medvedev. Only Aleksandr Solzhenitysn declined to join, explaining that he could not take an active part while he was in exile. With this foundation of patronage, Memorial activists were ready to try to form a legal independent mass organization.

As Memorial grew in membership and stature, however, it faced great internal and external pressures. Old internal debates about the form of the movement persisted and blossomed into disputes about the group's independence and political agenda. The struggle over the consolidation of a mass movement reflected not just the usual conflicts between radicals and moderates but a new factor—the introduction of relatively conservative establishment figures into the movement as representatives of founding institutions or through their election to the Social Council.

Close cooperation with officially recognized organizations increased the risk that the movement might be co-opted with strategic offers of aid to victims and symbolic recognition through sponsorship of a monument. The first such conflict arose in August when the members of Memorial debated whether to join a demonstration sponsored by another informal group to protest new restrictions on public demonstrations. When the majority of members voted that Memorial should participate as an organization, the newly formed Executive Committee, made up of representatives of the sponsoring organizations, protested that they alone could decide such questions. The incident was smoothed over, but it demonstrated both the need for a formal charter to spell out the society's rules and the danger of conflict over democratic principles. Meanwhile provincial groups that had formed in response to coverage of Memorial in the central press were pushing for a national conference to give them legitimacy and leverage with their local officials.

As Memorial started to plan its founding conference, Communist Party leaders expressed their apprehensions about a mass organization inspired by the regime's shortcomings in the past. Both the implied criticism of Communist rule and the form of that criticism—an independent group—challenged the leaders' control over reform. If they recognized the utility of a mass movement, they in effect admitted that the Party alone could not effectively represent or reconcile all social interests. The Party could re-press Memorial but at the expense of its new reputation for tolerance. It had to adapt its tactics to cope with Memorial's popularity, well-placed allies, and perceived occupation of the moral high ground.

Memorial's goals and tactics made it less open to slander than DS, for instance, so the regime had to move quietly as it tried to strong-arm activists into disbanding. Paradoxically, the Party exerted the most pres-sure on Memorial through those famous figures and prestigious unions that the moderates had expected would protect the organization. These people's close connections with the Party made them both receptive to its input and vulnerable to its pressure—after all, their careers and status depended on the Party's approval. Under pressure from the Central Com-mittee, the creative unions moved to postpone the conference planned for the fall of 1988. The group's radicals and moderates were determined to organize, however, so they sent out invitations to a conference in October before the issue of timing was resolved.[29]

The next stage in the battle over the founding conference revealed the depth of both the state's hostility and the group's internal divisions. The day before the founding conference, Memorial's Executive Committee, which included Samodurov, Ponomarev, and Viacheslav Glazychev of the Architects' Union, surrendered to the Central Committee's demands that the upcoming gathering be some kind of working meeting, not a "found-ing conference." In justifying its retreat to a general meeting of the mem-bership, the committee argued that the provincial organizations had not had time to prepare; some of them had not seen drafts of the charter. The radical faction, however, brought with them a dozen delegates from other cities who had already arrived in Moscow. With great agitation these delegates insisted that, on the contrary, they needed a central founding conference immediately to give them leverage against local officials who were trying to drive them out of existence. The crisis escalated into a shouting match when a representative of the Filmmakers' Union declared that if the society would not accept the compromise, his union would

29. Interview with Viacheslav Igrunov, 14 April 1991.

withdraw its auditorium as a meeting place. The activists retorted that they would sooner meet on the street. Barely averting a total split in the organization, the two sides worked out a more radical compromise: the meeting would be called a "preparatory conference," but the date for a founding conference would be announced and published. Moreover, the sponsors promised to publish a draft of the charter in the union press at least a month before the next conference convened.

## FROM CONFLICT COMES RADICALISM

The preparatory meeting, attended by 500 delegates and guests from 58 cities, began in a mood of pride and celebration.[30] Both activists and camp survivors felt they had won a long battle for recognition. The conference, however, also provided a forum for further formative clashes. As if in anticipation of conflict on the conference floor, Glazychev, in his opening remarks as a representative of the sponsors, admitted the existence of two factions: "One—this is the initiative movement—they brought with them great zeal and energy, enormous experience of a certain kind of direct interaction with people on the streets, but they lacked experience in constructive creative work. Others—representatives of the creative unions—they brought experience in social work, constructive, energetic organization on a whole range of tasks, and shortcomings in relations outside their contacts and professional circles." Larisa Bogoraz, a longtime dissident, rushed to contradict Glazychev, arguing that the real distinction between the two groups was the sponsors' access to material resources. The unions had no monopoly on organizational experience; the activists had invented a new form of activity—nonstate organization.[31] Thus conflict surfaced immediately between those eager to carve out a larger role for Memorial in the public sphere and those who rejected any radical political suggestions as bound to cause unnecessary trouble with the authorities. Division over the politicization of the movement affected

---

30. Of the 58 cities represented, 13 groups had 10 or fewer members, 14 had 10 to 20 members, 16 had 20 to 50 members, and 13 had more than 50 members. These figures give only a very rough picture of Memorial's strength, as no agreement had been reached on how to define "members." See "Stenogramma organizatsionnoi konferentsii obshchestva 'Memorial,'" 30 October 1988, p. 1, Moscow Bureau of Information Exchange Archives.
    31. Ibid., p. 3.

the nature of the Memorial movement and revealed to the participants a growing gap between official and popular understandings of Stalinism.

The first key debate centered on the presence of radicals in the association. It was sparked by Iurii Skubko's announcement of an unsanctioned demonstration to be held later that evening in Pushkin Square to mark Soviet Political Prisoners Day and his demand that the central KGB building in Moscow be turned over to Memorial to house a museum of the repressions. A few members of the audience accused Skubko of dangerous provocation, of suggesting a "war with the KGB." They urged a resolution banning members of DS from Memorial. Skubko successfully defended himself by reminding the audience that he spoke as a founding member of Memorial, not just as a member of DS, and by restating his view that a political police force was incompatible with democracy.[32] The meeting resolved not to exclude members of DS or any other group from Memorial, but though most agreed with Skubko about the KGB in principle, they voted not to confront the KGB directly.

A second sharp controversy arose when Viktor Aksiuchets, a radical Christian Democrat and longtime supporter of Solzhenitsyn, proposed that Memorial call for the rehabilitation of Solzhenitsyn and the publication of his works in the USSR.[33] As the resolution was about to be voted upon, the *Literaturnaia gazeta* representative interrupted to protest that his paper had evidence that Solzhenitsyn had been a KGB informer. This attempt to slander Solzhenitsyn provoked outrage. Many delegates, including the leader of the Vorkuta camp uprising, protested that anyone who thought they would believe such a story was insulting their intelligence. The very attempt by an establishment figure to defame Solzhenitsyn heightened the perception of a tremendous gap between more radical public perceptions of Stalinism and the official version. The majority of participants opted for a brave liberal stance and supported the resolution to honor Solzhenitsyn.

A final conflict arose over how to respond to reports of violent dispersal of an antistalinist rally in Minsk. Martiralog, the Belorussian equivalent of the Memorial Society, had gathered thousands of people outside Minsk at the site of mass graves of purge victims to mark the Belorussian traditional national day for remembering one's ancestors. The authorities attempted to prevent the demonstration, and when that effort failed, they dispersed

32. Ibid., pp. 49, 70.
33. Interview with Viacheslav Igrunov, 14 April 1991.

the crowd with tear gas and clubs. When this news reached the Memorial conference, it was met with fear and disbelief. Radical delegates proposed sending a telegram of protest to the Soviet government, while moderates and conservatives, doubting that the Party would use such force against peaceful marchers, argued that an uninformed complaint could be used as an excuse to shut down Memorial. The radicals and Martiralog delegates scrambled to verify the story, and ultimately a moderately worded telegram of protest was dispatched to Gorbachev.

The shape of Memorial was forged in these conflicts at the preparatory conference. The participants chose to form an inclusive, democratic organization with a liberal-radical agenda. The grass-roots activists, for the most part, showed a willingness to confront the authorities and take on a political role. Delegates proposed that Memorial nominate its own candidates to the USSR Supreme Soviet, investigate mass grave sites, and challenge the application of the statute of limitations to the purges because they were "crimes against humanity."[34] Activists' optimism about their ability to work with the system, however, was shaken by the level of disagreement between the representatives of the establishment and the activists over the direction Memorial should take. The events in Minsk heightened fears that the regime might move forcibly to disband the organization, but the conference pushed ahead with a radical agenda for independent antistalinist activity.

In each of the skirmishes during the preparatory conference, the more radical faction won out. Yet the struggle to shape and control Memorial was far from over. The founding conference had been set for 17–18 December 1988, contingent on publication of a draft charter in the union press a month beforehand. External pressures and internal divisions continued to plague Memorial as it entered this second round of the fight over the founding conference. Two key issues emerged: whether an all-union conference would be held at all if the Party objected, and what kind of charter would be adopted.

From the first, moderates attempted to keep control over the drafting of the organization's statutes out of the hands of the radicals. Only one "radical," Pavel Kudiukin, was elected by the organizing committee (which was composed of representatives of both the sponsoring organizations and the early initiative group). The moderates and sponsors envi-

34. V. Zelkin, A. Mil'chakov, Iu. Morkovin, and E. Mendeleevich in "Stenogramma organizatsionnoi," Moscow Bureau of Information Exchange Archives.

sioned a centralized organization, with issues of membership and agenda decided in Moscow; the radicals supported a hyperdemocratic, decentralized, federated structure with the central organization functioning only as coordinator. The radicals also proposed a clear statement of Memorial's moral and political principles, that is, of its commitment to participation in the democratic movement.

The contrast between the two conceptions of Memorial may be seen in the factions' proposed charters. The official, moderate draft begins, "Memorial is a social organization, conducting its activity in accord with the Constitution of the USSR, with the laws of the USSR and the union republics, and with the present charter." An alternative charter drafted by a group of thirteen radicals, including Kudiukin, opens thus: "Memorial is an independent social organization, created by citizens for active participation in and recruitment of broad sectors of the population for activity to restore and preserve the historical truth about Soviet society. This condition is necessary for the USSR to become a state ruled by law, which is one of the guarantees of the irreversibility of the democratization process."[35] The radicals thus immediately tackled the questions whether the organization should be political and whether to interpret Stalinism as a unique historical event or as a persistent institutional condition of the Soviet system. The resolution of these questions would determine whether Memorial became a special interest group or part of the democratic movement.

Before Memorial could debate its future, however, it had to convene a new conference. But even the restrained language of the official draft of the charter could not make Memorial palatable to all Party and state officials. *Literaturnaia gazeta* had pledged to publish the draft charter, but under pressure from above it delayed publication from week to week. Finally at the end of November, without consulting Memorial, the paper printed a notice declaring that the conference was postponed indefinitely. Simultaneously Central Committee officials summoned the representatives of the sponsor organizations to a confidential meeting. Samodurov and Ponomarev learned of the meeting at the last moment and managed to crash the session. The Central Committee representatives demanded that the all-union conference be canceled, but settled for another postponement.

35. "K obsuzhdeniiu proekta Ustava Vsesoiuznogo Obshchestva 'Memorial,'" 9 January 1989, ibid.

At the next meeting of the whole organizing committee in early December, moderates and radicals coalesced in their fury over the perceived sellout of Memorial. Exclusion from the decision-making process forced moderates to admit the ineffectiveness of a conciliatory stance. United in the face of the Party's intolerance, the group's founders demanded—but did not receive—the sponsors' support for a founding conference despite official opposition. Finally, one participant recalls, a respected member of the Social Council voiced the sentiments of the movement's ordinary members: "Then Adamovich got up—he didn't even sit with the sponsors there on the stage, though in principle he was one of them; he sat in the hall with us—and he said, 'You know, most likely [the members] are right. You've got to listen to these guys. Of course we have our positions, we have our Party cards, but we don't have the courage to start all this, so probably we should listen to them.' This was like a bomb exploding!"[36] The sponsors called for a break, then proposed to dissolve the Executive Committee and hence to release themselves from responsibility for Memorial's daily activities. The initiative group seized the opportunity and the more active members of the Social Council—Adamovich, Sakharov, Evtushenko, Kariakin, and Afanas'ev—took on the crucial roles of negotiators between the movement and the authorities.[37] Soviet leaders still did not recognize ordinary citizens as spokesmen; to the extent that the Party would negotiate, it would do so only with members of the elite.

Having decided to go ahead with the conference, the organizers proceeded with plans for a big gathering. Ignoring signs of trouble, the organizing committee had worked steadily to develop and formalize relations with the rapidly multiplying local societies. It had sent out invitations for a conference at the end of January—again without seeking the authorities' approval. And Afanas'ev promised to procure an auditorium large enough to seat a thousand delegates even if the Central Committee disapproved.

Indeed, the Central Committee took offense at Memorial's defiance and launched a new series of attacks. In what looked like a concession to the movement, the Ministry of Culture announced an official competition to select a design for a monument to the victims of repression "during the years of the cult of personality." But the ministry made no mention of Memorial, and it envisioned only a statue honoring the victims of Stalin's purges, not a research center and a monument to all victims of Soviet

36. Interview with Viacheslav Igrunov, 14 April 1991.
37. Andrei Sashin, "Khronika Memoriala," *Panorama*, no. 10, October 1989, pp. 6–7.

terror. A few days later, the minister of culture noted that an account for construction of the monument already contained over half a million rubles; he did not mention that this account had been opened for Memorial and built up by large contributions from its sponsors and hundreds of thousands of smaller donations by individuals. He also dodged a question about the potential loss of the "democratic nationwide nature of the movement to create a monument."[38]

The ministry's brazen attempt to usurp and distort Memorial's most identifiable goal showed Memorial's liberal patrons the limits of their influence. The disillusioned Evtushenko later admitted that he, unlike Adamovich, had believed that the ministry would accede to his personal request and postpone any announcement about the competition until after the Memorial conference.[39] New direct access to the top leadership and Gorbachev's repeated efforts to bring liberal intellectuals into the reform camp had given Memorial's patrons confidence that they could really protect the organization from the state's interference. In the final reckoning, their prestige combined with the potential international scandal did save Memorial from being forcibly disbanded.

As the day of the conference approached, the Central Committee summoned Afanas'ev, Adamovich, and several other members of the Social Council to demand that the conference be canceled. Meeting resistance, the Party representatives threatened to deny Memorial access to any auditorium. In exasperation Sakharov vowed that Memorial would meet in private apartments if it had to, and the Central Committee surrendered.[40] By some reasoning, the Central Committee decided that the costs of repressing Memorial—bad publicity and splits among the elite—outweighed the risk of sacrificing a little more control over the reform process. Sakharov certainly had the power to draw the attention of the international media to the spectacle of elderly survivors trudging through the icy streets to meet in crowded apartments. Gorbachev's own attitude toward Memorial remains unclear. Adamovich spoke to him several times about Memorial and reports that Gorbachev was supportive. But Adamovich and others continued to be called on the carpet by high-level

38. "Zakharov on Stalin Victims Memorial Competition," *Izvestiia*, 4 January 1989, in *Federal Broadcast Information Service Daily Report on the Soviet Union*, 5 January 1989, pp. 50–51.

39. "Stenogramma press konferentsii," 29 January 1989, Arkhiv Uchrezhditel'noi Konferentsii, Interregional Memorial Society Archives.

40. Interview with Viacheslav Igrunov, 14 April 1991.

officials, including the chief ideologist, Vadim Medvedev.[41] And Gorbachev never honored Elena Bonner's request, made at Sakharov's funeral in December 1989, to register Memorial.[42]

Delegates from 108 cities, almost double the number present at the preparatory conference, finally convened on 28 January 1989 and the next day adopted a greatly modified version of the draft charter. Led by Leningrad delegates, the provincial representatives won a radical charter that decentralized the organization, reduced the sponsors' role, and elevated the status of local branches.[43] The delegates also passed twenty-one resolutions, ranging from calls for material aid for victims of Stalin-era repression to a demand for the release of the jailed leaders of the Armenian Karabakh and Krunk committees. The conference did not stop at outlining policy goals; it also declared support for Sakharov's election platform and for the candidacies of sixteen Memorial members nominated to run in the first elections to the Congress of People's Deputies.

The diverse resolutions of the first conference foreshadowed Memorial's future activities. Memorial societies across the country pursued human rights, charitable, historical, and political work simultaneously. Despite continuing state opposition, Memorial publicized the cause of the repressed and their survivors, and provided them with material, medical, and legal aid. Through its research, Memorial advanced knowledge about the Soviet past. It spread its findings through exhibits, publications, and educational programs. Its human rights sector investigated current persecutions such as the imprisonment of the liberal journalist Sergei Kuznetsov and mass human rights violations in Northern Ossetia and Nagorno-Karabakh. Though Memorial did endorse and campaign for candidates for political office, the society had decided early on not to become a political party. From the start, as Skubko put it, "Memorial was not so much an opposition group as a civil rights society."[44] Memorial activists lacked the opportunity and the resources to take on the serious and dangerous task of forming an overt political opposition. Instead, they would try to work through the system—using the official press and establishment patrons to push for democratization—without working with it.

41. "Stenogramma press konferentsii," 29 January 1989, Interregional Memorial Society Archives.

42. Remnick, *Lenin's Tomb*, p. 287.

43. "Ustav Vsesoiuznogo dobrovol'nogo istoriko-prosvetitel'skogo obshchestva 'Memorial,'" in *"Memorial" informatsiia i dokumenty* (Moscow: Memorial, 1990), pp. 8–13.

44. Quoted in McFaul, "Last Hurrah for the CPSU," p. 11.

At Memorial's founding conference Galina Lewinson, a survivor of the Gulag, clutches her membership credentials. Moscow, January 1989. *Courtesy Interregional Memorial Society Archives, Moscow.*

Memorial members march in a pro-democracy demonstration. *Courtesy Interregional Memorial Society Archives, Moscow.*

Brezhnev's suppression of destalinization ended public discussion of the issue, but the official silence only exacerbated the pain and grief of survivors and the families of victims. Their pent-up emotions and the curiosity of those too young to remember the terror burst forth in demands for exploration of the past and repudiation of repression even decades after the height of the purges. And, given the trend in intellectual evolution from condemnation of the cult of personality to criticism of the totalitarian system during the 1970s and 1980s, Memorial quickly broadened its agenda from pleading for official recognition of past injustices to mobilizing the public to demand political accountability now.

Liberalization under Gorbachev changed the political opportunity structure for social mobilization. It increased access to institutional participation, divided the elite, and provided new allies for oppositionists. Gorbachev's reforms, however, created only a small window of oppor-

tunity for independent initiatives. The reformers wanted to mobilize public support, not public criticism. The regime itself introduced authoritative
self-criticism to justify reform, but it did not endorse spontaneous, potentially delegitimating calls from below for a thorough reassessment of Soviet history. Authorities therefore reacted with alarm to attempts from
below to capture the initiative on destalinization.

Originally optimistic about the Party's commitment to reform, activists
petitioned for commemoration of past injustices. In the process of refining
their ideas and searching for support from above, activists began to forge
a new identity for themselves: they became protesters. If the Party had
been willing to negotiate with its perceived opponents, it might have
capitalized on the clear internal divisions within the antistalinist movement. But it never tried to co-opt Memorial by inviting its leaders to join
its own destalinization efforts or by making concessions that might have
disarmed the radicals and won over the moderates. Official hostility fed
radicalization and a growing sense that victimization by hostile authorities was not a thing of the past but an ever-present danger. The
formation of a truly independent organization became part of Memorial's
moral agenda. "One of Memorial's tasks," Afanas'ev explained, "is to
transform itself into a model for new social movements that will become
the polar opposites of Stalinism. The more movements that appear, the
more strongly Soviet society will be structured, and the greater will be the
guarantee against a return to the old times."[45] Collective action thus not
only rewarded participants with a new sense of efficacy but became another bulwark against arbitrary rule.

Truth-telling proved to be a powerful catalyst for recruitment, but the
incompleteness of liberalization made organization difficult. Memorial
succeeded in forming a national movement because it found ways to work
with reformist elements of the Soviet system—the liberal press and liberal
intelligentsia—without being absorbed into the establishment, and because it developed a consistent, coherent, progressive agenda. Official
repudiation of Stalin's repressions created at least the potential for action,
and the widespread sentiment against the terrorist policies of the past
made Memorial attractive to people of many political persuasions. Because the implications of condemning Stalinism were open to very
different interpretations, Memorial could attract the timid without totally

45. Quoted in *Sovetskii tsirk*, 4 February 1989.

alienating people who rejected any form of Soviet rule. Memorial brought together both revolutionaries and petitioners to work for change within the Soviet system. Radical and moderate tendencies sustained Memorial at different moments in its development and helped it find a balance between confrontation and conciliation—the balance it needed if it was to survive the official hostility toward politicized independent associations.

# 6 THE MOVEMENT
## AND THE STRUGGLE

In the early years of perestroika, many Western Sovietologists were confident that liberalization from above had opened a space for the development of a civil society—that is, a spectrum of independent social organizations. Russian society, they contended, was not passive by nature; it had matured with education, industrialization, and urbanization and could be "activated" by a liberal leader.[1] And indeed, independent groups of all sorts, from charities to trade unions, proliferated wildly between 1988 and 1990. But it would be a serious mistake to assert, as two observers did, that under Gorbachev one could "express discontent virtually without fear of retribution."[2] Memorial's experience shows that the dominant feature of informal organizational life under Gorbachev was official resistance and occasional repression. Legacies of totalitarian rule and contemporary state policies created only the most tenuous opportunity for social mobilization. Given the Party-state's capacity to repress informal groups, Memorial societies strove to balance preservation of

1. Jim Butterfield and Judith B. Sedatis, "The Emergence of Social Movements in the Soviet Union," in *Perestroika from Below: Social Movements in the Soviet Union,* ed. Butterfield and Sedatis (Boulder, Colo.: Westview, 1991); James Scanlan, "Reforms and Civil Society in the USSR," *Problems of Communism,* March–April 1988.
2. Butterfield and Sedatis, "Emergence of Social Movements," p. 3. At one point, they seemingly qualify this assertion by noting that Democratic Union organizers were subject to harassment and brief administrative arrests, but were not sent to prison camps.

Pavel Negretov, an amateur historian and camp survivor, stands with his grandson at the foot of a cross erected to mark the graves of prisoners at the Vorkuta camps. *Photo by Kathleen E. Smith.*

their independence with development of a working relationship with the authorities.

Liberalization orchestrated from above does not generally involve the state's active promotion of critical independent associations, but to liberalize is by definition to expand civil and political rights. As we have seen, central Party officials met initial civic efforts to organize around antistalinism with hostility at worst and grudging tolerance at best. Continued ambivalence toward nonstate initiatives combined with sensitivity to the negative aspects of the Soviet past often led the central authorities to resist Memorial's efforts to organize and operate. Party policies also exploited two other stumbling blocks to civic activism: the short supply of resources and long-suppressed ethnic tensions.

While Memorial was gathering momentum in Moscow, where it benefited from the presence of international correspondents, similar antistalinist groups were springing up in other large cities and at the sites of former labor camps. Across the Soviet Union Memorial's agenda proved a powerful catalyst for social mobilization. Memorial attracted young and old, men and women, victims of Stalinism and those untouched by the purges. Moscow, while not exempt from adversity, was not representative of the poverty and conservatism prevalent in the regions. The nationwide movement took off only after the Moscow organization broke through the barrier of censorship to get coverage in the central media. Out in the provinces the word about Memorial spread through articles in *Literaturnaia gazeta* and letters in *Ogonek*.

Representatives of 53 cities attended Memorial's first national meeting in October 1988, and three months later 108 cities sent delegates to the founding conference in Moscow. The charter adopted at the conference supported regional autonomy; Memorial's only central organs were the Social Council of luminaries and a "working collegium" for coordination of everyday business. This loose structure permitted flexibility in choice of activity, degree of politicization, and extent of interaction with other informal groups. Some branches of Memorial concentrated their efforts on charitable activities to support the survivors of Stalinist prisons; others resembled political parties, and still others focused on historical research. The majority of Memorial societies pursued all three of these objectives simultaneously, and they all shared basic needs. Independent organization required freedom of association, material resources, and means of attracting new members—an appealing set of goals and principles, a coherent and feasible program of action, and some method of communicating with potential members. In all of these realms, save for an appealing set of goals, Memorial faced stumbling blocks that differed in degree but not in substance.

## LACK OF RESOURCES

Resources for collective action include not just money and materials, such as paper, typewriters, and meeting places, but human resources in the form of members, networks, and leaders. Memorial suffered from a shortage of both kinds of resources. At the time Memorial arose, it emerged into a near organizational vacuum. In many small cities Memorial organized the first open, independent political actions, usually public meetings or demonstrations. Being the first to organize created several problems, including lack of experienced organizers and the need to find potential members.

Finding like-minded people to join an organization requires some form of advertisement. In the West social movements often draw supporters from other groups with similar goals. Indeed, in Moscow and Leningrad the founders of Memorial met in socialist discussion clubs that brought together freethinkers, intellectuals, and former dissidents. Outside of the major cities, however, there were virtually no dissidents or clubs in 1988 and hence no organized independent bases to which Memorial could appeal for support. Most of the clubs that did exist were small, loose coalitions of "supporters of perestroika" who met infrequently and operated semiofficially, in the sense that the authorities permitted them to meet as long as they confined themselves to discussion. In Tula, for example, the earliest group, Grazhdanskaia Pozitsiia (Civic Position), was a political discussion club recognized by local authorities and headed by a worker from the city department of culture; its main activities consisted of lobbying the local people's deputy on ecological and social issues.[3]

The obvious alternative to drawing on previously mobilized groups or networks for support was to publicize the cause—a task that required either private material resources or access to the public arena, generally through the media. Technological backwardness and the general low level of disposable income in the USSR greatly limited the means available to informal groups to gain publicity. Many groups lacked even a typewriter. More significant, Gorbachev's reforms did little to weaken the state's monopolies on property and resources. Individuals had only limited ac-

---

3. Georgii Levin, president of Tula Memorial, to All-Union Memorial, 18 May 1989, Interregional Memorial Society Archives, Moscow. Much of the evidence for this chapter comes from a survey of Memorial groups I conducted by mail. The Appendix provides the questionnaire and sample responses.

cess to such organizational necessities as copying equipment and auditoriums. And lack of private business made fund-raising difficult. The Murmansk Memorial showed rare entrepreneurial talent in successfully soliciting money from new cooperatives; in other cities, authorities threatened potential contributors.[4] Furthermore, Soviet law prohibited the publication of materials by unregistered organizations. The combination of scarcity and monopoly sometimes drove Memorial out into the streets to demonstrate for attention, but the authorities considered demonstrations confrontational.

The Moscow and Leningrad Memorial societies originally obtained coverage in a variety of media by cultivating personal contacts with writers and artists and through their powerful liberal sponsors, principally *Ogonek* and *Literaturnaia gazeta*. Most provincial cities, by contrast, had a single large-circulation paper under the tight control of local Party and state officials. In some large cities a few independent publications, most of which had started life as samizdat journals, emerged in the 1980s. Articles in the central press brought basic information about the all-union organization to the provinces, but numerous local newspapers refused to carry stories about the Stalinist repressions, let alone announcements about regional branches of Memorial. Occasionally an editor agreed to publish an article on Memorial but was forced to remove it when the Party intervened. The Iaroslavl' Memorial, for instance, waged a long, unsuccessful struggle over publication of an article about its sponsorship of a Week of Conscience.[5]

The picture here, however, is not uniformly negative. A few local newspapers actively assisted Memorial. In Novorossiisk, Tselinograd, and Omsk, for instance, Memorial worked closely with local journalists, and in Vorkuta the local paper *Zapoliar'e* sponsored Memorial.[6] Occasionally interference redounded to Memorial's advantage. When two representatives of the Syktyvkar Memorial arrived for a scheduled interview on the

4. Interview with Aleksandr Zhosan, president of Murmansk Memorial, Murmansk, 8 February 1991; Robert Buinov, president of Chuvashiia Memorial, to the author, 19 April 1991.

5. "Khronika vzaimootnoshenii iaroslavskogo 'Memoriala' s partiinymi i sovetskimi vlastiami," manuscript, Interregional Memorial Society Archives.

6. G. Kurov, member of Novorossiisk Memorial, to the author, 21 March 1991; M. Chalimov et al., "'Memorial' v Tselinograde," 16 June 1989, Interregional Memorial Society Archives; S. Angarskaia, "Pervyi den' 'Memoriala,'" *Molodoi sibiriak*, 10 June 1989; L. Shutova and L. Petrova, "Dolg i pamiat' (Istoriia vorkutinskogo 'Memoriala')," manuscript, author's collection.

local youth channel, the order came from above that one of them—Revolt Pimenov, a well-known human rights defender and candidate for USSR people's deputy—was not to appear. The second representative went on the air, announced what had happened, and refused to participate further. The youth channel aired viewers' protests live until the deputy head of regional television shut down the broadcast. Later he fired the show's producers, and in doing so sparked the city's first public demonstrations.[7]

Publicity through the official media, however, often carried a price: to secure cooperation, Memorial had to exercise restraint in describing its agenda. By allowing publicity of this sort, officials could, to some extent, shape Memorial's public image into a less threatening form. Even the central press tended to play up Memorial's support for a monument and deemphasize its political goals.[8] Thus in the regions as well as in the center, the introduction of sponsors helped Memorial get publicity but made the group dependent on resources vulnerable to Party pressure.

Ultimately, Memorial groups in the provinces were likely to spring from the efforts of single individuals and chance meetings of like-minded citizens inspired or facilitated by the central press and the All-Union Memorial Society. Activities sponsored by the Moscow and All-Union Memorial created opportunities for dissemination of information and facilitated organization in the provinces by providing a forum where people could meet. Iurii Dzeva, who became president of the Pskov Memorial, recounted that while he was in Moscow for the Week of Conscience he "met yet another child of an 'enemy of the people' . . . [who also] lived in Pskov. On the way home we agreed to try to appear on local television. We managed to do that, and by the end of December we'd gathered a group of people who met every month."[9] A native of Tselinograd in Kazakhstan learned about Memorial from the central press and became a one-man advertisement for the association: he collected signatures on the street for the appeal for a monument, petitioned the city council for meeting space and assistance, and eventually attracted some support.[10]

7. A. Bobrakov, Syktyvkar Memorial, to All-Union Memorial, n.d., Interregional Memorial Society Archives.

8. Interview with Karina Musaelien, editor of the Moscow Memorial newspaper *Svoboda*, Moscow, 5 May 1991.

9. Iu. A. Dzeva to the author, 25 March 1991.

10. Marat Chalimov, president of Tselinograd Memorial, to All-Union Memorial, 30 March 1989, Interregional Memorial Society Archives.

Memorial activists gather signatures on a petition in Tselinograd, Kazakhstan. *Courtesy Interregional Memorial Society Archives, Moscow.*

Others resorted to organizing through the work collective or through friends. The founder of the Tula Memorial Society used his correspondence as secretary of the oblast division of the official all-union philatelist society to seek out others who might be interested in Memorial.[11] Many Memorial groups sought and found support from local teachers' institutes, libraries, and museums. Positive coverage in the central press and the support of local liberals helped provincial Memorial groups establish a reputation and attract members, but difficulties with resources persisted as the societies tried to begin work. Memorial could alleviate scarcities by attracting more and more members and soliciting donations, but it could not break monopolies on meeting space and media without the acquiescence of the local authorities.

11. Georgii Levin to Orgkomitet of All-Union Memorial, 22 November 1988, ibid.

## ETHNIC DIVISIONS

A second obstacle to Memorial's activity away from the center was ethnic conflict. Growing national consciousness had the potential either to reinforce antistalinism or to create divisions among Memorial activists. In some places the authorities played on ethnic divisions to try to split the movement; in other areas national independence movements overshadowed or swallowed up Memorial. The role of national identity in social mobilization is complex. Memorial's experience merely shows several ways in which the growth of national consciousness had a detrimental influence on antistalinist organization.

In the Belorussian capital of Minsk, independent associational activity began in the mid-1980s with the formation of tiny informal youth groups dedicated to preserving the Belorussian language, culture, and environment. In the autumn of 1987 these youth groups sponsored the first public commemoration of the victims of Stalin on *Dziady*, the traditional Belorussian holiday for honoring the dead. Mobilization around the Stalin question per se was sparked in June 1988, when a Belorussian-language newspaper published an article in which the archeologist and former dissident Zenon Pozniak described the mass graves of purge victims in the Kuropaty forest outside Minsk. Less than three weeks later, despite an official ban, 10,000 people marched on Kuropaty to commemorate the dead.

When a republican government commission to investigate the identities of the people buried in Kuropaty did little to pursue its task, the local, largely Belorussian creative intelligentsia formed Komitet-58, named after the article in the criminal code under which many of Stalin's victims were convicted. In a meeting sponsored jointly by nationalist youth groups and Komitet-58, some 400 people met and created Martiralog Belorussii, an organization almost identical to Memorial, which later joined the all-union association. Pozniak, who consistently equated Stalinist repressions with the destruction of the Belorussian intelligentsia, language, and culture, was elected president of the new organization. More significant, a committee for the creation of a Belorussian Popular Front (BNF), on the model of the Baltic nationalist movements, was formed at Martiralog's founding meeting.[12]

---

12. Interview with Vladimir Kriuchkovskii, co-president of Martiralog; Aleksandr Lukashuk, member of Martiralog and the BNF; and Alesa Semukha, member of Talaka, Minsk, 18 March 1991.

From the first Martiralog was linked with and overshadowed by the overtly political and nationalist BNF. In reclaiming the history of past atrocities, the non-Russian peoples of the Soviet Union found reason to reject not only Stalin and totalitarianism but the whole concept of a Russian-dominated central government. Outside of Russia, the purges were often viewed as acts of genocide, and each ethnic group claimed to have suffered more than the others. The introduction of the idea of unequal suffering, however, divided victims and their supporters along ethnic lines, and made Russians feel excluded. Moreover, as Belorussians became radicalized, they shifted their political activity to the Popular Front. After all, the BNF aimed specifically to mobilize political, including electoral, opposition to the regime. Martiralog continued to exist, but nearly all of its members also belonged to the BNF. In early 1991 Martiralog still had not been registered by the city officials and it limited its activities to gathering historical information informally. As one activist put it, "Martiralog does everything in people's souls rather than carrying out concrete acts, whereas the BNF does the opposite."[13]

The interaction of ethnic and civic goals was most complex in Ukraine, in part because of the republic's mixed ethnic Russian and Ukrainian populations and the historical differences between its eastern and western regions. The sheer number of Memorial associations in Ukraine—more than fifteen—makes it difficult to generalize about their involvement with national movements; nevertheless, a common developmental path may be seen until late 1990. From the start the Ukrainian Memorial chapters pursued objectives specific to the republic, most notably commemoration of victims of the 1932 famine. In March 1989 they formed a republican coordinating council, but the election platform it drafted that November made no nationalist demands.[14] Neither the inclusion of famine victims nor the creation of a republican body caused rifts in Memorial; dissension began only in 1990, when growing interest in some regions in an independent Ukraine created pressure for Memorial to take a stand on Ukrainian sovereignty.

Some branches of Memorial split over the question of participation in and cooperation with the Ukrainian independence movement known as RUKh. At its second annual conference, held in September 1990, the

13. Ibid. (Semukha).
14. "Predvybornaia platforma Ukrainskogo dobrovol'nogo istoriko-prosvetitel'nogo obshchestva 'Memorial' k vyboram v respublikanskie i mestnye Sovety narodnykh deputatov 4 marta 1990 goda," 28 November 1989, author's collection.

president of the Odessa Memorial chapter proposed that the group join RUKh as a collective member. When some delegates resisted the idea of uniting with what they saw as an overly political and ethnically exclusive organization, the president walked out, taking part of the membership with him.[15] The Kiev Memorial also split over the issue of Ukrainian self-determination and the use of the Ukrainian language at Memorial meetings and in documents.[16] Divisions over resources and status considerably weakened Memorial in Odessa as well. Other regional chapters successfully negotiated relations with the national movement without coming to blows or losing their separate identity. They found a way to commemorate the distinctive travails of Ukraine while embracing all victims of Stalinism, regardless of ethnic background.

Unlike Martiralog, Ukrainian Memorial groups developed simultaneously with but separate from the nationalist movement; and though many of its members belonged to other independent associations as well, Memorial recruited a solid membership base of its own. Memorial often cooperated with new political parties and other informal groups to sponsor meetings on larger political themes, but did not carry the burden of organizing a broad political or national opposition. In Mariupol', Memorial, DS, and an ecology club rallied 6,000 for a meeting about the spring 1990 elections. Other informals also participated in activities involving Memorial's themes. RUKh and Memorial in Poltava organized a requiem meeting to honor victims of the famine; International Human Rights Day was marked jointly in Khar'kov by RUKh, the Christian Popular Front, Memorial, and the Ukrainian Helsinki Union.[17]

In Kazakhstan it was republican officials, not ordinary citizens, who introduced ethnicity into the debate about antistalinism. When supporters of Memorial in Alma-Ata gathered in December 1988 to form a committee to organize a local society, a Kazakh member of the Communist Party, allegedly a provocateur, disrupted the proceedings by proposing that the committee be made up solely of Kazakhs. The idea of a multinational

---

15. Interview with Nikolai Danilov, member of Odessa Memorial, Moscow, 13 February 1991; untitled account of 29 September 1990 conference, Moscow Bureau of Information Exchange Archives.

16. Interview with Izrail Reznichenko, president of Kiev Memorial, Kiev, 22 April 1991; interview with Valerii Rubtsov and Nikolai Lysenko, members of Ukrainian Republican Memorial Coordinating Council, Kiev, 23 April 1991.

17. *Ekspress-Khronika*, no. 8 (133), 20 February 1990; no. 46 (119), 12 November 1989; no. 51 (124), 17 December 1989.

committee prevailed, but still Kazakhstan's Party-state leadership pressed for creation of a republican-level organization, which they apparently believed would be more isolated, susceptible to manipulation, and prone to splits.

In the weeks leading up to the April 1989 founding conference, the leader of the Memorial organizing committee, the Kazakh writer Bulat Gabidov, had two of his screenplays rejected. Afterward he began to urge creation of a Kazakh Adilet (Justice) Society. As a result, the organization split at its founding conference, with a majority joining Adilet and a smaller group of activists forming the Alma-Ata Memorial Society. One Russian participant explained, "If we created Adilet with only Kazakhs and Memorial with only Russians, then the Party had won, so some of the people of other nationalities went with Adilet."[18] Despite the Party's intention to isolate and split the antistalinist movement, both groups sought affiliation with the All-Union Memorial and eventually cooperated with each other.

Pressure to split and "nationalize" the movement extended out into the provinces of Kazakhstan as well, where the authorities were more heavy-handed. In Tselinograd, representatives of the city authorities serving on the Memorial organizing committee tried to get activists to join the republican Adilet. The majority refused, and won a promise from all the members of the organizing committee not to speak of Adilet at the local founding conference. Yet the local Party bosses carried out a series of measures designed to undermine Memorial. First, they placed a notice in the major city paper announcing the formation of Adilet and inviting everyone interested in a historical educational society to the local conference—giving the coordinates of the Memorial conference. Second, the day before the conference, the city committee of the Party, which had promised to print credentials for the delegates, demanded that the word Memorial be omitted, so Memorial activists had to write credentials by hand.

On the day of the conference, the Tselinograd authorities handed out copies of the Adilet program, while Memorial supporters handed out the Memorial charter. Inside the hall, Party workers, members of the city executive committee, representatives of the Procuracy, and veterans of the militia and KGB shouted down the organizing committee's representa-

18. Interview with Viktor Snitkovskii, member of governing board of Alma-Ata Adilet, Moscow, 14 March 1991.

tives and gave the podium to a series of well-rehearsed speakers, who spoke about Adilet and appealed to nationalist feelings. At last the Memorial supporters walked out and held their own meeting. Again two organizations with presumably identical goals formed, though in Tselinograd, Adilet was so much a creature of the Party that it never mustered real public support.[19]

The confrontational relations between the state and the informal groups in Kazakhstan did not serve nationalist movements above others, as in Belorussia. Here nationalism was thrust upon the movement from above and failed to take root. Adilet did not succumb to pressure to take a strong nationalist stand, and thus did not limit its potential alliances. When genuinely nationalist political parties eventually emerged in Kazakhstan, Adilet and Memorial had consolidated their positions and were able to cooperate with new groups without being absorbed by them. On the whole, Adilet maintained good relations with the full spectrum of independent associations. Its petition for the KGB building in Alma-Ata to be turned into a memorial museum and for construction of a monument to famine and purge victims was also signed by representatives of Memorial, the Social Democratic Party of Kazakhstan, the nationalist Zheltoksan and Alash parties, the Russian Edinstvo Society, and the Ukrainian and German cultural centers.[20] Adilet played to a multinational constituency by publishing materials in the Russian-language press and cooperating with local and other Memorial chapters; and when Adilet talked about Kazakh victims of the famine of the early 1930s, it shunned the Ukrainian nationalists' inflammatory words and rarely spoke of "genocide."

The Party's relaxation of its monopoly on political discourse and activity unleashed a multitude of long-suppressed grievances at once. In many non-Russian areas civic groups of all stripes were pressured to take a stand on the issues of ethnicity and national sovereignty. Though national sentiments may at first have heightened public interest in exploring the history of repression, the resurgence of nationalist sentiment ultimately complicated informal associations' pursuit of an antistalinist agenda. Whether markers of ethnic identity were introduced from above

19. Marat Chalimov to All-Union Memorial, 30 March 1989, and Chalimov et al. to All-Union Memorial, 16 June 1989, Interregional Memorial Society Archives; "Skazat' pravdu o repressiiakh," *Tselinogradskaia pravda,* 15 June 1989.
20. Viktor Snitkovskii, "Dom na krovi," *Gorizont* (Alma-Ata), 9 February 1991.

or below, their adoption limited the constituency from which antistalinist groups could draw members; otherwise the impact of national consciousness on antistalinist organizing depended on the choice of alliance made by the individual groups.

## THE COMMUNIST PARTY INTERVENES

Both in the republics and in the Russian provinces direct sabotage by Communist Party and state officials far outweighed all other obstacles. Given its control of the legislative, police, and court systems, as well as of all forms of media and property, the Party-state apparatus's attitudes toward social mobilization carried enormous weight. The relaxation of central power and the strains of reform did expose differences of opinion within the Party on a range of issues, including how best to deal with informal groups and the merits of destalinization. But despite the leadership's pronouncements on pluralism and democratization, local officials remained almost uniformly hostile toward informal associations. They differed, however, in the extent of their displeasure and in their choice of tactics to manage the situation. Some leaders spared no efforts to squash independent associations, while others attempted to co-opt the groups, or ignored them in the hope that they would fade away.

Before we examine the tactics available to the authorities and evaluate concrete cases, it is necessary to lay out the issues involved. Fundamental to Memorial's whole program was its existence as a representative of survivors and as a bulwark against a return to repression. The Soviet state had the power to deny any organization the legal right to exist. Without official registration, an association could not legally open a bank account, rent space, or publish its materials. City authorities found many grounds for refusing to register Memorial. Some claimed to be waiting for a new law on associations—passed by the USSR Supreme Soviet only in October 1990—to replace the 1932 law. Others maintained that branches of an all-union association could not be registered until the all-union society was legally recognized.

Though the authorities were not directly to blame for the poverty of independent associations, they limited such groups' ability to raise funds both by withholding permission to open bank accounts and by exerting pressure on would-be institutional contributors. City officials could further control an association by refusing to authorize its public meetings and demonstrations, barring it from public halls, and threatening organizations that were willing to rent or donate space to it. Unauthorized meetings might be dispersed by militia and security forces. Organizers of unsanctioned demonstrations and distributors of samizdat could officially be fined or held under administrative arrest.[21] Unofficially, they were often harassed, threatened, or fired.

The Party also restricted formal political participation; during new "democratic" elections, for instance, it often instructed electoral commissions not to register independent candidates.[22] Finally, policy matters such as assistance to the repressed fell under the overlapping jurisdictions of Party and state. In 1989, after the Politburo decreed the creation of local commissions to help rehabilitate victims and secure social assistance for them, decision making shifted to local officials, who chose the local commission's members and set its agenda.

It is extremely difficult to evaluate the state's relations with informals rigorously. First of all, the "authorities" include a mixed bag of institutions, ranging from Party committees to city legislatures to the KGB. In this analysis I treat these bodies as unified. I do not attempt to assess the relative strengths of democrats in local soviets; such data are not readily available, and the lack of clear criteria for determining who should be considered a democrat makes them problematic. In 1990 many independent candidates ran under broad anticommunist coalitions. Once in office, these deputies could not easily identify with their constituents and rarely felt tied to any specific program. This lack of identity wreaked havoc even in the Oktiabr'skii regional council in Moscow, one of the few legislatures in the country to have a majority of "democrats."[23]

Most important for our purposes, early elections rarely put more than a handful of independent candidates into provincial soviets and had little effect on the treatment of informals. Splits between reformers and conservatives in the Party which were evident at the center undoubtedly existed in the provinces as well, but I lack the detailed information necessary to evaluate them. Thus I measure "conservatism" solely on the basis of

21. Francis X. Clines, "What's the Latest in Soviet Oppression? Routinely 15 Days in Jail," *New York Times*, 2 November 1989, p. A9.
22. Michael Urban, *More Power to the Soviets: The Democratic Revolution in the USSR* (Aldershot: Edward Elgar, 1990), pp. 100–103.
23. Interview with Shota Kakabadze, legal assistant to the president of the Oktiabr'skii *raispolkom*, 4 May 1991, Moscow.

policies toward the limited range of issues I have identified as concerning the development of Memorial.[24] The intensity of the authorities' opposition, however, should not be taken as absolutely indicative of an association's failure or success.

We can best observe the Party's capacity to restrain or manipulate independent associations by examining a situation in which the local Party fiercely opposed independent activity and antistalinist initiatives. Party-state officials in Belorussia won well-deserved renown in the Gorbachev era as guardians of the old order. Allegedly they hoped their republic would remain a slumbering island in a sea of radical reforms. Official attitudes and tactics toward Martiralog demonstrate the depth of hostility that some Party members felt toward the antistalinist movement and the full range of state powers that could be turned against independent activists.

In Minsk, the authorities began to pressure the informals by interfering with activists in much the same way that the Brezhnev regime persecuted dissidents. They harassed activists and their relatives by threatening to fire them or to withhold bonuses and promotions. If the activists were students, they threatened to stop their university stipends, to lower their grades, and to withhold their diplomas. Several young men involved in the new movements were called back into active military service from the reserves for several months; all young men who had completed their compulsory service were technically in the reserves and hence vulnerable to recall. As supporters of political reform organized, the authorities maligned their leaders in the press and orally. One participant recalled that Party officials liked to slander the informals in talks to work collectives—such talks not only generated rumors effectively but left no concrete traces.[25]

The conflict between Party-state officials and informal groups in Belorussia came to a head over the issue of antistalinism in 1988, when Tuteisha, a group of young writers affiliated with the Soviet Cultural Fund, applied to the Minsk city authorities to conduct a public meeting for the *Dziady* holiday. (Tuteisha applied instead of Martiralog because it

24. Interestingly, the governments of many oblasts that had been extremely hostile to informals—including Saratov, Chita, Lipetsk, and Tambov—supported the August 1991 coup.

25. Interview with Ales' Susha, member of Talaka and editor of BNF publications, Minsk, 19 March 1991.

was already sponsored by a legally recognized entity.) The authorities had no intention of permitting dissemination of information about the new organizations and they withheld permission, though they had no legal grounds to do so. The meeting's organizers decided to proceed nonetheless.

On 30 October 1988 all public transport in the direction of the cemetery where the meeting was to be held was stopped for "technical reasons" and the militia seized and detained a number of well-known cultural figures and activists as they marched toward the meeting site. After warning the crowd to disperse, the militia broke up the demonstration with tear gas and clubs. Many of the ten thousand who had gathered, however, broke through the cordon and headed toward the mass graves in the Kuropaty forest. There they were again blocked by a chain of militiamen and soldiers and ranks of fire engines. As a last resort, the approximately five thousand remaining participants knelt in a field off the highway and, despite falling snow and wind, listened as Zenon Pozniak read the declaration of the Martiralog Society. When several people unfurled the Belorussian national flag, the militia and troops pushed into the crowd and beat the "troublemakers." They continued to harass the demonstrators as the crowd dispersed and headed back to the city.[26]

The brutal treatment of this crowd of citizens, which included many elderly people, women, and children, shocked those Belorussians who had hoped that perestroika would bring liberalization. It also intensified mistrust of the government, especially when the authorities persisted in claiming afterwards that neither tear gas nor undue force had been used. One participant recalls, "People saw this kind of [attack] during the war or maybe before the war during the Stalinist arrests, but we had seen nothing like this and it was a shock to our social consciousness. . . . [Open confrontation] was a tremendous help in the development of political consciousness in the republic of Belorussia. Nothing stimulates political development like clubs and gas."[27] The negative publicity that resulted from the use of force against demonstrators perhaps persuaded the authorities to deploy less conspicuous means of choking informals' ac-

---

26. *Belorusskaia tribuna* excerpted in M. Iu. Roschin, "Neformal'noe dvizhenie sredi belorusskoi molodezhi (podborka materialov)," in *Molodezhnyi renessans,* ed. A. G. Bystritskii and M. Iu. Roschin (Moscow: Nauka, 1990), pp. 176–80; Aleksandr Borin, "Minsk, 30 Oktiabria. Do i posle sobytiia," *Literaturnaia gazeta,* 26 December 1988, p. 10.
27. Interview with Aleksandr Lukashuk, 18 March 1991.

tivities, but in no way dissuaded them from attempting to undermine democratic reform.

Minsk officials refused to register the new groups, persecuted and smeared individuals who attempted to keep the informals' money in their personal accounts, and restricted meeting space. The Belorussian National Front had to hold its founding conference in Vilnius, Lithuania—a situation that even the central press decried.[28] The authorities physically threatened Martiralog organizers throughout Belorussia. In Brest they raided the apartment of one activist to confiscate display stands prepared for an exhibit about the Stalinist repressions.[29]

Nevertheless, the BNF and Martiralog persisted and even supported delegates in the local election campaigns. Here, too, they encountered official opposition at every turn. Michael Urban has noted that "the intensity of the electoral contest, a head-to-head struggle for power between the apparatus and the emergent democratic forces, was epitomized by events in Minsk, where the police administered beatings to peacefully assembled pickets, jailed scores of them, and carried out illegal raids on the offices of independent political groups, confiscating their materials and destroying their property."[30] Despite official attempts to paint Pozniak as a member of the "Jewish Mafia," a "fascist," and the grandson of a Nazi collaborator, the leader of Martiralog and the BNF won a seat in the republic's supreme soviet. After a letter allegedly from a group of war veterans asked how Pozniak had time for work when he was engaged in so many civic activities, the Central Committee even issued orders to check up on Pozniak's work performance with a view towards dismissing him.[31] The few seats won by democrats hardly softened official opposition. In 1989 the press continued to malign the BNF, especially for its antistalinist and anticommunist stance.[32]

The depth and persistence of Belorussian conservatism on the Stalin question can be seen in a 1991 article in a journal of the Belorussian Communist Party in which the author argued that Stalin pursued the

28. A. Sumerov and A. Ulitenok, "Ne nashli soglasiia," *Pravda,* 17 January 1989.

29. Elena Maz'ko, Brest Martiralog, to All-Union Memorial, and Mogilev Martiralog to All-Union Memorial, Interregional Memorial Society Archives.

30. Urban, *More Power to the Soviets,* p. 105.

31. Interview with Vladimir Kriuchkovskii, 18 March 1991.

32. I. Grishan, "Ob"edinilis', chtoby protivostoiat', ili o tom, komu vygoden novyi vitok konfrontatsii," *Sovetskaia Belorussia,* 30 March 1991; Anatolii Maisenia, "BNF: Dva goda spustia," *Znamia iunosti,* 23 April 1991.

correct line in punishing real enemies of the state. He provided the following assessment of current events: "The impression is that the members of the 'right-Trotskyite-centrist bloc' were not really shot, and, not succumbing to the effects of time, have launched a second [attempt] to crush socialism and restore capitalism. Only they have changed their names and are acting not clandestinely but fully legally, gathering together in the Democratic Union, 'Popular' fronts, the Interregional [group of deputies], Memorial, 'Democratic' Russia, and even the Union of Zionists."[33]

## Evaluating the Sources of Efficacy

### Worst-Case Scenarios: Orel and Pskov

In contrast to the turbulent first steps of Martiralog, Memorial in Orel began ordinarily enough in March 1988 with the collection of signatures on an appeal to Gorbachev for construction of a monument to Stalin's victims. People interested in the history of the 1930s also arranged for a reading of Anatolii Rybakov's *Children of the Arbat* at the local library. Orel had a special place in the history of Stalinist repressions. In 1941, as the Germans advanced on the city, the NKVD took almost two hundred political prisoners from their cells and executed them. On the anniversary of this event in September 1988, Memorial organized the first tiny, independent, and unsanctioned public meeting in the city at the walls of the Orel prison. There activists posted lists of the names of those killed under Stalin to the walls. The authorities tore down the lists the next day. They also tried to deny Memorial's competence to represent the interests of the victims: they refused to register the organization and excluded it from the oblast commission on the affairs of the repressed. This commission first announced that Memorial had no branch in Orel, then conceded that it did, but "the city does not need Memorial."[34] The commission itself meanwhile did nothing to assist the repressed.

By late 1989 the Orel authorities had yet to authorize a single independently organized public demonstration. But in the face of opposition from several weak democratic proto-parties, they began to look more favorably on Memorial. They decided to try to turn public sympathy for Stalin's

33. S. Zhdanov, "Tak byl ili ne byl sostav prestupleniia?" *Politicheskii sobesednik*, no. 1, January 1991, p. 61.

34. E. Mendelevich to All-Union Memorial, n.d., Interregional Memorial Society Archives.

victims to their advantage by working with Memorial—if Memorial would accept the Party's control. Thus in September 1989 the Party allowed commemoration of the Orel massacre—in a city auditorium under official guidance. After the head of the city commission on the affairs of the repressed prevented representatives of democratic organizations from speaking, approximately seventy people quit the hall and held an unofficial demonstration.

In July 1990 the city council actually declared 11 September the Day of Remembrance of Victims of Repression, but did not announce its decision in the media. Despite this concession, the 1990 commemoration followed the same pattern as that of the year before: the presiding city official diverged from the agreed-upon list of speakers, allowing Memorial a word but denying other democratic representatives, and an unsanctioned demonstration ensued.[35] Relations between Memorial and the authorities continued to deteriorate in 1991. The authorities still refused to recognize the existence of Memorial and other informals, except the ultraconservative, Communist Edinstvo Society, whose newspaper regularly published paeans to Stalin.[36] In sum, for two years the authorities attempted to ban, ignore, and preempt Memorial, then made a brief unsuccessful attempt to co-opt the group before reverting to hostility. The level of repression in this case kept the base of activists small, and so severely limited their capacity to organize that they could not independently gain publicity, let alone achieve any concrete goals.

Another organization stunted by pervasive Party-state interference can be found in Pskov. This branch of Memorial formed very early and was meeting regularly by the end of 1988. When the Pskov Memorial sought to formalize its status, however, it encountered cleverly masked resistance from above. The leader of the Pskov group recalls: "In my naiveté, I turned for help to the city committee of the Party. . . . They lovingly put meeting space at our disposal and prepared 250 credentials [for the founding conference]. But the city committee itself distributed 167 of them. . . .

---

35. See *Ekspress-Khronika,* no. 38 (111), 17 September 1989; E. Mendelevich, "Byt' li perestroike [*sic*] v provintsii?" ibid., no. 48 (121), 26 November 1989, and "Godovschina Orlovskoi tragedii," *Svoboda* (Moscow), no. 11, 1990.

36. Edinstvo was allegedly sponsored by the oblast Party committee and its newspaper featured such items as a long essay on "antistalin hysteria," in which the author argued that there was no proof that anyone arrested under Stalin was innocent. See V. Krylov, "K voprosu o repressiiakh," *Edinstvo* (Orel), no. 4, September 1990. A later issue included a satire in which the devil is asked if there are real enemies of Stalin today and he replies, "Of course there are. And not just in Moscow. They've even formed a society. It's called Memorial." See "Skazka pro to, kak chert v Moskvu zlodeia vozil," ibid., no. 14, March 1991.

When it became apparent that the Party would not be able to place a majority of its candidates on the governing board, it tried to wreck the meeting."[37] Here the Party permitted activists to begin to organize either under the impression that it could control the group or because at first it did not see Memorial as a threat to the Party's legitimacy. When co-optation failed, however, the local Party apparatus used new tactics to limit its activity. During the election campaign, it refused to register a priest who had received the backing of Memorial and other small independent associations. By and large, Party officials simply turned their backs on Memorial. They did not register the society, form contacts with it, or grant any of its petitions. Memorial's failure to win benefits for Stalin's victims greatly weakened its credibility among the city's residents, and without capital or access to resources, Memorial could not itself offer meaningful financial aid to anyone.

### Best-Case Scenarios: Apatity and Mariupol'

It is difficult, perhaps impossible, to find places where the Party-state apparatus welcomed popular initiative to uncover the hidden history of repressions. Indeed, when the Party readily proffered assistance, it often did so out of a desire to co-opt and channel antistalinist activity. Thus the best terms the informal groups could realistically hope for seem to have been mutual tolerance forged out of initial suspicion. Such was clearly the case in both the small northern town of Apatity and the city of Mariupol', in southern Ukraine. In both cases, authorities initially reacted to Memorial with mistrust. The KGB in Mariupol' called Memorial representatives on the carpet over a telegram they had sent to the KGB chief in Moscow to protest the local KGB's refusal to open archives on the purges. After negotiations, however, Memorial gained limited access to the KGB's regional archives in Donetsk.[38] The Apatity Memorial had to wrangle with local authorities for months to obtain permission to erect a memorial cross on a piece of unused land.[39] Eventually both Memorial branches

37. Iu. A. Dzeva to the author, 25 March 1991. A similar fiasco occurred in Rostov, where a near riot broke out when officials refused to admit some activists and turned away scores of survivors. See G. A. Fomenko, "Nokdaun 'Memorialu,' ili demokratiia po-Rostovskii," 21 April 1989, manuscript, Interregional Memorial Society Archives.

38. Galina Zakharova, member of governing board of Mariupol' Memorial, to the author, 22 May 1991.

39. Interview with Elena Balaganskaia, co-president of Khibin Memorial, Apatity, 5 February 1991.

managed to involve city officials in their work, at least to the extent of getting representatives to speak at meetings in commemoration of Stalin's victims.

What made officials in Apatity and Mariupol' so accommodating? There may have been significant liberal elements within the local Party organizations, but other factors played a role as well. First, both Memorial societies had quickly gained access to the media through sympathetic journalists: the Mariupol' Memorial received a monthly page in the major local newspaper, and the Apatity society published its own newspaper more or less monthly and used the profits to fund its charitable activities. Publicity helped Memorial attract sizable numbers of activists by Soviet standards—approximately 60 in Apatity (population about 80,000) and more than 100 in Mariupol' (population about 517,000).

Moreover, both Apatity and Mariupol' boasted several informal associations, some of them overtly political, and compared to them, Memorial seemed quite moderate. A representative of the Murmansk oblast committee of the CPSU praised Memorial in comparison with more political and "immodest" groups.[40] With a wide base of activists with a range of interests, the chapters avoided the obsolescence to which single-issue groups are prone. Large numbers of activists also translated into practical results as they worked to gather historical materials, set up exhibits, and lobby for privileges for the rehabilitated. In Apatity this process was aided by the election of two Memorial members to the city council and their service on the Social Welfare Committee.

Finally, in each city special conditions improved Memorial's resource base. Apatity was an "academic city" and thus home to many intellectuals, who proved to be the most enthusiastic participants in informals. In Mariupol' social forces were emboldened by success in their first battle—a campaign to undo the naming of the city for one of Stalin's associates, Andrei Zhdanov.

### Intermediate Cases: Tomsk and Voronezh

Tomsk was home to an active yet struggling Memorial society. The group began with two advantages: it was founded on the basis of an existing informal organization, the Soiuz Sodeistviia Revoliutsionnoi Pe-

---

40. Iu. Mal'tsev, "Vstrecha ideologov s neformalov," *Vestnik ODD* (Apatity), no. 5, November 1989.

restroike (Union for Cooperation with Revolutionary Perestroika), and it found sponsors in the Tomsk divisions of the Soviet Writers' Union and the Russian Artists' Union. This sponsorship protected Memorial from harassment but did not shield it from the authorities' attempts to disenfranchise it. The oblast executive committee reacted to the creation of Memorial by setting up a commission to assist victims with rehabilitation. It allowed two members of Memorial to join the commission, but started its own account for building a monument to victims. It then refused to register Memorial in April 1989, in part because the executive committee's legal consultant declared that the society's efforts to collect money for a monument and create an information center were unnecessary. But one member noted with pleasure that there had been "no repressions linked to membership in the Memorial movement."[41]

Constant lobbying plus cooperation with other informals won the Tomsk Memorial publicity and renown. The chapter attracted national attention when it criticized Egor Ligachev for his callous cover-up of the Stalin-era mass graves exposed by flooding during his tenure as first Party secretary of Tomsk oblast.[42] Despite its aggressive pursuit of the truth, the Tomsk Memorial eventually secured registration and the authorities' cooperation in placing a "stone of sorrow" at the site of a future monument. This stone became a focal point for democrats, who gathered there to mark International Human Rights Day and the anniversary of the massacre of unarmed demonstrators in Novocherkassk in 1962, and to stage an alternative commemoration of the anniversary of the October Revolution.[43]

Another moderately successful Memorial society emerged in Voronezh. This chapter had no special assets—no sponsors, allies in the media, or concentration of intellectuals—but it did have carefully nurtured relations with the local authorities. Its president asserted, "I consider the 'introduction of a bridge' between the authorities and people who suffered from repression and who need to turn to these authorities as a success."[44] He

41. N. Kashcheev, co-president of Tomsk Memorial, to All-Union Memorial, n.d., Inter-regional Memorial Society Archives.

42. V. Zapetskii, "Iz Nekrologa odnoi politicheskoi biografii, ili eshche raz o kolpashevskom zakhoronenii," *Posev*, no. 6, 1990.

43. *Ekspress-Khronika*, no. 51 (124), 17 December 1989; no. 23 (144), 8 May 1990; no. 46 (171), 13 November 1990.

44. Viacheslav Bityutskii, president of Voronezh Memorial, to the author, 23 March 1991.

The "stone of sorrow" dedicated to victims of Stalin's terror in Tomsk. *Courtesy Interregional Memorial Society Archives, Moscow.*

recognized that informals had to depend on the people in power if they were to achieve such goals as material aid for survivors. Nevertheless, except in rare instances when a Memorial society occupied itself solely with charitable aims, the political nature of Memorial's primary task of revealing the history of repressions in the USSR led to conflict with the representatives of Soviet power.

Thus the Voronezh Memorial, formed in late 1988, managed to gain registration only in May 1990. And a year later members of new political parties still sought to avoid persecution by "us[ing] their membership in Memorial to give constitutionality to their actions: observing during elections, referendums, and using the bank account."[45] While striving to maintain political independence and integrity, the Voronezh Memorial

45. Ibid.

used both deliberate tact and public support mustered through its investigation of local mass graves to form "constructive" relations with city
authorities including the KGB.

The success of some Memorial societies in creating and maintaining an independent and forceful voice for democratic change and defense
of victims of Stalinism cannot be attributed to any single factor. Allies in
the media, recruitment of skilled members, strong leadership, lack of
ethnic tension, and good relations with other informal groups all bol-
stered the movement in some areas. Perhaps the greatest determinant of
the movement's development, however, was a factor that lay far beyond
activists' control—that is, relations with local Party-state authorities.
Representatives of the Mariupol' Memorial admit that credit for their
success must be attributed not only to their own substantive endeavors
but to tact and pragmatism in building a relationship with the Party. At a
meeting of the All-Union Memorial the Mariupol' delegate argued: "The
building occupied by the Party's city committee is called the Mariupol'
White House. Today all power is centered there. And if Memorial needs
offices, we can't take them by storm, like the Winter Palace in 1917. . . .
That means we must go to the local authorities and reach an agreement
with them."[46] The Mariupol' Memorial safeguarded its independence
while it negotiated a relationship with the authorities based on peaceful
coexistence.

How could an organization find or win over reasonable members of the
city administration while retaining its integrity? Memorial societies had to
exploit the cracks in the system to survive, and most often mutual tolerance emerged only after significant confrontation. In Iaroslavl', for instance, Memorial gained status and strong allies by piggy-backing on the
local Popular Front, which served as a lightning rod for the Party's hostility. There, as in Tomsk, the authorities came to regard Memorial as the
least unacceptable part of a strong informal movement.[47] Through indus-
trious organization building, the Iaroslavl' Memorial could report growth

46. L. D. Iarutskii, quoted in G. Zakharova, " 'Vse zavisit ot nas samikh . . .': Na pervom
plenume pravleniia Vsesoiuznogo obshchestvo 'Memorial,'" *Priazovskii rabochii* (Mariupol'), 17 November 1989.

47. The authorities showed their favoritism for Memorial in January 1991 when they
evicted all other parties and clubs from the Social-Political Center (formerly the House of
Political Enlightenment of the Obkom of the CPSU) for "activity harmful to the Party": Iurii
Markovin, president of Iaroslavl' Memorial, to the author, 25 November 1991.

in membership and influence even in 1991, when branches in many other cities were losing members to new political parties.

The most obvious failures occurred in those cities where Party inter- ference was so intense as to stunt all organizational growth and activism. In Saratov, Stavropol', Orel, and Chuvashiia, membership in Memorial averaged ten persons in 1990–91, in large part because the authorities in these places allowed no meetings or press coverage, threatened potential sponsors, and arrested and fired potential activists. Since few people dared to act, and since the situation received no sympathetic media coverage, the population remained ignorant of the authorities' abuses of power and so never became polarized.[48]

Unyielding official opposition in Pskov made Iurii Dzeva pessimistic about his group's future: "The Party simply doesn't need to battle with us, it's enough for it simply to take no notice of us. What does this mean? That we won't be heard or understood, as all levels of power from brig- adier to president are 95 percent filled by members of the CPSU." Memo- rial itself could not provide the material help that victims needed, nor could it rouse the authorities to do so. When the Pskov group tried to set up a charitable fund, it was told that it had to pay 2,000 rubles for registration and that any enterprise created under this fund would be subject to taxes. Dzeva admitted that his Memorial alone was practically helpless—it even had trouble collecting oral histories without tape re- corders, typewriters, or a place to store its records.[49]

The majority of Memorial societies fell between the two extremes of relations with the local authorities. Most Memorial leaders in 1991 judged local authorities' attitudes toward them as "indifferent" or "busi- nesslike." In fact, by the time the Communist Party was outlawed in the wake of the attempted coup in August 1991, even in Orel and Pskov the nascent democratic movements had won the battle for free association by the most crude measure: that is, the police no longer broke up their demonstrations or routinely jailed their organizers. But the Party's earlier interference had stunted the growth of these groups by disappointing public expectations for civic representation. Memorial bears the scars of more than a struggle against poverty. It became radicalized through con-

48. Interview with Iurii Chernyshev, Saratov Memorial, Moscow, 4 May 1991; Taisiia Kazacheeva, Stavropol' Memorial, to the author, 10 May 1991; Robert Buinov to the author, 19 April 1991.
49. Iu. A. Dzeva to the author, 25 March 1991.

frontation with the regime, but remained organizationally weak. Though their very existence testifies to the depth of resentment toward Stalinism, provincial branches of Memorial produced only erratic substantive accomplishments. Like the dissidents before them, Memorial activists were distracted from concrete tasks by the cycle of repression. Gorbachev's reforms changed the political opportunity structure to permit association, but as the history of Memorial reveals, the dominant feature of informal organizational life under Gorbachev was still official resistance even to goals that Gorbachev publicly endorsed. Liberalization from above did not equal destruction of the old system. New groups had not only to overcome a host of inherited obstacles to organization but also to operate in a largely unchanged political environment.

# 7 BATTLES OVER COMMEMORATION AND COMPENSATION

In the aftermath of grave abuses of human rights in Argentina, Uruguay, and Brazil, conflict focused on official documentation of specific offenses and on prosecution of offenders. Survivors saw official, public recognition of state crimes as real acknowledgment of the injustices done to them. And activists argued that failure to prosecute abusers would create a culture of impunity within the military and intelligence forces.[1] As in Latin America, battles over coming to terms with state crimes in the Soviet Union centered on changing political discourse and achieving some measure of justice. But the duration and the scope of repression in the USSR, as well as the unique position of reform Communists, ruled out the possibility of fully documenting human rights abuses and made the prospect of comprehensive prosecutions unlikely.

In the Soviet Union, four foci of controversy arose under Khrushchev and again under Gorbachev as part of the struggle to cope with a repressive past: acknowledging and compensating individuals through rehabilitation and reparations; shaping a new collective memory through the rewriting of Soviet history; enshrining new principles through symbolic politics; and retribution through settling of accounts with human rights abusers. The debates, policy choices, and public initiatives in these

---

1. Lawrence Weschler, *A Miracle, a Universe: Settling Accounts with Torturers* (New York: Pantheon, 1990), p. 4.

areas demonstrate both the difficulties of reform specific to the Soviet
state and the universal problems of justice for victims. How could the
government make reparations to victims without undermining its own
position, without casting itself in the role of a mass murderer? How could
survivors be compensated? Could historians adapt to demands that the
gap between official history and private memory be closed? What exactly
should a monument to victims of repression commemorate? And why was
judicial prosecution not a popular demand?

Analysis of specific union-level policy debates and their outcomes reveals the interaction between official stances and public pressures, and the
relative leverage or control of the various parties involved. After all, neither official preferences nor the effectiveness of Memorial in mobilizing
the public should be conflated with successful resolution of concrete issues in contention. When we compare policy battles across the decades,
however, several cautionary notes are in order. Official policies toward
previous state-sponsored abuses reflect the level of the government's general commitment to reform at the time in question, as well as the status of
ongoing confrontations over basic rights such as freedom of speech and
association. In comparing distinct periods one must also consider how the
passage of time has affected demands and constraints in efforts to come to
terms with the past. Finally, the secrecy surrounding policy making in the
USSR and the continued restrictions on access to archives preclude the
kind of deep policy analysis possible in more open societies. Because the
Communist Party laid claim to the "leading role," it rarely attributed
policy changes to suggestions or pressure from other groups.

## Individual Rehabilitations and Reparations

The top priorities of purge victims and their families in 1953 were
release and rehabilitation, neither of which was satisfied quickly or completely. Small waves of releases in 1939 and at the end of World War II had
prompted victims' relatives to flood the Procuracy with fruitless requests
for information about their loved ones and for reconsideration of their
cases. Stalin's death awakened new hopes for mass amnesties or rehabilitations. But the government marked the occasion with an amnesty
of only common criminals. While the Presidium refused to endorse any
sweeping measures, its members secured the release of their own relatives

and some close associates immediately after Stalin's death. Viacheslav Molotov's wife, for instance, was allegedly freed on the day of Stalin's funeral. By 1955 only a few thousand "politicals"—mainly former high-ranking Communists and prominent public figures—had been freed. This "silent destalinization" neither reduced the pressures in the camps nor alleviated concerns for the fate of purge victims.

Most political prisoners, with the exception of former POWS, were freed en masse in the aftermath of Khrushchev's 1956 "secret speech," but rehabilitation proceeded slowly, erratically, and covertly. The political elite hesitated in part because rehabilitation, unlike amnesty, conveys an admission of error. In a formal juridical sense, rehabilitation means not a pardon but a revised sentence. In the USSR, the judiciary based reversal of criminal convictions on lack of evidence of guilt or lack of evidence of a crime. One may also conceive of "social rehabilitation"—that is, restoration of property, position, pension, and, in the USSR, Party membership, as well as compensation for lost wages and suffering. Finally, rehabilitation may be understood in terms of reputation, restoration of the victim's good name.[2]

After Stalin's death, controversy first emerged among top leaders over the methods of juridical rehabilitation. Disputes arose over the speed, agency, initiative, and formula behind the reversal of criminal sentences. Molotov, as head of the first commission to investigate Stalin's purges, opted for a long-drawn-out review process. His stance reflected the anxiety common among top Party officials that a wave of returnees would damage the Party-state's legitimacy and possibly damage the authority of current officials. According to one unofficial source, only 7,679 people were rehabilitated between 1954 and Khrushchev's secret speech in 1956, whereas 617,000 were rehabilitated between the 20th Party Congress and the end of 1957.[3]

When Khrushchev won the battle over the secret speech, he also triumphed in the matter of legal rehabilitations. In the spring of 1956, in order to process the huge number of prisoners, Khrushchev formed special traveling three-person commissions. Each commission was made up of an

2. These distinctions are adapted from Albert Van Goudoever, *The Limits of Destalinization in the Soviet Union: Political Rehabilitations in the Soviet Union since Stalin,* trans. Frans Hijkoop (New York: St. Martin's Press, 1986), p. 7.

3. Dmitrii Iurasov, quoted in Stephen G. Wheatcroft, "*Glasnost'* and Rehabilitations," in *Facing Up to the Past: Soviet Historiography under Perestroika,* ed. Takayuki Ito (Sapporo: Hokkaido University Slavic Center, 1989), pp. 201–3.

official from the prosecutor's office, a representative of the Party Central Committee, and—thanks to the intervention of a former prisoner—a Party member who had already been rehabilitated.[4] These commissions fanned out to camps and places of exile across the country, briefly reviewed each convict's file, held a short interview, and used their extraordinary powers to rehabilitate or pardon the prisoner on the spot. Thus the time and form involved in the reversal of a sentence often paralleled the manner of its imposition: ten minutes in front of a three-person commission with extralegal powers. Given the Party's circumspection about its errors and its strong hold on power, it naturally preferred to act unilaterally and quietly.

When the victim was dead, the government felt less pressure to act rapidly or generously. The Procuracy granted a posthumous rehabilitation only after receipt of a request from the victim's family or friends and an often lengthy review of the case. All rehabilitations proceeded behind closed doors, generally without the victim's participation, and without the right to appeal. The review of complex cases might involve the Procuracy, the KGB, the courts, long archival searches, even reexamination of witnesses, so the potential for intentional or unintentional delay was enormous. Anatolii Spragovskii, a former senior investigator for the Tomsk regional KGB, recalled that between 1955 and 1960 he and his colleagues traveled throughout the region interviewing witnesses and visiting sites of alleged crimes even after it became clear that the major case under which thousands of local residents had been tried was totally fabricated: victims had been convicted of blowing up bridges or factories that never existed. Cases with several defendants were complicated by the Procuracy's policy of rehabilitating only those persons who had filed appeals.[5]

When Spragovskii wrote to Khrushchev to propose streamlining rehabilitation with national-level legislation, however, he was censured by his superiors. Officials saw a national solution as predicated on an assumption of unacceptably broad error on the part of the government and as only drawing attention to the scope of the problem. National legislation was used for "mass rehabilitations" only to restore the rights of some deported ethnic groups. But because state decrees were published only in

4. "In Memory of Alexei Snegov," *Moscow News,* 22–29 October 1989, p. 5.
5. Unpublished interview with Anatolii Spragovskii by Adam Hochschild, Tomsk, April 1991.

the local press in the areas directly concerned, suspicion of deported nationalities remained strong in the 1990s.[6]

Far from all of those who applied for rehabilitation received it. Most notably, the government refused to rehabilitate the victims of the famous show trials of the 1930s, including the old Bolsheviks Nikolai Bukharin, Lev Kamenev, and Grigorii Zinoviev. Of those convicted in the great show trials only Akmal Ikramov, who confessed and was executed along with Bukharin, won posthumous rehabilitation. Ikramov's son Kamal had appealed to the first secretary of Uzbekistan, who brought the case to the attention of Khrushchev personally. Though Khrushchev then apparently gave Molotov a two-month deadline to resolve the case, Ikramov's legal rehabilitation took a year, and even then it was treated as top secret. The document reinstating him in the Party was stamped "Confidential" and kept locked in the Central Committee's safe.[7]

Like the causes for arrest, the criteria for rehabilitation remained subjective and shrouded in mystery. In 1988 Gennadii Terekhov, a former senior investigator for the USSR Procuracy, recalled his personal guidelines for rehabilitation: cases should be investigated to see (1) if the person had no record before arrest and suddenly began to "confess"; (2) if the case was built only on the confession of the accused; or (3) if the only testimony against the accused came from other prisoners. When he followed these guidelines, "it became clear whom to rehabilitate and whom not to rehabilitate. After all, during the period of baseless repressions they judged real criminals too."[8] Because there were no written guidelines and no one wanted conflict with the leadership, the Procuracy often refused to recommend rehabilitation in complicated or political cases.

Direct interference in rehabilitations came simultaneously from other agencies. According to the son of an executed old Bolshevik, Anton Antonov-Ovseenko, "the Stalinists tried to isolate the new leader from the rehabilitated Communists. They slandered them, had them followed. To Nikita Khrushchev's honor, when he was brought transcripts of 'seditious' conversations by figures who had suffered from the repression under

6. "'The Punished Peoples' of the Soviet Union: The Continuing Legacy of Stalin's Deportations," *Helsinki Watch Report,* September 1991.

7. Kamal Ikramov, *Delo moego otsa* (Moscow: Sovetskii Pisatel', 1991), pp. 56–60.

8. Anatolii Golovkov, "Vechnyi isk" (interview with former procurator G. A. Terekhov), *Ogonek,* no. 18, 1988, p. 31.

Stalin, he tore up the accusations and chased the accusers out of his office."[9] Khrushchev appointed two old Bolshevik former prisoners—Aleksei Snegov and Olga Shatunovskaia—to help with rehabilitations, but both encountered resistance in their work.[10] Another instance of foot-dragging, according to Antonov-Ovseenko, occurred when the Presidium adopted a resolution freeing deportees. The head of the KGB apparently intervened and it was discovered only a month later, after some old Bolsheviks complained to Mikoian, that the Supreme Soviet had not implemented the resolution.[11] In Tomsk, Spragovskii complained that KGB bosses, having themselves been promoted on the basis of cases they had fabricated in the 1930s, overrode the Procuracy's orders to interview witnesses who had since become high Party officials.[12]

Party-state officials also employed more subtle means to soften the impact of rehabilitation. First, they gave many families false information about the date and cause of death of the victim in question, to disguise the fact that execution had followed arrest almost immediately or that conditions in the labor camp had been responsible for the victim's death. Second, information on burial sites was completely taboo. No one was to know of the existence of mass graves, many of which lay near city centers.[13] Third, the courts often chose a rehabilitation formula that hid the utter baselessness of the arrests. Thus the poet Anatolii Zhigulin and his comrades in an underground youth organization were first amnestied in 1954, then rehabilitated for lack of evidence of guilt in the spring of 1956. Only in the autumn of 1956 did Zhigulin receive a document certifying what he considered "full rehabilitation," that is, dismissal of the case for lack of evidence that a crime had been committed.[14]

Full social rehabilitation was extremely rare. The government did provide assistance with housing and limited financial compensation for survivors of the purges or their families. Ikramov's sons received housing and were readmitted to their educational institutes even before their father's

9. Anton Antonov-Ovseyenko, *The Time of Stalin: Portrait of a Tyranny*, trans. George Saunders (New York: Harper Colophon, 1981), p. 316.

10. Sergei Khrushchev, *Khrushchev on Khrushchev*, ed. and trans. William Taubman (Boston: Little, Brown, 1990), pp. 13–15.

11. Antonov-Ovseyenko, *Time of Stalin*, p. 323.

12. Hochschild interview with Spragovskii, April 1991.

13. Aleksandr Mil'chakov, "Kak sobrat' ubityi narod," *Vecherniaia Moskva*, 18 February 1992.

14. Anatolii Zhigulin, *Chernye kamni*, in *Zarok: Povest', rasskazy, vospominaniia* (Moscow: Molodaia Gvardiia, 1989), pp. 229–32.

case was resolved.[15] According to decrees of the USSR Council of Ministers, all survivors received two months' wages from their old jobs, and could count their years of work in labor camps toward pensions and job seniority. Technically, a rehabilitated citizen who was physically fit to work had the right to be reinstated in his or her old job or school. A family that had lost its breadwinner could also receive two months' back wages and a special pension. Official documents confirming the former workplace and salary and the amount of time spent in detention were necessary before a survivor could claim a full pension or a family receive compensation for loss of the head of household.

Only in 1964 did an article by E. Efimov finally outline survivors' rights and procedures for securing financial compensation. The article specified numerous obstacles to obtaining proper documentation and many instances in which benefits were unjustly denied. Some officials refused to honor rehabilitation certificates, for instance, because the documents said the case against So-and-So had been dismissed (*prekrasheno*) but did not actually contain the word "rehabilitation."[16] Efimov cited only a few actual cases, but one may assume that he chose them because they represented larger problems and trends. This article appeared not in the mass media but in a professional legal journal. Efimov sought to help officials, not to empower victims. Unlike Latin America in the 1980s, the USSR had no human rights groups or independent lawyers to guide victims through the claims process. In an informational and associational vacuum individuals learned how to proceed by word of mouth.[17]

Moreover, Efimov's article said nothing about a victim's right to return to his or her old job or course of study. All of Zhigulin's codefendants were reinstated in their institutes, and one man's father, who had been second secretary of Voronezh, received his union-level pension. But despite their legal rights, apparently few former prisoners resumed their former positions, especially if they had held high office earlier. Of the three surviving top officials sentenced in the postwar "Leningrad affair," only one returned to Party work.[18] The Central Committee invited the former

15. Ikramov, *Delo moego otsa.*

16. E. Efimov, "Pravovye voprosy vosstanovleniia trudovogo stazha reabilitirovannym grazhdanam," *Sotsialisticheskaia zakonnost',* no. 9, 1964, pp. 42–45.

17. Evgenia Ginzburg, *Within the Whirlwind,* trans. Ian Boland (New York: Harcourt Brace Jovanovich, 1981), pp. 405–15.

18. "The So-Called 'Leningrad Case,'" *Political Archives of the Soviet Union* 1, no. 2 (1990): 163–65.

head of the Gold Trust to return to work there, but as a deputy to his former subordinate.[19] Lingering suspicion of "enemies of the people" may also have limited reinstatement in the Communist Party. The Party Control Commission reviewed more than 70,000 petitions between 1956 and 1961 but reinstated only 30,954 members.[20] And though a biographical note about a public figure might mention that he or she had been a victim of illegal repression, no article on rehabilitation per se appeared in the Soviet press.

Since the rehabilitation process was never demystified, some people were afraid to apply for review of their cases. Others became frightened during the process. A former employee of the militia recounted that in Leningrad the people who were being rehabilitated were to be given the news by young militiamen; the idea was that fresh young faces and the absence of secret police would alleviate any anxiety the former prisoners might feel. The procedure, however, was to issue a summons to the petitioner to appear at the militia office on a certain day. There the former prisoner was to be given a copy of the rehabilitation certificate and informed about housing rights and the possibility of compensation for confiscated property. But many people apparently misinterpreted the summons as the start of a new prison term, and showed up wearing layers of warm clothing, equipped with food packages, and accompanied by weeping relatives.[21]

Besides cloaking the legal and reparative aspects of rehabilitation in secrecy, the authorities censored press reports on the rehabilitation of individuals; one observer called the process "rehabilitation by stealth."[22] But pressure for public rehabilitations was exerted by foreign Communists, old Bolsheviks, scientists, and members of the military establishment who intervened on behalf of their former colleagues. In the 1960s the Central Committee received a steady stream of letters asking for commemorative articles on behalf of old Bolsheviks who had been legally

---

19. N. Mil'chakova, "Pisat' vse-taki nado! . . . ," in *Vozvrashchenie k pravde: Reabilitirovan posmertno,* vol. 2 (Moscow: Iuridicheskaia Literatura, 1988), pp. 80, 136.

20. "Iz 'otcheta o rabote komiteta partiinogo kontrolia pri TsK KPSS za period s XX po XXII s"ezd KPSS (1956–1961 gg.),'" in *Reabilitatsiia: Politicheskie protsessy 30–50-kh godov,* ed. Aleksandr Iakovlev (Moscow: Politizdat, 1991), pp. 80–91.

21. Letter from V. I. Savin, colonel of militia, Leningrad, in "*Dal'she . . . dal'she . . . dal'she!*" *Diskussiia vokrug odnoi p'esy,* comp. Gennadii Li (Moscow: Knizhnaia Palata, 1989), pp. 239–40.

22. Leopold Labedz, "Resurrection and Perdition," *Problems of Communism* 12 (March-April 1963).

rehabilitated. These petitions recounted the political and professional careers of the victims and asked for articles about them in the central press and occasionally suggested events to honor them at the Museum of the Revolution.

The Central Committee responded grudgingly to such requests, first carrying out its own investigation of each alleged victim through the Institute of Marxism-Leninism, then requiring that the article coincide with an important anniversary. In several cases the Central Committee refused requests on the grounds that the given anniversary was not important; the victim's sixty-fifth birthday, say, was not the "jubilee" that his eightieth birthday would be. Often the Central Committee would agree to publish a commemorative article, but not in *Izvestiia* or *Pravda*.[23] Most calls for commemoration of revolutionary figures came from old Bolsheviks such as Elena Stasova, a Party member since 1898 and member of the Central Committee secretariat under Lenin.[24] In several instances republican Party secretaries wrote to Moscow suggesting an article in *Pravda* to commemorate a local former high Party official who had been repressed.[25] Few applications from relatives found their way to the Central Committee, but those that did tended to be more demanding—asking for restoration of entries in the *Soviet Encyclopedia*, reissuance of the subject's works, and so forth.

Party authorities clearly sought to limit commemoration overall, yet to recognize leading Party, state, scientific, and military cadres who had suffered at Stalin's hands. Here the contradictions of Khrushchev's stance become evident. On the one hand, publications regarding the repression of outstanding figures reinforced the idea of the Party as martyr. On the other hand, the real extent of repression, especially among old Bolsheviks, cast doubt on Khrushchev's argument that the Party had always retained a Leninist core, that its revolutionary purity was intact.

The Party did not fluctuate between total silence and complete openness

23. I found forty-five petitions for commemoration of political figures in the Central Committee archives for the period January 1963–June 1964; only eight concerned people who had not been repressed. See fond 5, opis' 55, Tsentr Khraneniia Sovremennykh Dokumentatsii, Moscow.

24. Stasova's signature headed a petition for rehabilitation of Bukharin written in 1964 after a positive comment about him appeared in the published transcript of a congress of historians. See Wheatcroft, "*Glasnost'* and Rehabilitations," p. 206.

25. In the spring of 1964 the CPSU Central Committee received requests from the secretaries of the central committees of Azerbaijan and Belorussia and from the obkom first secretary of Buratiia: fond 5, opis' 55, Tsentr Khraneniia.

regarding the past, but rather struggled over how to use certain bits of the truth artfully to discredit Stalinism without undermining the Soviet regime. Stalinists such as S. V. Kossior, V. Ia. Chubar, R. I. Eikhe, and Ia. E. Rudzutak were granted some degree of rehabilitation, while the central press continued to condemn Trotskyites and others who had sided against Stalin in the intraparty struggles of the 1920s and 1930s. But standards shifted over time, and pressure from below sometimes had an effect. In 1957, for instance, the Presidium apparently drew the line at public rehabilitation of army leaders; yet at the 22d Party Congress, Khrushchev used this omission to tar the members of the antiparty group as neostalinists.[26]

In sum, under Khrushchev, public and legal rehabilitations were not entirely random, but neither were they strongly regulated by procedure or law. For the former Party elite, politics and highly placed allies played major roles in deciding who received public rehabilitation. The government publicized few norms regarding any aspect of rehabilitation, and individuals had no other sources of information about how to proceed or what their rights might be. The totalitarian state's restrictions on social organization also impeded the formation of self-help groups, vital in an informational vacuum and when rehabilitation had to be initiated from below.

During the first eighteen months after Khrushchev's ouster, little change could be discerned in policies toward rehabilitation. But soon thereafter, mention of repression began to disappear from biographical notes. References to the dates of purge victims' deaths suddenly omitted the formula "during the period of the cult of personality." And on the fiftieth anniversary of the October Revolution in 1967, no new rehabilitations of old Bolsheviks were announced.[27] Under Leonid Brezhnev, legal rehabilitations gradually slowed to a trickle and special assistance to survivors ceased. Roy Medvedev cites the case of two old women who had benefited from preferential treatment in housing upon their release from camp in 1956. When they asked for help twenty years later they were told, "The fashion for rehabilitated people is now dead."[28] The president of the

26. Wheatcroft, "*Glasnost'* and Rehabilitations," p. 204.

27. Jane P. Shapiro, "Rehabilitation Policy under the Post-Khrushchev Leadership," *Soviet Studies* 20 (April 1969): 490–98.

28. Quoted in Roy Medvedev, *Khrushchev: A Biography,* trans. Brian Pearce (Garden City, N.Y.: Doubleday/Anchor, 1984), p. 98.

Supreme Court admitted that between 1964 and 1987 only 240 people had been rehabilitated.[29] The change in sentiment was clear to the public; as one longtime employee of the Moscow Procuracy put it, "There were few of these appeals [in the 1970s and 1980s], obviously because the social-political situation wasn't right."[30]

Interest in rehabilitations rose as Gorbachev's policy of glasnost allowed journalists some leeway in choosing their own topics. Beginning in 1987, the liberal press devoted considerable attention to Stalin's persecution of famous political and cultural figures. In many cases, the media revealed legal rehabilitations that had taken place under Khrushchev but had never been disclosed to the general public. Lack of access to official documents, however, limited coverage of the purges. In one well-publicized case, a *Moscow News* reporter was denied access to his own parents' case files. Only after considerable negotiation did the KGB and Procuracy allow him to photograph the mug shot of his father preserved in their files.[31] As the initiative in public rehabilitations shifted to journalists, they chose their subjects with discretion, and at first political oppositionists such as Bukharin and Trotsky remained taboo. Slowly, however, journalists and writers chipped away at the Party's restrictions. For instance, an *Ogonek* interview with Bukharin's widow and an extremely positive analysis of his life and work in *Moscow News* preceded Bukharin's official rehabilitation in February 1988.

Spontaneous and uncoordinated media reports about past atrocities led officials to search for a means to reassert control over revelations about the purges without reversing glasnost. In 1987 the Politburo formed the Commission on Additional Studies of Documents Pertaining to Repressive Measures of the 1930s-1940s and early 1950s. With a monopoly on archival materials, the commission became the authoritative source of rehabilitations. It used its jurisdiction to resolve the scandal over Bukharin and other sensitive cases. Significantly, investigation of repressions remained the province of the Party, not the government or an independent committee. And Party-state archives remained closed to other researchers.

The public rehabilitation of famous figures prompted citizens to appeal for rehabilitation on behalf of themselves or their relatives. At first rehabilitation proceeded as before—slowly, only after a specific request had

29. Quoted in Wheatcroft, "*Glasnost'* and Rehabilitations," p. 218.
30. Interview with Olga Matlash, Moscow City Procuracy, Moscow, 21 May 1991.
31. Grant Gusakov, "Closely-Guarded Secrets," *Moscow News,* 24–29 July 1989, p. 16.

been filed, and without much publicity. Gradually the Procuracy began to spread information on where and how to appeal for rehabilitation. At the same time, a shortage of personnel and resources and the lack of criteria for granting or denying rehabilitation created long delays in responses to public inquiries. Two official decrees, one in 1988 and one in early 1989, however, radically changed the process. First, the local KGB and procurators' offices were ordered to review all cases from the 1930s to the mid-1950s, whether or not a complaint had been registered. The Politburo also asked local Party organizations to accelerate their review of petitions for reinstatement. Most important, the Politburo decreed that all sentences that had been decided by "troika" (a three-person committee set up to alleviate the burden on the courts during the height of the repressions) or other nonjudicial bodies be annulled and the people sentenced be rehabilitated.[32] This order allowed the KGB and Procuracy to resolve a great many cases in a short time. By the spring of 1991, a representative of the Moscow Procuracy claimed that it had resolved 90 percent of its cases that involved sentences by nonjudicial bodies—a large share of its 100,000 cases subject to review.[33]

The timing of these two decrees is noteworthy. The first was issued after Memorial had held its first sanctioned meeting and at the same time that history exams were canceled. The second was passed just weeks before Memorial's founding conference. Gorbachev and other lawmakers did not consult Memorial on the new decrees, but they clearly sought to defuse public complaints and dampen the impulse behind the organization of a nationwide movement.

Despite the streamlining of rehabilitation by executive order, complaints continued. Victims of dekulakization and of persecution for religious beliefs or dissident activity sought to be classified as victims of repression. The informal or samizdat press helped to raise public awareness of repressions beyond the official time span of 1930–53. Independent newspapers such as *Ekspress-Khronika* and the Democratic Union's *Svobodnoe slovo* published accounts of political prisoners of the 1970s and 1980s, and their columnists reminded readers of the Red Terror of

32. "O dopolnitel'nykh merakh po zaversheniiu raboty, sviazannoi s reabilitatsiei lits, neobosnovanno repressirovannykh v 30–40-e gody i nachala 50-kh godov" (11 July 1988) and "O dopolnitel'nykh merakh po vosstanovleniiu spravedlivosti v otnoshenii zhertv repressii, imevshikh mesto v period 30–40-kh gody i nachala 50-kh godov" (5 January 1989), both in Iakovlev, *Reabilitatsiia*, pp. 16–18.
33. Interview with Olga Matlash, 21 May 1991.

1918. In August 1990, President Gorbachev implicitly recognized a broader definition of repression when he ordered that full rights be restored to people who had suffered exile or arrest as a result of forced collectivization in the 1920s.[34] He also restored citizenship to twenty-two dissidents who had been exiled abroad under Brezhnev. He did not, however, admit to a past pattern of human rights violations, which would have implied that Soviet institutions had contributed to the abuses.

The official press, meanwhile, functioned as a watchdog, responding to individual complaints and at one point reporting that officials in the provinces had continued the old practice of issuing false information about causes and dates of death.[35] And Memorial assisted people who needed help in writing appeals for rehabilitation or filing claims for compensation. The Moscow Memorial even organized a group of lawyers who volunteered their services to people who needed assistance. Thus official decrees and citizen initiatives in this area coincided to some extent: both wanted to help individuals obtain legal rehabilitation. In comparison with other demands, legal rehabilitation was a relatively painless concession for the state.

While Gorbachev overhauled the rules governing legal rehabilitation, he did not alter the existing statutes on reparations to victims of illegal imprisonment. They stipulated revision of pension status and awarded two months' pay at the rate in effect at the time of arrest—which currency reform now had reduced to a pittance. Many angry letters appeared in the Soviet press from newly rehabilitated survivors who rejected such compensation (often around 60 rubles, or about $20 at that time) as an insult.[36] Moreover, those who tried to collect compensation again encountered officials who were ill informed about the law. And the passage of time made collecting the money more difficult because back wages were to be paid by the former employer or its heir or, as a last resort, the responsible ministry.[37]

34. "Vosstanovlenii prav vsekh zhertv politicheskikh repressii 20–50-kh godov" (13 August 1990), in Iakovlev, *Reabilitatsiia*, pp. 332–33. In May 1991 the Council of Ministers had still not worked out a procedure for restoring the rights of dekulakized peasants, so the Procuracy and courts were powerless to resolve questions about the return of confiscated land.

35. G. Izhbul'din, "Nazvat' vse imena," *Ogonek*, no. 7, 1989.

36. For instance, letter from K. Shishlok in *Izvestiia*, May 1989, in *Federal Broadcast Information Service Daily Report on the Soviet Union (FBIS-Sov)*, 17 May 1989.

37. O. Laptev, "Kompensatsii reabilitirovannym," *Narodnyi deputat*, no. 3, 1990, pp. 115–17.

The extremely low standard of living of many victims sparked innovative proposals from the public. One former prisoner suggested that all the money collected for monuments could be better spent on housing and aid for victims.[38] Another radical proposal came from USSR People's Deputy A. Shchelkanov, who proposed that rehabilitated survivors of repression receive 1,000 rubles per year of incarceration, the funds to be drawn from the Party's coffers. Using figures supplied by Memorial, he estimated that total compensation would require less than one-fourth of the Party dues collected in a year. Memorial itself appealed to the Congress of People's Deputies in a more moderate tone, requesting revision of the law on compensation and higher pensions and better medical service for survivors.[39]

The national legislature failed to respond, so in 1989 a few local councils took steps to assist former purge victims. Some cities reacted to moral outrage stirred up by the media and to pressure from local Memorial branches by awarding survivors (and sometimes their spouses as well) the same privileges accorded war veterans, including special food rations, free passage on local transport, and access to better housing and medical care.

By 1991 the initiative for controlling legal and social rehabilitation had shifted to the republican parliaments. Beginning in 1988, the Baltic republics adopted a whole series of measures regarding rehabilitation, compensation for suffering, and restoration of confiscated property for victims of Soviet occupation and deportation. In part because the nature of repression in the Baltics differed substantially from the experience of other Soviet republics, Baltic laws did not serve as direct models for legislation elsewhere. But the idea of republican-level legislation to satisfy the popular demand for uniform privileges spread. In December 1990 the Belorussian Supreme Soviet tried to calm the public outcry over the purges by adopting a law rehabilitating victims of repression from the 1920s to the 1950s and granting them reparations. Ukraine followed Belorussia's example in April 1991, while Russia and Kazakhstan were discussing their own laws. In Ukraine and Russia victims' associations cooperated with legislators to produce workable laws that included gradual payment of monetary compensation based on time spent in prison, labor camp or

38. F. Eremenko, "Luchshii pamiatnik," *Argumenty i fakty,* no. 39, 30 September–6 October 1989.

39. A. Shchelkanov, "Obrashchenie Obshchestva 'Memorial' k narodnym deputatam SSSR," typescript, author's collection.

exile.[40] The USSR Supreme Soviet moved so slowly that by the time of the coup in August 1991 it had only just produced a draft law on rehabilitation and reparations.

By the late 1980s, individual legal and public rehabilitations seemed to have lost their sting as far as the government was concerned. On the contrary, the Party-state apparatus took credit for having speeded up and brought candor to the rehabilitation process. By strengthening the procedural base and rapidly resolving individual cases, the government sought to capitalize on the moral outrage over Stalinism and at the same time to show that the Gorbachev administration differed qualitatively from its immediate predecessors. Nevertheless, the regime still reacted defensively to discussion of the extent and roots of repressions. One can contrast the Politburo commission that reviewed famous cases at its own discretion with Latin American "truth commissions," comprising representatives of official and civic groups, which documented the nature and extent of repression. The most notable improvements in benefits for Soviet survivors resulted from pressure from below channeled through new political opportunity structures. Victims benefited from glasnost in the media, from advocacy by newly permitted civic groups, and from pressure on local and regional legislatures for material assistance to survivors.

## REWRITING SOVIET HISTORY

A second venue for restoring justice to victims is historiography. Unlike rehabilitations, revision of history has a broad public impact. Traditionally, historians have been expected to preserve the memory of public events and bring the lessons of the past to new generations. Yet historians choose what to remember and what to consign to oblivion. Historians' activities are socially conditioned and shaped by conscious and unconscious principles of selection. In the Soviet Union, remembrance and forgetting were governed not only by social and personal factors but by the dictates of Party-state officials and the criteria of *partiinost'*. History, like

40. Interview with Izrail Reznichenko, president of Kiev Memorial, Kiev, 22 April 1991; interview with Anatolii Kononov, deputy of the Russian Supreme Soviet and member of its Committee on Human Rights, Moscow, 13 May 1991. For a comparison of republican laws, see L. V. Boitsova and V. V. Boitsova, "Vosstanovlenie i okhrana prav zhertv massovykh repressii: Sostoianie i perspektivy zakonodatel'nogo regulirovaniia," *Gosudarstvo i pravo*, no. 6, 1992, pp. 15–26.

the arts, was expected to serve the people's interests as defined by the Party. The Party used history to support its legitimating myths, enshrine its heroes, and promote social cohesion by whitewashing conflicts. With its extraordinary control over the means of communication, the Party had a monopoly on the transmission of public memory.

From 1938 until 1956 all Soviet schools used the *Short Course on the History of the CPSU(b),* which exalted Stalin's role and minimized the contributions of other old Bolsheviks. The *Short Course,* designed to produce a single vision of the past, became a catechism for students. Not surprisingly, Khrushchev singled out the *Short Course* as one of the main vehicles of propaganda behind Stalin's cult of personality. While a generation of Soviet citizens had been raised on a textbook that deified Stalin, a generation of historians had been devastated by the purges and by pressures to conform to the vagaries of Party ideology. A Western observer noted shortly before Stalin's death, "Histories succeed each other as if they were being consumed by a giant chain smoker who lights the first volume of the new work with the last of the old. Historians appear, disappear, and reappear; others vanish without a trace."[41] The purges affected both written works and their authors. Historians learned to work without access to important archives and documents. The survivors developed sophisticated internal censors to allow them to shift with changing political trends.

In the years after Stalin's death, the historical profession continued to suffer a crisis of credibility and courage. Despite the Party's condemnation of historians' role in creating the Stalin cult, few historians readily engaged in serious self-criticism. Older historians were compromised by their earlier writings. As we saw earlier, Anna Pankratova, who spoke out at the 20th Party Congress and afterward urged revision of historical studies, endured harsh criticism from audiences who were skeptical of her ability to overcome her participation in falsifying history. The questions from historians in her audiences also suggested that many of her colleagues were still preoccupied with more mundane matters linked to their own survival. Could they continue to quote Stalin? Which of Stalin's works could be considered classics of Marxism-Leninism?[42] Even younger scholars had grown accustomed to responding to commands from

41. Bertram D. Wolfe, "Operation Rewrite: The Agony of Soviet Historians," *Foreign Affairs,* October 1952, p. 39.

42. A. M. Pankratova, "Dokladnaia zapiska" (report to Presidium of Central Committee, CPSU), March 1956, TsK KPSS, obshchii otdel, fond 5, opis' 16, Tsentr Khraneniia.

above rather than seizing the initiative in choice of topic and tone for their works.

In 1956 a few liberal historians repudiated the command system, arguing that since the 20th Party Congress had mandated reform of historical studies, historians no longer needed to await orders from above. Led by the editors of the journal *Voprosy istorii*, Pankratova and E. N. Burzhdalov, reform-minded historians embraced a broad notion of how to overcome the cult of personality. They tried to create an atmosphere for scientific debate and to restore the names of Party figures who had been erased from Stalin-era historiography. Reform included rewriting the history of the Revolution itself to include the participation of rehabilitated old Bolsheviks, Mensheviks, and members of other political groups. Burzhdalov called for a more realistic view of Party history, one that did not attribute all errors to "enemies" and all successes to leaders. He forthrightly asserted that historians were more truthful in the 1920s than in the 1930s, yet more truthful in the 1930s than in the 1940s. Historians today, he urged, should pay attention to the role of the masses, seek greater access to archives and documents, and engage in discussions without name-calling.[43]

Attacks such as Burzhdalov's on Stalinism and on the work of living Soviet historians raised considerable controversy. Though Burzhdalov rejected one reader's call for organized measures against living holdovers of the cult of personality—he noted that all historians made mistakes and that there was no need for name-calling or worse in what was an ideological battle—his whole reform program threatened the status of orthodox Stalinist historians.[44] And conservative scholars and ideologists fought back against *Voprosy istorii*. Privately, the journal's opponents wrote to the Central Committee accusing Burzhdalov of denigrating the central leadership in ideological work and contending that his call for "100 percent truth" ignored the dangers presented by capitalist encirclement of the USSR. Others charged Pankratova with supporting politically questionable historians and consorting with Trotskyites.[45] Publicly, conservatives

---

43. E. N. Gorodetskii, "Zhurnal 'Voprosy istorii' v seredine 50-kh godov," *Voprosy istorii*, no. 9, 1989, pp. 69–79.

44. "Doklad E. N. Burzhdalov o sostoianii Sovetskoi istoricheskoi nauki i rabote zhurnala 'Voprosy istorii' (na vstreche s chitateliami 19–20 iunia 1956 g. v Leningradskom otdelenii instituta istorii AN SSR)," *Voprosy istorii*, no. 11, 1989, p. 123.

45. Director of Institute of History of the Party, Leningrad obkom, to Central Committee, 2 July 1956, fond 5, opis' 35, and A. M. Rumiantsev, deputy director of Department of Science and Culture, report marked "Secret," 17 April 1955, sec. 2, "Ob otnoshchenii k

questioned the journal's political orientation, accusing it of "bourgeois objectivism," catering to enemies of socialism, and fostering "nihilism" among the young. An article in *Leningradskaia pravda* even charged Burzhdalov with subverting the study of history under the guise of carrying out the resolutions of the 20th Party Congress.

Burzhdalov's attempts to publish a response to the attacks on him and to have his opponents penalized by the Party Control Commission for slander failed. In the wake of the Hungarian uprising, the Central Committee refused to recommend publication of his response. It agreed that *Leningradskaia pravda* had distorted Burzhdalov's words in some places, but noted that it would be wrong to use the press to settle accounts.[46] Pankratova also attempted to defend the journal and its reformist line, but in March 1957 an alliance of conservative historians and Party ideologists persuaded the Central Committee to remove the journal's liberal editors. The triumphant orthodox Party press exulted: "While criticizing Stalin's mistakes, the Party at the same time defends him against the attacks of revisionists."[47] The new editorial board of *Voprosy istorii* interpreted the resolution on overcoming the cult of personality "in the spirit of neostalinism"; that is, it condemned the cult but praised Stalin.[48]

On a practical level, history teachers struggled in the aftermath of the 20th Party Congress to restructure their lesson plans. During her 1956 lectures Pankratova was besieged by questions from teachers about how to react to revelations about Stalin and the *Short Course*. Pankratova reported to the Central Committee that "a great many teachers in Leningrad wonder if exams shouldn't be postponed this year, in light of the lack of textbooks and the great confusion in students' minds." She supported that idea. "By the fall semester the teaching of history in the USSR will have to be completely overhauled. As things stand now, exams in the middle schools could do more harm than good."[49] The government did indeed cancel history examinations rather than leave teachers to cope individually with touchy ideological questions. This vacuum in the social-

litsam, politicheski skomprometirovanikh sebia," pp. 2–3, fond 5, opis' 17, both in Tsentr Khraneniia.

46. V. Kirillin's response to Burzhdalov's letter of 8 February 1957 to Pospelov, Kirillin, and Konstantinov, 25 February 1957, fond 5, opis' 35, Tsentr Khraneniia.

47. *Partiinaia zhizn'*, no. 6, March 1957, quoted in Merle Fainsod, "Soviet Russian Historians, or: The Lesson of Burzhdalov," *Encounter*, March 1962, p. 86.

48. Gorodetskii, "Zhurnal 'Voprosy istorii,'" p. 79.

49. Pankratova, "Dokladnaia zapiska."

ization of Soviet youth could not be permitted to last, and a series of textbooks was prepared. At the end of the 1960s, however, the government returned to the format of a single book.[50]

Conservative historians successfully defended the idea that history should be written to serve the Party's goals, however they might be defined, against the notion that historians should present the facts and let readers make their own judgments. In 1957 the struggle to write the whole truth was lost, and as a consequence literary writers and memoirists, who required less institutional support and training than historians did, took the lead in publishing the most revealing and thoughtful accounts of the purges. After Khrushchev's ouster, neostalinist historians consolidated their position and grew bolder in their positive assessments of Stalin. Senior historians criticized Khrushchev's secret speech for its "subjective, incorrect, antileninist evaluation of the whole period of constructing socialism" and for fostering nihilism and disrespect for the older generation.[51] Individual historians who continued to criticize Stalin suffered career setbacks or even imprisonment.[52]

By the beginning of perestroika, the reimposition of strict censorship of negative aspects of Soviet history had sharply reduced popular knowledge of the Stalin-era repressions. The history textbook in use in 1986 barely reflected Khrushchev's destalinization campaign. It mentioned that Stalin had made "serious errors" and cited the Central Committee's resolution of 1956 condemning the cult of personality, but did not discuss Stalin's role in collectivization or in the famine of the 1930s.[53] Gorbachev himself criticized the "paradox" that interesting historical and social scientific questions "often become dry, banal, and formal" in lectures and textbooks. He urged creation of an "honest, brave, appealing book, laying out the heroic journey of the nation and Party in all its glory . . . not bypassing the drama of events and human fates."[54]

50. N. N. Maslov, "Kakim dolzhen byt' novyi uchebnik po istorii KPSS?" *Voprosy istorii KPSS*, no. 7, July 1987, p. 52.

51. Speeches by the historians Likholat, Aleksandrov, and Borodin at a June 1965 seminar sponsored by the Central Committee's Department of Science and Educational Institutions in "Stenogramma soveshchaniia po voprosam istorii KPSS," 21 June 1965, fond 5, opis' 35, Tsentr Khraneniia.

52. "While Clio Was Asleep . . . Soviet Historians: Where Were They Yesterday?" *Moscow News*, 13–20 November 1988, p. 8.

53. R. W. Davies, *Soviet History in the Gorbachev Revolution* (Bloomington: Indiana University Press, 1989), pp. 180–81.

54. Quoted in Maslov, "Kakim dolzhen byt'," pp. 47, 62.

As during the thaw, liberal historians engaged in self-criticism, bemoaning their profession's loss of prestige and public confidence. They attributed the shortcomings in Soviet history to historians' personal failings, such as opportunism, as well as to structural problems, such as editors' unwillingness to publish original ideas.[55] Glasnost permitted historians to quarrel over how much perestroika they needed. Iurii Afanas'ev took a very radical position, criticizing those who hid behind half-truths or created artificially balanced views of the past: "On the one hand there were crimes, repressions, and [the] moral degradation of our society. On the other hand, however, there were joy, enthusiasm, and great accomplishments. Thus everything appears normal—some sort of balanced construction is produced . . . Fair enough, but where is the whole? Where is the totality?" Others argued that history needed to be improved, but not totally rewritten. Liberals concurred, however, that historians needed to explore the cult of personality more fully than they had done in the past, to speak openly about Stalin's crimes.[56]

The historians' recognition of their shortcomings did not translate into immediate results. Popular writers might write novels and memoirs "for the drawer," without expectation of publication, but antistalinist historians had had no access to the materials that might have led to high-quality studies during the years of stagnation. In the short run, a Soviet historian wrote, history "spilled out of the academic auditoriums . . . into the pages of the popular press."[57]

Meanwhile, history teachers were clamoring for professional guidance and new materials. Public debates over the interpretation of Stalinism led the authorities to cancel exams in Soviet history again in the spring of 1988. Instead of taking a written exam, students participated in an "ungraded individual interview" or "free conversation." These interviews revealed that students were interested in history but that they often disagreed with their teachers—a finding that suggests they were acquiring most of their information and opinions outside the classroom.[58]

55. Interview with Iu. Poliakov, *Literaturnaia gazeta,* 29 July 1987, p. 10, in *FBIS-Sov,* 4 August 1987, pp. 22–27.
56. See the historians' roundtable, *Nedelia,* no. 52, 27 December–3 January 1987, pp. 14–15, in *FBIS-Sov,* 11 January 1988, pp. 65–69.
57. V. A. Kozlov, "The Historian and Perestroika," *Voprosy istorii KPSS,* no. 5, May 1987, in *Soviet Historians and Perestroika: The First Phase,* ed. Donald J. Raleigh (Armonk, N.Y.: M. E. Sharpe, 1989), p. 33.
58. Davies, *Soviet History,* pp. 183–84.

After the Ministry of Education announced an official competition for a new textbook for high school students in May 1987, a lengthy debate broke out in the historical press. Nikolai Maslov urged historians to stop presenting history as a "straight line," to end the "depopulation" of history, and to pay more attention to facts and events.[59] The journal *Voprosy istorii KPSS* monopolized discussion of the proposed textbook, and kept it firmly within the bounds of *partiinost'* à la Gorbachev. Participants agreed that both the positive and negative sides of Soviet history must be exposed, and one out of two materials submitted in the textbook debate suggested ways to improve the discussion of Stalin's cult of personality.[60] Overall, however, students' and even teachers' opinions seemed to play a small role in the debates; historiography remained the province of professional historians.

Given the pressure to produce a revised educational program immediately, as one observer noted, the educational system "faced the unenviable task of making definitive statements about topics under intense debate in society at large."[61] Indeed, the first new history textbook came under fire for being out of date by the time it came off the presses.[62] The book failed to incorporate teaching methods that would encourage students to draw their own conclusions from primary source material, and teachers continued to face a tremendous credibility problem because of what Afanas'ev called a gap between popular oral history and history as it was taught in the schools. It was this contradiction, he argued, not depressing revelations about the past, that led young people to distrust authority.[63]

But could a new textbook narrow the gap between popular and public history? Every society distinguishes between people's literal memories and the social construction of public memory of larger events; this is the difference between autobiographical memory of events experienced by the individual and historical memory communicated to the individual about remote events important in the national experience.[64] Official cen-

59. Maslov, "Kakim dolzhen byt'," pp. 55, 57–58.

60. V. K. Gorev and A. V. Bedov, "Uchebnik pravdy, uchebnik zhizni," *Voprosy istorii KPSS*, no. 7, July 1988.

61. William B. Husband, "Rewriting Soviet History Texts: The First Phase," in Ito, *Facing Up to the Past*, p. 84.

62. Obsuzhdenie shkol'nogo uchebnika po istorii SSSR," *Voprosy istorii*, no. 1, 1990, pp. 188–91.

63. Citied in Davies, *Soviet History*, pp. 182–83.

64. Maurice Halbwachs, *The Collective Memory*, trans. Francis J. Ditter and Vida Yazdi Ditter (New York: Harper & Row, 1980), pp. 50–51.

sorship exacerbates contradictions between private memory and public history; and a rift in interpretations of the past, as Paul Connerton points out, causes alienation: "Images of the past commonly legitimate a present social order. It is an implicit rule that participants in any social order must presuppose a shared memory. To the extent that their memories of a society's past diverge, to that extent its members can share neither experiences nor assumptions."[65] The Soviet regime eliminated public contention over interpretation of national history by creating uniform textbooks and imposing orthodoxy on historians, but in doing so it aggravated the alienation produced by selective official amnesia about historical figures and events.

Victims of Stalinism in particular felt the disparity between their personal experiences and the public celebration of the period of "the construction of socialism." Torturers rob victims of their voices by persuading them that no one will ever know their fate.[66] Soviet survivors knew from experience how easily politicians could erase once-famous figures from history. Even during the thaw many felt that their individual voices would never be heard. To counter this possible loss of historical records, Memorial's Scientific Information Center brought together victims and amateur historians to collect oral histories and memoirs, and to create data bases of statistical information garnered from independent sources. Following the lead of the young archive worker Dmitrii Iurasov, who had lost his job for covertly gathering data for a card catalog of victims, many Memorial chapters tried to compile comprehensive lists of local victims.

Only in late 1988, however, did Party historians seem to accept the need to incorporate first-person accounts and literary treatments of the past into their own debates. In November 1988 the Central Committee Academy of Social Sciences and *Voprosy istorii KPSS* at last included nonscholars in a historical roundtable, among them Dmitrii Shepilov, accused of participation in the antiparty group, and the novelist Anatolii Rybakov.[67] Official attention also turned to creative methods for teaching history. One article explained in minute detail how teachers could use various game scenarios to engage students.[68] Interestingly, the author neglected to

65. Paul Connerton, *How Societies Remember* (New York: Cambridge University Press, 1989), p. 3.

66. Elaine Scarry, *The Body in Pain* (New York: Oxford University Press, 1985), p. 49.

67. "Problemy istorii i sovremennost'," *Voprosy istorii KPSS,* no. 2, February 1989.

68. Zh. Iu. Knyrkova, "V poiskakh netraditsionnykh form prepodovaniia," *Voprosy istorii KPSS,* no. 3, March 1990.

mention a mock trial, which many liberal teachers employed to assess Stalin's activities and other controversial events.

Even in debates over the textbook, a somewhat esoteric subject, one sees shifts in the definition of competence. The popular conception of history gradually expanded to include reminiscences, documents, and oral interviews of ordinary people. Shaping collective memory became a task for nonprofessionals—amateur historians, novelists, journalists, memoirists, and ordinary citizens. Under Khrushchev, historians tried to break away from the command system, under which they essentially performed research on demand and within strict political guidelines; under Gorbachev, people asserted their competence and reassessed the value of private memory against distorted official history. Moreover, distress over blank spots in history led the public to question the role of historians as selective guardians of the past. Mass repressions, in particular, had a tremendous impact on people's lives but found little place in history governed by Marxist class-based theory and periodization based on the tasks of CPSU congresses. Under new programs survivors of repression themselves contributed their stories as bulwarks against oblivion. And independent intellectuals aired the idea that Stalinism was not an aberration but an extension of Leninism.

## COMMEMORATING VICTIMS: SYMBOLIC POLITICS AND CIVIC ACTIVISM

Besides condemning Stalin in words, Khrushchev took numerous steps to dismantle the trappings of his cult. After Khrushchev's secret speech, authorities at all levels, from ministers to school principals, took down portraits of Stalin and banners bearing his words. In some schools, students cut Stalin's picture out of their textbooks, just as they had removed pictures of "enemies of the people" in the past. Similarly, in the wake of the 22d Party Congress, Stalin's body was unceremoniously removed from Lenin's mausoleum. But nothing came of the proposal to officially honor victims.

During perestroika the issue of commemorating victims reemerged, and once again attention focused on monuments and graves. In 1987, however, the idea of commemorating victims of repression arose not at a Party congress but among young people and through the independent Memorial society. Neither Gorbachev's sanction of a monument nor Memorial's inclusion on the design commission actually settled the basic problem of what kind of monument should be built. Given the subject matter and Soviet attitudes toward *partiinost'* in the arts, the content and form of a monument commemorating repression were subject to varying political and personal calculations. As diverse concepts for a monument began to pour in to Memorial and competition organizers, art critics and social observers focused on such crucial unresolved issues as who was to be commemorated and for whom this monument was intended.[69]

The range of projects submitted in the fall of 1988—piles of bones, giant statues of Stalin with the Soviet people crouched at his feet, parks with fountains of tears, museums—revealed that society did not even approach consensus on the purpose of the monument. The concepts and designs submitted reflected the interests and perceptions of different groups. When Khrushchev conceived of a monument to Stalin's victims, he imagined some sort of sculpture dedicated to loyal citizens who had shown some special merit before their arrests. Khrushchev's elevation of a subset of victims chosen on the basis of their loyalty to socialism (and even to Stalin) glossed over inherent contradictions. Though by 1988 the idea of the martyrdom of ordinary people had been firmly established, the notion of dividing the pure from the impure still remained a part of social consciousness. As one Memorial activist noted, many people inserted the word "innocent" before "victims of repression" in Memorial petitions.[70] Selectivity would permit conformity with the Soviet tradition of gigantic, heroic monuments—one might immortalize the good Communist victim with an enormous sculpture of the "brave prisoner."

Another problem was how to commemorate people who had been cogs in the system; one critic compared them to the Jews at Auschwitz who stoked the fires of the crematoria while waiting their own turns.[71] The real-life mix of complicity and innocence did not lend itself to triumphal art.[72] By the Party's standards both in 1961 and in 1988, the concept of Party and society as both victims and victimizers was unacceptable. The

69. Aleksandr Melik-Pashaev, "Dolgo budet rodina bol'na . . . ," *Dekorativnoe is-kusstvo*, no. 4, 1989, p. 6.

70. Nina Braginskaia, "Slava besslav'ia," *Znanie—sila*, January 1991, pp. 14–15.

71. The psychologist Leonid Radzikhovskii in the roundtable "Memorial zhertvam Stalinskikh repressii," *Dekorativnoe iskusstvo*, no. 8, 1989, p. 15.

72. It could not be "shouted," commented Aleksandr Rubtsov, "Mezhdu dvumia konkursami," *Dekorativnoe iskusstvo*, no. 3, 1989, pp. 13–14.

The artist V. I. Soldatov's conception of the Stalin era. *Courtesy Interregional Memorial Society Archives, Moscow.*

Party wanted to single out noble victims and vile executioners and leave it at that; and though survivors and relatives of victims differed on the form the monument should take, many of them shared the impractical view that victims must be sorted into good and bad, that the monument must honor something lest it promote nothing but despair.

The early stages of the competition revealed that many victims and their friends and relatives had not been able to think through the experience of Stalinist repressions. Prevented from learning about the scope and mechanisms of the purges, many people simply focused on their own undeserved and incomprehensible pain. Survivors tended to propose designs that directly reflected their experiences. A plethora of designs reproduced the prison cell or labor camp, complete with barbed wire, guard towers, and guard dogs, or showed interrogators and torturers from the prisoner's viewpoint. Suffering is inherently difficult to express, and a literal rendering produces a chamber of horrors. An early attempt (during Khrushchev's thaw) by the sculptor Ernst Neizvestny showed a downtrodden, broken victim on a stark plain marked with the numbers of camps. Neizvestny's more recent efforts portray the impact of Stalinism on Russian civilization, but his first project, according to the journalist Nina Braginskaia, "testifies to suffering, empathizes with pain; his position is as close as possible to the position of the victim, unable to understand the reason for such torment; an attempt to comprehend the vastness of the phenomenon leads to extensive use of space and enumeration."[73] Ultimately, the perspective of Ivan Denisovich is moving but unsatisfying, especially for members of the younger generation.

Another design favored by people of the purge generation was a grave. A symbolic grave would serve the need of survivors and relatives for a place to gather and mourn. But, as Braginskaia noted, a symbolic grave would allow each person to nurse his or her private grief in isolation. At such a monument "one has no need to rethink anything, in general one has no need for ideas. My father (mother, brother, husband, son, sister, grandmother, etc.) was tortured for nothing, and he hasn't got a tombstone, so now there will be one for everyone. And that's it."[74] A tombstone is comforting and uncontroversial, but it cannot convey the scope or complexity of the terror.

In the 1980s appeals for a monument began to reflect a more sophisti-

73. Braginskaia, "Slava besslav'ia," p. 14.
74. Ibid., p. 15.

A monument design inspired by the film *Repentance* shows women waiting outside a prison window on one side and a girl reaching out to the future on the other. Collage by Sergei Losev. *Courtesy Interregional Memorial Society Archives, Moscow.*

cated, civic-oriented conception of how to commemorate Stalin's victims. Memorial based its appeals on the concept of a research center, library, and archive to promote continuing interpretation of the terror and of a monument to all the victims of repression. Some Memorial activists looked at a monument as merely something to complement civic action—the real guarantee against a return to totalitarianism—and the Scientific Information Center, which embodied the continuing search for truth.

If Soviet artists wished to help "enlighten" people, they needed, as one critic framed it, to break away from Brezhnev-era gigantism and triumphalism and find an image that promoted catharsis. Citing Aristotle's dictum that tragedy produces pity and terror in the audience, Arsenii Chanyshev hoped for a monument that evoked terror and even anger, which then would be converted into spiritual renewal and a bulwark against the return of repression.[75] Another artist called for a monument with an "all-human" element, a point of view that crossed the bounds of time and space.[76] Future generations would benefit from a monument with a preventive message. Thus some artists tried to conceive of "antimonuments"—maelstroms, pits in the ground leading to the underworld. Others suggested multiple monuments, with a variety of media and sites across the country, to slay the multiheaded hydra of repression.

The first stage of the formal competition focused on site selection, and this matter revealed a full range of opinions. Many people wanted the monument to be put on "sacred ground," variously interpreted as Red Square, the Kremlin wall, or a religious location such as the site of Christ the Saviour Cathedral (demolished on Stalin's orders in the 1930s). Choice of sacred ground and symbols, depending on their content, affirmed victims' innocence by appealing either to religious sentiments or to loyalty to the Soviet regime. A minority, however, argued that the monument not be allowed to mar Moscow's historic center. They saw politics as a dirty and shameful blot on an otherwise glorious national history. A more popular proposal was to place the monument within or in front of the Lubianka prison, to contrast with the statue of Feliks Dzerzhinskii, founder of the Soviet secret police. Braginskaia called this choice "an apotheosis of symbolic revenge." Permission to build at this location would serve as a sort of substitute Nuremburg to affirm the innocence of victims, and for

75. Arsenii Chanyshev, "Ochishchenie cherez vozmedie," *Dekorativnoe iskusstvo*, no. 4, April 1989, p. 2.
76. Melik-Pashaev, "Dolgo budet rodina bol'na," pp. 5–7.

An entry in the competition to select a design for a monument to Stalin's victims. *Courtesy Interregional Memorial Society Archives, Moscow.*

some people would also function as a kind of magical taming of terrible forces.[77]

Dzerzhinskii's statue is gone now, and a boulder from the first political concentration camp in the USSR marks the spot in front of the Lubianka where a monument will be placed, but a winning design has yet to be selected. Despite delays and disappointment with the predominance of crude or Brezhnevite proposals, the inclusion of Memorial on the jury reassured many people that a creative design would eventually be chosen. Moreover, a consensus emerged among art critics, at least, that the competition for a monument had revealed that "living human memory has nothing in common with this gigantic mass of petrified official memory, which has embodied the state and Party apparat's directives about what to

77. Braginskaia, "Slava besslav'ia," pp. 16–17.

remember and how to remember. The competition for a monument presents an opportunity to embody popular memory, which is sincere, quiet, stern, humble, versus propaganda history, which is wordy, didactic, grandiose, and aggressive."[78] Having rejected the old monumental style, however, people still await the construction of a new idiom.

Another aspect of commemoration—the creation of new holidays and rituals—centers on civic action. In 1974 Soviet political prisoners declared 30 October to be their holiday—Soviet Political Prisoners Day—which they marked in camp with hunger strikes.[79] Under perestroika, radical groups led by former political prisoners took their celebration of this day to the public. In 1988, DS staged tiny protests in Moscow, Leningrad, and Novosibirsk; two years later the number of their demonstrations had quadrupled. DS's preferred tactic was to picket KGB headquarters and to crown statues of Dzerzhinskii with wreaths of barbed wire—an ironic reversal of the official proclivity for laying flowers at the feet of its monumental heroes.[80]

For DS, Soviet Political Prisoners Day was an occasion for defiance and rebellion. Memorial, in contrast, began to celebrate the holiday in 1989 with a civic action described as a "living chain" around the Lubianka. Memorial activists and survivors of Stalin's camps brought candles to the Lubianka and honored prisoners with a silent demonstration. A year later, Memorial members gathered in Lubianka Square to dedicate the site of the future monument and to hold a requiem for victims of repression. DS rejected a funereal meeting as too passive; its members held a separate protest nearby, and addressed the topic of past guilt and present accountability with such slogans as "Half of the nation were executioners, half informers. Shame on us all!" and "Only a change of regime will free the remaining prisoners."[81]

Whether as a day of sorrow or a day of contempt for the authorities, Soviet Political Prisoners Day remained a civic holiday, unrecognized by

78. Evgenii Ass in "Memorial zhertvam stalinskikh repressii," p. 14.

79. Ludmilla Alexeyeva, *Soviet Dissent: Contemporary Movements for National, Religious, and Human Rights*, trans. Carol Pearce and John Glad (Middletown, Conn.: Wesleyan University Press, 1985), pp. 319, 329.

80. On patterns of officially sanctioned commemoration, see Nina Tumarkin, *The Living and the Dead: The Rise and Fall of the Cult of World War II in Russia* (New York: Basic Books, 1994).

81. "Demonstratsii v den' politzakliuchennogo SSSR," *Svobodnoe slovo*, 11 November 1988; *Ekspress-Khronika*, no. 45, 6 November 1990; Vadim Kushnir, "Konsolidatsiia v Lubianki," *Svobodnoe slovo*, 13 November 1990.

Memorial members form a "living chain" around the Lubianka prison in downtown Moscow to mark Soviet Political Prisoners Day, 30 October 1989. *Courtesy Interregional Memorial Society Archives, Moscow.*

the Communist authorities. In fact, the militia routinely dispersed DS demonstrators. The authorities did not disrupt Memorial's ceremonies, but they had ways to discourage attendance. During the "living chain" they blocked the entrances to the square to people who arrived even a minute after its starting time; the state radio announced the wrong time for the dedication ceremony; and both years the official press proclaimed

Mourners observe Soviet Political Prisoners Day in front of the Lubianka, 30 October 1991.
*Photo by Tanya Smith.*

the KGB's participation in the ceremony and failed to mention the significance of the date.[82]

Citizen initiative also paved the way for discoveries in a third battlefield of symbolic politics: the uncovering of mass graves. Starting in 1989, revelations of common burials of purge victims seemed to emerge from all corners of the Soviet Union as Memorial and individual citizens drew on the testimony of witnesses to uncover the sites. Between 1989 and 1991 mass graves were uncovered in Moscow, Leningrad, Odessa, Kiev, Alma-Ata, Minsk, Cheliabinsk, Iaroslavl', Kursk, Tula, Lugansk, and several smaller cities. As in Belorussia, such shocking discoveries proved a strong stimulus for antistalinism. Once discovered, such graves and old camps became sites for pilgrimages by victims' families, centers for protests, and powerful symbols for radical politicians.

Unwilling to wait for graves to be discovered by accident, one journalist began a crusade to locate mass graves in Moscow and to identify the anonymous corpses. Aleksandr Mil'chakov's interest in secret burials was sparked when, while doing research for a novel in 1961, he learned from cemetery employees that in the 1930s hundreds of bodies with bullet holes in their foreheads had been thrown into unmarked common graves in central Moscow cemeteries. His own father had survived a long term in the camps; now Mil'chakov was struck by the thought of those who had disappeared. "After all," he noted, "they couldn't really have vanished, their remains had to be somewhere."[83]

Under glasnost, Mil'chakov made his knowledge public, and in cooperation with Moscow's main evening newspaper, *Vecherniaia Moskva,* he published a series of articles recounting the progress of his quest for official confirmation of grave sites and asking for new information. What *Vecherniaia Moskva* labeled "Mil'chakov's duel with the KGB" led to a flood of letters and phone calls. Mil'chakov even got a few tips from liberal officers in the KGB and remorseful former NKVD workers. The public furor and Mil'chakov's reputation became so great that in 1990 the

---

82. "Tsepochka pamiati," *Pravda,* 1 November 1989; "O sobytiiakh 30 Oktiabria," undated Memorial leaflet regarding protests of 30 October 1989, author's collection; *Ekspress-Khronika,* no. 45, 6 November 1990; Karina Musaelian, "Muchenikam zemli sovetskoi," *Demokraticheskaia Rossiia,* no. 5, November 1990, pp. 8–9.

83. Interview with Aleksandr Mil'chakov, Moscow, 13 April 1991.

Excavation of a mass grave of purge victims in Cheliabinsk. *Courtesy Interregional Memorial Society Archives, Moscow.*

newly elected, more liberal Moscow City Council created a commission on mass graves and voted the exemption necessary to make Mil'chakov its president, though he was not a deputy. The committee contributed little of practical significance to the search for graves, but it gave Mil'chakov more clout in his dealings with the KGB.

After months of silence, stalling, and deception, the KGB finally yielded to public pressure and not only confirmed the sites discovered by Mil'chakov but produced lists of the people secretly buried there.[84] Beginning in December 1990 *Vecherniaia Moskva* published a weekly column

84. Ibid.; "Duel': Aleksandr Mil'chakov protiv KGB," *Vecherniaia Moskva*, 14 April 1990; "KGB: Rasstrel'nye spiski naideny," *Vecherniaia Moskva*, 27 November 1990.

of photographs and short biographical sketches of the victims. Mil'chakov's lists, with their haunting black-and-white photos and terse obituaries, created moving images of the victims, far more powerful than dry statistics. The lists shattered the myth fostered by Khrushchev that the Party was Stalin's main victim. Chauffeurs and professors, blue-collar workers and executives, Party members and nonmembers, young and old, all appear in the execution lists. Though the majority of the first 800 victims pictured were engaged in "intellectual labor," 10 percent were blue-collar workers and another 10 percent were unemployed at the time they were arrested. Moreover, no correlation could be found between victims' execution and their level of education, profession, political affiliation, or ethnicity.[85]

Most important for the growing movement toward public empowerment, an ordinary citizen had broken down the defenses of the once-omnipotent secret police. In continuing to hide mass graves, the authorities tried both to block the creation of physical foci for demonstrations and to hide potentially delegitimizing symbols. After the Communist Party was banned in the wake of the failed August coup, Mil'chakov expressed the belief that knowledge of secret burial sites inevitably led to doubts about the one-party system. It was fear of just that outcome if people ever looked squarely at the mechanisms and results of the Party's rule that kept it from disclosing the burial sites as long as it could.[86]

By building statues, opening up archives, creating rituals of remembrance, and uncovering mass graves, members of the public took advantage of glasnost to carve out a niche in the public realm for mourning and commemoration. Grave markers, demonstrations, monuments, and published lists of victims all served to rescue the individual from oblivion and to reverse the stigma associated with repression. Though repentance and catharsis may be impossible to achieve, there is a generally shared belief that public commemoration can serve as a barrier against future abuses of human rights. Monuments have no magical powers, even if one could be placed in front of every prison and mass grave, but civic involvement in governing the public realm does preserve private memory as an alternative to official propaganda.

85. V. Poletaev and I. Kornakovskii, "Absurd, stavshii normoi: Popytka sozdaniia sotsial'nogo portreta na osnove rasstrel'nykh spiskov," *Vecherniaia Moskva,* 30 March 1992.
86. Aleksandr Mil'chakov, "Kak sobrat' ubityi narod," *Vecherniaia Moskva,* 27 February 1992.

TRIALS

In Latin America the pursuit of justice for victims of human rights abuses focused on prosecution of secret police and military perpetrators. In the USSR, neither the authorities nor the public relied on the judicial system for redress. Khrushchev engaged in both legal reform and selective prosecutions of human rights abusers to reassert control over the secret police. But in prosecuting Lavrentii Beria, chief of the secret police, the Presidium was acting out of fear that he would install himself as a new Stalin, not out of outrage at his role in carrying out the purges. That role was a convenient excuse to sentence Beria and his six codefendants to execution. Four more closed trials followed, in which, according to the Soviet press, twenty-three high police officials, all Beria's protégés, were sentenced to execution or long prison terms.

The fates of other former NKVD officers tried in the 1950s remain obscure. One Memorial historian has discovered that at least fifty other high-ranking NKVD investigators—whose names surfaced during the review of cases of major Party and cultural figures—were also arrested for bringing false charges or torturing prisoners.[87] According to an official of the Procuracy, "If facts came to light showing that one or another state security officer was mixed up in baseless accusations against Soviet people . . . then such workers, depending on the degree of their guilt, were expelled from the Party, removed from their posts, or judged by law . . . There were no special purges, the staff was not reduced."[88] The Party did admit to expelling 347 of its members (including 10 ministers of internal affairs and state security at the union and republic levels and 72 senior NKVD officials) for violations of socialist legality between 1956 and 1961; but no data have come to light on the number of secret police subjected to penalties.[89]

Investigations under Khrushchev had to be initiated from above. Memoirs of the time tell of numerous complaints to officials at all levels

87. N. Petrov, "Spravka-dopolnenie (sudy nad rabotnikami NKVD-MGB)," in *Zven"ia*, ed. N. G. Okhotin and A. B. Roginskii (Moscow: Progress, 1991), pp. 430–36.

88. Quoted in Golovkov, "Vechnyi isk," p. 31.

89. "Iz 'otcheta o rabote komiteta partiinogo kontrolia pri TsK KPSS za period s XX po XXII s"ezd KPSS (1956–1961 gg.),'" in Iakovlev, *Reabilitatsiia*, pp. 88–89; T. Men'shikova and Iu. Solomonov, "Moment istiny" (interview with the military procurator V. Provotorov), *Sovetskaia kultura*, 25 February 1989, p. 8.

about torture and abuse by NKVD investigators, with little result. Aleksandr Mil'chakov's father "appealed from the camp darkness with unanswered applications to the Party Central Committee, the USSR Supreme Soviet, the Procuracy, and the USSR Supreme Court. Later, when I returned to Moscow after I was rehabilitated, I saw some of these declarations, written on odds and ends of paper, including cement bags and soap wrappers, in my personal file."[90] The state preserved these petitions, but it did not use them to prosecute anyone. Rehabilitation of victims did not include an opportunity to file legal complaints against the people responsible for their illegal arrest and sentencing. In fact, according to one witness, "All Moscow heard the news that a Party organization at an academic institute had been disbanded because of demands that all those guilty of the mass repressions be prosecuted."[91] Such rumors undoubtedly served to kill hopes for accountability before the law. Moreover, by 1956 many of the people who carried out the purges had themselves become victims or had retired. The introduction of a statute of limitations as part of a new criminal code in the late 1950s ended the possibility of prosecutions for crimes of the 1930s.

During perestroika, however, the idea of a trial of Stalin and Stalinism became a subject of public debate. Many Memorial activists pointed to the Nuremburg trials as a precedent for prosection.[92] International law, they further noted, mandates that there can be no statute of limitation for crimes against humanity. But when the Tomsk branch of Memorial tried to prosecute Party officials, including Ligachev, for crimes against humanity for the cover up of mass graves in the 1970s, the courts refused to hear the case.[93] A public furor also arose when the press revealed that Khrushchev's imposition of a statute of limitations had led to the release of several former investigators who had been indicted for torture and fabrication of cases, and that those men still held high civilian posts in

90. Quoted in Mil'chakova, "Pisat' vse-taki nado! . . . ," p. 155.

91. Fedor Burlatsky, *Khrushchev and the First Russian Spring,* trans. Daphne Skillen (New York: Scribner 1988), p. 72.

92. See, for instance, Elena Zelinskaia, "Pepel klaasa stuchit v moe serdtse!" AS 6132, *Materialy samizdata,* 22 January 1988.

93. Adam Hochschild, "The Secret of a Siberian River Bank," *New York Times Magazine,* 28 March 1993, pp. 29–31, 38, 40, 78; Yegor Ligachev, *Inside Gorbachev's Kremlin,* trans. Catherine A. Fitzpatrick, Michele A. Berdy, and Dobrochina Dyrez-Freeman (New York: Pantheon, 1993), pp. 254–56.

Moscow. The publicity cost them their positions and decorations, but they remained immune to prosecution.[94]

Oddly enough, one of the few cases to gain a preliminary court hearing was based on a citizen's initiative to *defend* Stalin. A former prosecutor charged a liberal writer and newspaper with slandering Stalin and his defenders. Stalin could not be called a "criminal," the plaintiff argued, because he had never been tried or convicted of any crime. The proceedings really were nothing more than a media event, with both sides struggling to present their opinions before the judge ultimately dismissed the suit. The popular press celebrated the suit's dismissal as a defeat of modern-day incarnations of Stalinism, but admitted that the plaintiff's spirited defense of Stalin's honor had great resonance for some members of the older generation.[95]

The press continued its "slander" of Stalin, and support for the idea of exposing the names of his NKVD henchmen remained strong. Publication of the names of executioners has often been proposed as an alternative to a Nuremberg trial, but such a proposal assumes that the identity of the guilty can be determined without benefit of legal procedure. Controversy over using secret police files to screen public servants in Czechoslovakia and elsewhere has demonstrated that "outing" informers without due process may increase distrust of the judiciary.

Lack of respect for the Soviet legal system is one of the reasons behind public support for an extraordinary forum. The idea of a mock "social trial" of Stalin and Stalinism gained popularity during perestroika. In school classrooms and public auditoriums across the Soviet Union history teachers and various clubs experimented with a trial format to reach moral and historical judgments of Stalin. In early 1991, the most elaborate and pointed mock trial was held by a group of Moscow City Council deputies, who charged not Stalin but the Communist Party with grave crimes, ranging from systematic violations of human rights beginning in 1917 to the invasion of Afghanistan. According to the accusers, the Party not only had put itself above the law but had committed crimes against

94. Yevgeniya Albats, "Not to be Pardoned," *Moscow News*, 16–23 May 1988; "Negative Selection," ibid., 23–30 October 1988; and "Will There Be an End to the Lubyanka?" ibid., 18–25 March 1990.

95. Lyudmila Saraskina, "I Shall Defend Comrade Stalin's Honour and Dignity as Long as I Live," *Moscow News*, 9–16 October 1988; Bill Keller, "Stalin Has Lots of Friends in Court," *New York Times*, 30 January 1989, p. A4.

A banner reading "Bring Stalinism to public trial!" hangs over a map of the Gulag. *Courtesy Interregional Memorial Society Archives, Moscow.*

humanity.[96] Ultimately, the trial was a one-sided affair and it had little public impact (though it turned out to be a harbinger of postcoup charges against the Communist Party). The idea of a "social" or "moral" trial still appealed to radicals, though, because it sidestepped the Soviet judicial system and tapped into what they felt were shared basic moral standards not always embodied in written law. Moreover, a social trial empowered ordinary people by encouraging them be the judges of their national past.

Aside from the legal obstacles to real prosecutions, many liberal intellectuals cited the possibility of a return to inflammatory rhetoric and political purges as reasons not to pursue a Nuremburg-style trial. If prosecutions attained the same scope as persecutions, the Soviet Union would be awash in a sea of lawsuits. The scale of the hostility that could be unleashed by mass prosecutions deterred even those who in principle would have liked to see the perpetrators of repression held to account. Still, many people considered a legal trial or investigation vital if the country was to break with the repressive past. One letter writer was concerned about the possible results of condoning impunity: "How can we talk about perestroika if all these crimes are never subjected to judicial examination?" Another asked how one could accept the idea that all these terrible things happened but that no one was guilty.[97]

Why have trials—whether prosecutions of individuals or grand affairs—not been among the major efforts to come to terms with the Soviet past? Obviously, the scale of the crimes involved, as well as the passage of time, is an obstacle. Second, there is the problem of prosecuting persons whose defense would be that they were following orders or that they believed they were acting in the state's interest. An equally important factor stems from the society's deep lack of respect for the legal system. On the whole, the courts were never the first choice of recourse for Soviet citizens seeking justice. They expected change to come from the central authorities, so petitioners addressed their grievances to the real source of power in the USSR, the Party and its representatives. Former prisoners in particular still viewed Soviet laws as subject to manipulation by the Party and as not so different from the laws under which the original abuses were committed. A new government has the chance to validate itself and

96. S. Sulakshin, *KPSS: Vnezakonnost', prestupnost', otvetstvennost'* (Tomsk, 1990); "Obshchestvennyi sud nad KPSS," *Volia Rossii*, no. 1, December 1990, pp. 1–2; "Obshchestvennyi sud nad KPSS," *Gospodin narod*, no. 1, 1990, p. 11.

97. T. Reprintseva in *Ogonek*, no. 42, 1989, p. 25; A. Abel'skii, ibid., no. 45, 1989, p. 4.

discredit the old regime by holding a special trial. But, given the continuity of Communist Party rule under Khrushchev and Gorbachev, the leadership had no desire for what Paul Connerton has labeled "trial by fiat of a successor regime," which "is like the construction of a wall, unmistakable and permanent, between the new beginnings and the old tyranny."[98] Soviet rulers tried to rework symbols and history to serve new positive goals and to end public debates, but their inability to sever ties to the past made it impossible to restore legitimation through the courts.

The same issues of commemoration and compensation arose under Khrushchev and Gorbachev, but the balance of power clearly shifted over time. Soviet society was traumatized and atomized after Stalin's death. The thaw introduced Soviet citizens to the first open analyses of the terror. Readers devoured all sorts of literary treatments of the purges and began to contemplate the ramifications of state-sponsored repressions. But the Party tightly controlled all aspects of rehabilitation and restitution. The Gorbachev era, by contrast, was characterized by gradual civic empowerment and politicization. Glasnost revolutionized the means by which Soviets could criticize the regime and challenge official interpretations of the past. The Party-state authorities, by recognizing pluralism, relinquished their monopoly on discourse. And whereas during the thaw the survivors of the purges were too frightened to express their feelings about repression, during perestroika citizens began not only to talk openly about the past but to publicize the status of victims, to challenge historians' competence, and to demand compensation for past injustices. Drawing a lesson from past abuses, citizens tried to reclaim the public arena and to reassert their competence in many realms of policy making.

Khrushchev-era liberalization, because it did not extend the right of free association, severely limited the public's influence on policy. Rehabilitation and reparation procedures were designed to disguise the extent and arbitrariness of the repressions, and they reinforced social atomization and impeded the process of mourning by forcing individuals to appeal privately for assistance. The government did not employ sweeping legal measures to rehabilitate the mass of victims, nor did it create a single fund to cover reparations. Ordinary survivors had to pursue rehabilitation alone; they had no opportunity to combine forces to gain public recognition and political clout. Only old Bolsheviks, who could draw on their

98. Connerton, *How Societies Remember*, p. 7.

revolutionary and Leninist credentials, managed to unite and influence the Party elite in the matter of legal and public rehabilitation. Khrushchev did seek to address the material complaints of survivors by promoting social rehabilitation, but his government would not tolerate the revelations that would have been unleashed by open prosecutions of secret police officials or by independent historical or journalistic accounts of past events. Khrushchev himself took steps to reform and subdue punitive institutions, but he did so unilaterally and often clandestinely. He found it impossible to balance criticism and authority without sharply limiting the flow of information about the purges.

Gorbachev, for his part, unleashed a wave of spontaneous debate about the past by lowering restrictions on expression and association. Giving voice to popular desires, however, did not automatically translate into constructive state responses. Survivors and their allies were now able to organize and lobby the state for public rehabilitations and revision of official history, and when that effort failed, to protest publicly and to start self-help programs. They collected funds to help survivors, recorded their own versions of history, and solicited designs for a monument. Legal rehabilitation, reparations, textbook revision, and prosecutions, however, remained contingent on the authorities.

The passage of time had removed the threat of charges against the governing elite, and Gorbachev and other reformers recognized that it would reflect well upon them to rehabilitate Stalin's victims. But they continued to try to control the pace of public rehabilitations and to limit the definition of victims. They did not open the archives or initiate an official investigation of the purges. Though they catered to individual requests for rehabilitation, they shrank from discussing the scope of the purges and from commemorating the victims on a grand scale. For ideological reasons, the Party tried to preserve a positive view of Soviet history. Propagandists stressed the heroic not just for patriotic reasons but to support the notion that Communist rule had been a boon to the populace. For the heirs of Lenin and Stalin, the inverse link between authority and criticism still made any acknowledgment of the real scope of past errors unthinkable.

Ultimately, Memorial had an effect on the realm of cultural change but not on the realm of institutional reform. With the authorities' forbearance, organizations and individuals remade discourse among both specialists and citizens. They informed and educated society about state-sponsored repressions and created their own rituals of mourning and defiance. But during reform from above, policy changes still had to come from the top. And while officials occasionally reacted to try to ease pressure from below, they did not consult, negotiate, or work with informal associations. Without the initiative of politicians, issues of acknowledgment and reparations could not be addressed formally. The institutional legacies of Leninism were a physically powerful but ideologically vulnerable state and a shattered, marginalized society. That state did not wish to investigate the past officially, make restitution to victims a national policy, or prosecute offenders; and civic forces did not have the clout to compel them to do so.

# 8 THE DECLINE OF ANTISTALINISM

With radical attacks proliferating on many fronts, the reformist leadership of the Soviet Union conceded an ever-greater public realm to civic groups in 1990. Yet as opportunities for protest increased, both participation in Memorial and public concern with the need to come to terms with past repressions declined. Had a conservative backlash arisen against digging up the painful past? Or had liberals' attention shifted toward more revolutionary projects? Had the stalemate between Memorial and the authorities discredited the movement? Or could success in some items on its agenda have created the impression that the Stalin question had finally been resolved? The causes for the waning of Memorial's activities and the drop in interest in the purges may be found in both the evolution of social movements and the unique environment for politics created by the liberalizing totalitarian regime. The decline in antistalinism began with emotional overload and was exacerbated by the consolidation and routinization of a once "informal" movement. The changing political environment also raised new obstacles for Memorial, such as competition with new political parties for members.

The traditional approach to the development of social movements envisioned their transformation in Weberian terms, from charismatic movements to routinized, bureaucratic organizations. In theory, over time such organizations shift their goals in the direction of consensus with the greater society, becoming less ambitious and more conservative. As a primary goal becomes maintenance of the organization itself, leaders are motivated to avoid costly conflicts with the authorities. Moreover, with greater organization comes concentration of power, which in turn alienates members and depletes the organization's radical base. Mayer Zald and Roberta Ash challenge the determinism of the Weberian model, arguing that it does not take into account other possible internal processes or environmental conditions that might produce alternate outcomes, including radicalization.

Zald and Ash distinguish between external factors (an "ebb and flow of sentiments" among potential supporters, clarification of potential success or failure in achieving goals, and competition with other organizations within the larger movement) and internal factors (splits, changes in the type or style of leadership) that may pull movements in different directions.[1] Social movements are also affected by larger cycles of protest, which promote and then drag them down. Considerable historical evidence leads Sidney Tarrow to contend that infrequent and unpredictable waves of civic activity amplify the impact of resource-poor movements that might never attract notice under normal circumstances. In the "descending phase" of such waves, new participants have been socialized, the boundaries of conventional politics stretched, and new social movements institutionalized, but activists may be frustrated by the rising costs of disruption, exhausted, and disenchanted with organizational splits. Disruptive unconventional tactics also produce official displeasure, imitation and competition, and radicalization, all of which may be costly to the movement in the long run.[2]

I am concerned here not with the dynamics of the development of social movements for its own sake but its impact on the movement as a political actor. Admittedly it is difficult to evaluate the "success" of a social movement. One can distinguish between two kinds of success that do not necessarily go hand in hand: efficacy in achieving an agenda and success in maintaining the group's organizational coherence and legitimacy. An agenda could be fulfilled by the state's preemption of the social movement's goals; or, on the contrary, a movement could gain acceptance but

1. Mayer N. Zald and Roberta Ash, "Social Movement Organizations: Growth, Decay, and Change," in *Protest, Reform, and Revolt: A Reader in Social Movements,* ed. Joseph R. Gusfield (New York: Wiley, 1970), p. 517.

2. Sidney Tarrow, *Struggle, Politics, and Reform: Collective Action, Social Movements, and Cycles of Protest* (Ithaca: Center for International Studies, Cornell University, 1989), pp. 42–55.

be co-opted without having achieved its radical aims. Or a radical movement could achieve its more mundane objectives without ever accomplishing its transformational, system-changing goals—and in this regard one must consider to what extent broad social changes that occur during an era of reform should be attributed to the social movement.[3]

As to whether the evolution of a social movement into an interest group may be equated with success, theorists are divided. For some, enfranchisement in the existing political system equals co-optation and betrayal of revolutionary means and ends. Adoption of a formal structure and participation in "normal" politics sacrifices the social movement's unique power to influence through disruption.[4] Others, however, see the creation of stable networks and the transformation of a social movement into an interest group as a sign of success. After all, when an organization that develops out of a social movement acquires legal recognition and the advantages that go with it, it may achieve lasting influence.[5] A movement that has won representation for formerly disenfranchised or disadvantaged constituents has only to supervise the distribution of benefits. But movements by their nature seek to restructure society; it is bureaucracies that provide regular services.[6] Thus this mode of "success," while possibly preserving the organization, signals the end of the movement phase of activity. Let us focus on how changes in *Memorial* affected its achievement of its concrete and transformational goals and its basic survival.

## External Pressures on the Movement

### Shifts in Popular Sentiment

The so-called ebb and flow of sentiments may be defined as "the extent to which there are large numbers of people who feel that the [movement's] goals and means are in harmony with their own" and the extent to which they "feel neutral toward, reject, or accept the legitimacy and value of the

3. Ibid., pp. 71–73.
4. Frances Fox Piven and Richard A. Cloward, *Poor People's Movements* (New York: Pantheon, 1977), pp. 1–14.
5. Ronald M. McCarthy, "Institutional Development and Nonviolent Resistance," in *Research in Social Movements, Conflicts, and Change*, vol. 5 (Greenwich, Conn.: JAI Press, 1983), p. 2.
6. Zald and Ash, "Growth, Decay, and Change," p. 519.

social movement and its organizational manifestations."[7] Though the authorities ceased to question openly Memorial's right to exist as a political, charitable, and historical organization after the Moscow chapter's official registration in January 1990, Memorial faced criticism from a rival group and a growing conservative backlash. More significant, in 1990 Memorial organizers began to experience a drop in popular attention and sympathy toward victims of the purges.

The conservative backlash against perestroika and antistalinism arose slowly. Tiny pro-Stalin groups operated more or less underground in the late 1980s,[8] but no nationwide coalition formed until after Nina Andreeva's famous letter appeared. On the basis of the positive responses from readers, Andreeva created a conservative "Bolshevik" movement— Edinstvo (Unity), which held its founding conference in May 1989 and by 1991 boasted at least a dozen regional branches. Andreeva and her followers opposed what they saw as Gorbachev's betrayal of Communist ideals, in particular the restoration of capitalism. While focusing on current political and economic events, Edinstvo's leaders freely proclaimed their admiration for Stalin.[9] Andreeva herself downplayed the significance of the purges and sought to justify them. Baseless repressions were certainly criminal, but she argued that Stalin had reacted to real threats from a potential "fifth column" in the USSR.[10] Despite its Stalinist sympathies, Edinstvo did not clash directly with Memorial. Perhaps fearing that no good could come from attacks on survivors of repression, Edinstvo concentrated its vitriol against the new political parties and the reformist Soviet leadership.

The one group that did challenge Memorial's legitimacy as an organization was a rival survivors' group, the Assotsiatsiia Zhertv Nezakonnykh Repressii (Association of Victims of Illegal Repression). Apparently, the Assotsiatsiia formed with the blessing of the authorities—they registered it immediately and granted it access to meeting places—specifically to split Memorial. It challenged Memorial's right to speak for victims of the purges, claiming that Memorial had lost sight of the survivors' real needs

7. Ibid., pp. 520–21.
8. "Obrashchenie," Soiuz Sovetskikh Stalinistov, n.d., and *Bolshevik,* no. 3, n.d., author's collection.
9. Interview conducted by M. Steven Fish with Boris Gun'ko, president of Moscow Edinstvo society, Moscow, 14 January 1991.
10. Andrei Petrov, "Nina Andreeva: 'Nas gorazdo bol'she chem vy dumaete!'" *Moskovskii komsomolets,* 3 April 1990.

in its quest for political influence. The group's leaders charged Memorial with essentially being a part of the radical DS and of slandering Lenin.[11] In contrast to Memorial, the Assotsiatsiia accepted only those survivors who had been officially rehabilitated and focused almost exclusively on obtaining charitable aid for them. Its exclusiveness, internal scandals over financial irregularities, and anti-Memorial rhetoric, however, alienated many of its intended constituents and prompted them to form an alternative survivors' group, Ob"edinenie Lits, Postradavshikh ot Repressii (Union of People Who Have Suffered Repression), under the aegis of Memorial.[12]

Thus Memorial responded to the popular interest in a separate survivors' organization by incorporating the idea in a constructive manner. But Memorial continued to face challenges by the Assotsiatsiia's leaders, who tried to undermine Memorial's reputation by spreading disinformation through the press. The Assotsiatsiia took credit for placing the cornerstone for the future monument to purge victims, for instance, and claimed that Memorial had received aid packages from Germany but not distributed them. Memorial and its survivors' group constantly had to devote precious time to formulating responses to false charges and placing them in the press.[13] On the whole, however, the Assotsiatsiia, which arose in 1989, seemed unable to distract attention from Memorial, which had established itself when public interest in antistalinism was at its peak.

As for the harmony of Memorial's interests with public opinion, though it is extremely difficult to measure burnout or to pinpoint its causes, letters to the press indicate a trend toward intolerance. In 1987–88, many citizens burned with curiosity about what official propaganda and orthodox historiography had hidden from them. The early dialogue among citizens, journalists, and historians was marked by pleas, especially from young people, for more information, "more light." Typical of such correspondence during the dawn of glasnost was a 1988 letter from a twenty-four-year-old student asking the editors of the political magazine *New Times* for "more historical features—say, a series on the Stalin period." Yet already the writer felt compelled to explain, "I'm not just being curious or trying to follow the current craze for history. All I want is to know

11. "Protokol zasedaniia pravleniia Moskovskoi assotsiatsii zhertv repressii," 2 December 1989, author's collection.
12. "Otkrytoe pis'mo chlenov ob"edineniia lits, postradavshikh ot repressii," manuscript, ibid.; A. Nadezhdina, "Nikto ne budet zabyt," *Literaturnaia gazeta,* 23 August 1989.
13. Meeting of the Working Collegium of Moscow Memorial, 26 February 1991.

more about the most difficult period of my country's history."[14] Most print media responded eagerly to readers' demands; even technical scientific and artistic magazines profiled famous figures in their respective fields who had been purged.

From the very first, media coverage of the purges drew criticism from a small minority, who denied that they had ever occurred. Over time, doubters were joined by people who objected to constant negativism—a radical change from the usual aggressive optimism of the Soviet press. The new style of journalism also created the impression that interest in Stalinist repressions was part of a general craving for "sensation." For many members of the older generation, the "crimes" of the past seemed exaggerated, especially in comparison with what they considered the barbarity and chaos of the present day. But even liberals came to criticize the press for its treatment of Stalinism. In the spring of 1991 the organizer of the 1988 Week of Conscience exhibit argued: "Too many people are writing about Stalin now. There are a lot of superficial judgments. . . . We've reached a sort of saturation, unfortunately. . . . Now when a reader sees Stalin's name in a newspaper or magazine, he or she may flip through the pages without reading them."[15]

Elements of both informational overload and distaste for dwelling on the past surfaced in the wake of Aleksandr Mil'chakov's publication of lists of victims in *Vecherniaia Moskva*. From the first appearance of the lists, the newspaper received some negative responses. Unhappy readers did not challenge the veracity of the lists, but they complained that they had heard enough about Stalinism. Only journalists greedy for honoraria needed those lists, one reader claimed; only relatives cared about seeing the photographs and biographies of individual victims.[16] Some even charged that Mil'chakov's work hurt the nation's progress: "At this difficult time you spread rumors about the issue of victims of repression, you talk about the past, about executions and burials. The country has so many problems. It's not right to upset people now. Enough!"[17] This complaint led another commentator to wonder why the Soviets tired of their

14. *New Times*, no. 3, 1988, p. 3.

15. Interview conducted by Adam Hochschild with Aleksandr Vainshtein, organizer of the Week of Conscience, Moscow, 1991.

16. Aleksandr Mil'chakov, "Stalin: 'Ikh vsekh nado rasstreliat,'" *Vecherniaia Moskva*, 26 February 1991.

17. Aleksandr Mil'chakov, "A KGB molchit . . . ," *Vecherniaia Moskva*, 20 October 1990.

The Week of Conscience exhibit, Moscow, 1988. *Courtesy Interregional Memorial Society Archives, Moscow.*

newly uncovered horrors so quickly, in contrast to Armenian and Jewish remembrances of genocide. And why did people take such offense at those humble lists and not at the gruesome crime stories that had become the rage?[18] He could not answer his own questions, but perhaps part of the intolerance stemmed from the fact that some Soviet citizens were uncomfortably reminded of their roles as dupes, informers, or torturers. Many West Germans combined a "willed amnesia" about Nazi atrocities with a pragmatic desire to close the book on the past.[19] Here one sees similar resentment at being reminded of the past, and the same call to stop wallowing in guilt and grief.

18. Aleksandr Vorshchagovskii, "Smert' po nakladnoi," *Vecherniaia Moskua,* 26 March 1991.
19. Judith Miller, "Erasing the Past: Europe's Amnesia about the Holocaust," *New York Times Magazine,* 16 November 1986, pp. 30–36, 40, 109–11.

Such impatience with reminders of past horrors was certainly not universal. Mil'chakov received many supportive letters, including one that argued that the execution lists sensitized one to current injustices. He reminded readers that perestroika required the whole truth and that society owed it to victims to restore their good names. Of course, rehabilitation could not bring the dead back to life, but their memory was sacred. Adopting a sharper, more radical political stance, Mil'chakov even began to claim that his lists were necessary to discredit both Stalinism and Brezhnev-style socialism.[20] The concerned public seemed to be polarized about coming to terms with past events. But perhaps the majority were becoming desensitized to the whole debate about Stalinism and more interested in other aspects of reform. This was certainly the impression of some purge survivors, and it made them fear that their stories might not be welcome.[21]

### Failure and Success in Achieving Goals

Social movements, as we have seen, have trouble balancing practical and ideal goals. Paradoxically, if movements set realistic goals and attain them, they make themselves unnecessary; yet if they set unattainable goals their members become frustrated and the organization fails. "In a sense," write Zald and Ash, "the perfectly stable movement organization which avoided problems of organizational transformation, goal displacement and the like, would be one which over time always seemed to be getting closer to its goal without quite attaining it."[22] Thus a successful social movement organization must constantly set new reasonable goals or face extinction. The political, social, and economic environment under Gorbachev severely limited Memorial's choice of activities. The difficulty of finding openings for protest other than street demonstrations and electoral campaigns, plus official disapproval of radical activism, channeled Memorial's action into certain spheres.

The first area in which Memorial met almost no direct challenges was charitable activities. Memorial excelled in the collection of small dona-

20. Mil'chakov, "Stalin: 'Ikh vsekh nado rasstreliat'"; "A KGB molchit . . . "; "Kak sobrat' ubityi narod," *Vecherniaia Moskva,* 27 February 1992.

21. In an interview in Moscow in February 1991, the survivor Susanna Pechuro noted that when she spoke to school classes, she was always careful to begin by inviting students who were not interested in the purges to excuse themselves.

22. Zald and Ash, "Growth, Decay, and Change," p. 525.

tions, and the Moscow chapter frequently received humanitarian aid from abroad. Provincial chapters also achieved considerable results by lobbying local legislatures to extend privileges to the repressed. Granting free passage on local transport, access to veterans' stores, and so forth provided local authorities with good publicity and often served as a relatively uncontroversial way to defuse public interest in destalinization. In such cases, Memorial received some credit for having raised the idea of restitution and could turn its own scarce financial resources to other ends.

Immersion in charitable activities had two clear effects on Memorial. Fair, efficient allocation of humanitarian parcels required substantial investments of time and administrative energy. In Moscow the victims' group within Memorial developed a strong system of regional coordinators, who devoted their energies almost exclusively to evaluating the needs of their constituents and distributing aid. Though the Ob"edinenie group did not abandon its interest in Memorial's political activities, it took on the characteristics of a bureaucratic institution. Branches of Memorial involved in lobbying for privileges underwent the same sort of bureaucratization: either they shared in the administrative tasks of registering survivors for aid if they were successful or they found that the authorities had created sham commissions to tie up their time and energy. By funneling requests for aid through commissions attached to the local city councils and inviting Memorial activists to sit on these boards, the authorities increased their control over informal activists. If activists failed to cooperate, they could be blamed for any lack of progress; if they did participate, they could be tangled up in red tape. Moreover, a few activists perceived their success in securing privileges as a reason to abandon antistalinist activities altogether. In Kaluga, busy democratic activists happily yielded this issue to authorities.[23]

A second area in which accomplishments transformed the direction of Memorial's activity was historical work. The president of the Moscow Memorial, Arsenii Roginskii, was a historian who had served time in prison for his samizdat activities. He recruited a solid core of independent historians interested in various aspects of Soviet repressions and initiated numerous contacts with foreign specialists. Memorial created NITs (the Scientific Information Center) in Moscow, complete with its own archive, computer system, and library. NITs worked closely with branches of

23. Valerii Safranskii, member of Aprel' and of the Republican Party of Russia, to the author, 6 May 1991.

Memorial—such as Krasnoiarsk, Tomsk, and L'vov—where interest in history was strong. In cooperation with foreign scholars, Memorial won grants from the West to fund specific projects regarding the history of the human rights movement in the USSR and the fate of Russians deported to work in Nazi Germany, and to create displays of antistalinist literature. In 1991 *Memorial* published an extremely professional first issue of its historical almanac, *Zven"ia* (Links), and materials for a second issue waited for paper to become available.

Again accomplishments reinforced attention to a particular sphere and diverted human resources to specific activities, away from transformational goals. Some politically minded activists bemoaned the decline of spontaneity and political activism in favor of budget discussions and research. Though Memorial never ceased to take stances on political issues, its growing preoccupation with nontransformational goals alienated its most politicized members. In both Leningrad and Moscow, some activists left the movement when groups formed within Memorial to concentrate on charitable, human rights, and historical activities. One former participant even argued that "the strongest went off into politics," leaving behind those interested in "sausages and intrigues." In particular, she blamed the changes in Memorial's activities for the decline in participation by young people.[24] Moreover, the fact that some grant money went to pay a permanent staff at the Scientific Information Center aroused envy. Now the organization had resources to quarrel over.

Though Memorial branches became more bureaucratic in the sense of providing regular services, institutionalization did not extend fully to the national leadership. Like the new Russian political parties, Memorial faced some unusual problems in aggregating members' interests. Suspicion of centralized hierarchic control—as in the battle over Memorial's charter—led to hyperdemocratic principles of decentralized organization.[25] In practice, the idea of independent local branches and a central coordinating council based on volunteers was inefficient and unreliable. The central group could not respond to requests from the provinces quickly or efficiently, and the central council lacked the resources to initiate programs. Local groups constantly asked for some sort of central

24. Interview with Marina Zhzhenova, founding member of the Leningrad Memorial, Leningrad, 4 June 1991.
25. M. Steven Fish, *Democracy from Scratch: Opposition and Regime in the New Russian Revolution* (Princeton: Princeton University Press, 1995), pp. 55–57.

clearinghouse to disseminate information about local events, activists' experiences, and practical legal and organizational advice, but no central press organ was ever set up. Individual correspondence and an annual plenum served as the only means for interaction on a somewhat systematic basis. Only a few local groups formed bilateral ties based on mutual interests or geographic proximity. Without a feeling of national mobilization and progress, whole branches lost faith in the movement and its capacity to transform Soviet society.

### Competition with Political Parties

Organizations interact with other organizations, potentially competing for material resources, membership, position, and legitimacy. Social movements are generally made up of a variety of organizations, which sometimes compete for resources and prestige, at other times share and cooperate; frequently carve out specialized niches for themselves, though they may merge in temporary coalitions; and from time to time declare war on one another. A dwindling of resources, the expansion of a group's agenda, and differences in radicalism may all increase competition. Cooperation is encouraged by specialization in complementary task, overlapping constituencies, threats by the authorities to quash the social movement, and a shared enemy.[26] Timing also plays a role, as early groups foster others that outstrip them in radicalism. As we shall see, Memorial went through periods of cooperation, coalition, and debilitating competition.

During the first stage of Memorial's development, the organization did not compete with any other informal society. In fact, it often served as an umbrella for democratic activists of all persuasions. Radicals whose real aim was to undo the whole Soviet system could evade immediate reprisals by identifying themselves with the less controversial antistalinist movement. Memorial's early emergence combined with its broad progressive agenda permitted the society to serve also as a "marriage bureau" for democratic activists and as a school for learning how to handle the tremendous practical difficulties of organizing under Soviet rule. Memorial

26. Mayer N. Zald and John D. McCarthy, "Social Movement Industries: Competition and Cooperation among Movement Organizations," in *Research in Social Movements, Conflicts, and Change*, vol. 3 (Greenwich, Conn.: JAI Press, 1980), pp. 1–20.

sometimes suffered from internal conflicts between radicals and moderates, but both sides brought innovative tactics to the organization. Moreover, Memorial's inclusiveness permitted members to participate in other nascent democratic organizations; since groups generally focused on debates or street politics, membership was not particularly demanding. In an environment of low organization and growing popular interest in antistalinism, Memorial attracted volunteers rapidly.

Soviet society in general became more politicized with the advent of multicandidate elections to the USSR Congress of People's Deputies in the spring of 1989. Because the first semidemocratic elections for national offices were held when political parties were still officially banned, civic activists struggled to identify, nominate, and elect democratic candidates. Given the lack of parties with clear political programs, membership in, affiliation with, or support from Memorial often became an important indicator of a candidate's commitment to democracy. For the 1989 elections, Memorial helped organize public meetings, supported individual candidates, and cooperated with popular fronts and other pro-perestroika coalitions to publicize democratic candidates. Many of the liberal luminaries who served on Memorial's Social Council—including Sakharov, Evtushenko, Yeltsin, Adamovich, and Afanas'ev—won seats in the new legislature. There was virtually no competition among democratic groups at this point. Few democratic candidates survived the nomination process, and the small number of democratic organizations joined forces to support any independent candidates nominated in their regions.

Memorial again cooperated with other democratic groups in the spring 1990 campaigns for the Russian Congress of People's Deputies and local city councils. Moscow Memorial's election literature demonstrates the depth of the organization's politicization and its linkage of its particular concerns and transformational goals: "There is a widespread and growing ultraconservative mood in the country which threatens a return to a regime of mass terror. Moscow Memorial calls on a broad union of popular forces to defeat the conservatives in these elections and overcome bureaucratic paralysis." Specifically, Memorial called for a multiparty system, the separation of powers, property rights, and market relations. It further reminded voters that it acted "in accord with the Interregional Group of People's Deputies of the USSR, and is a member of Elections-90, the voters' bloc of Moscow democratic organizations, and cooperates

A sign at Andrei Sakharov's funeral calls for repeal of article 6 of the Soviet Constitution, which enshrined the "leading role" of the Communist Party. Moscow, 1989. *Courtesy Interregional Memorial Society Archives, Moscow.*

with the Moscow Union of Voters."[27] Again Memorial supported many successful candidates for the RSFSR Congress of People's Deputies— Sergei Kovalev, Gleb Iakunin, Lev Ponomarev, Pavel Kudiukin, Ernest Ametistov, Vladimir Lysenko, and Viktor Sheinis—but many of these deputies already held leadership positions in other organizations.

In early February 1990, almost on the eve of the elections, the Central Committee agreed that the CPSU should surrender its constitutionally enshrined "leading role," thus opening the door for legalization of new proto-parties. Though parties could not be registered by law until January 1991, they gained legitimacy and security immediately upon the abolition of article 6. Despite its endorsement of democratization and civil society,

27. *Rossiia pered vyborom: Predvybornaia deklaratsiia Moskovskogo 'Memoriala'"* (leaflet), 1990, Interregional Memorial Society Archives.

Memorial disavowed the form of a political party as inconsistent with its goal of openness to all victims of repression. By accepting Communists and members of DS, Memorial preserved its credibility as a society tolerant of all who supported its goals, and gained access to the broadest pool of potential adherents. But by 1990 Memorial had lost much of its original appeal because its activities were no longer perceived as uniquely radical or topical.

In many ways Memorial's success fed its later decline. As forerunners in organizing under glasnost, Memorial and DS really served as what Sidney Tarrow has called "crucible[s] out of which the repertoire of contention evolve[d]."[28] While Memorial helped introduce the terms and articulate the basis for the debate on democratization, the new parties that arose had learned from Memorial and honed their goals and tactics. Memorial's broad democratic agenda made it possible for people of all political persuasions to work within the organization, but that same agenda proved unsatisfying for those who formed concrete, specific political goals and platforms. The issue of repressions originally concentrated attention on the lack of democratic guarantees; now political parties could (though they did not always) create more sophisticated programs that addressed pressing economic, social, and political issues. In the early years, many activists managed to combine their activities, but as organizations grew, so did the demands on their members. And even founding members, such as Lev Ponomarev, Vladimir Lysenko, and Pavel Kudiukin, let their participation in Memorial lapse as they took up leadership positions elsewhere.[29] Memorial's inclusiveness facilitated cooperation and coalition but it did not hold members.

The unbanning of alternative parties unleashed greater competition among groups for media attention and membership. Democratic organizations all drew support from the same social base—the urban intelligentsia—and the fight for these members intensified as parties developed. Moreover, the end of elections robbed democratic groups of a single urgent, unifying task. As competition for scarce material and human resources and splits became endemic among political parties, Memo-

---

28. Tarrow, *Struggle, Politics, and Reform,* p. 47; see also David A. Snow and Robert D. Benford, "Ideology, Frame Resonance, and Participant Mobilization," in *International Social Movement Research,* vol. 1 (Greenwich, Conn.: JAI Press, 1988).

29. Ponomarev helped found Democratic Russia, Lysenko headed the Republican Party of Russia (originally called Democratic Platform), and Kudiukin was a leader of the Social Democratic Party of Russia.

rial retained an important resource. Despite its bureaucratization and attempts by radicals to portray Memorial as having sold out to the authorities—an impression encouraged by Party media, which frequently and falsely reported that Memorial was cooperating with the KGB—Memorial retained an unparalleled reputation for strict moral principles and cohesion.[30] Memorial lost the spotlight, but not its legitimacy.

Overall, however, competition did not bode well for Memorial. By 1991 a typical complaint of Memorial leaders focused on an outflow of active members to politics or business. They frequently blamed the repeal of the ban on political parties for the drop in membership. One Memorial leader noted, "Young people who had come while [Memorial] was forming . . . left with the repeal of article 6 of the USSR constitution and created their own parties and movements."[31] And though many of Memorial's elderly members took part in both political and charitable activities, their numbers declined with every passing year. The legitimation of political parties also changed Memorial's focus. One local leader summed up the situation this way: "Up to the moment political parties were allowed, Memorial actively engaged in politics—agitating against the war in Afghanistan, offering alternative programs for the country's development, agitating against totalitarianism among the masses, doing organizational work to rally political groups. . . . Now Memorial supports the political campaigns of Democratic Russia through its members but itself takes political initiative much less often."[32]

Some activists greeted the division into more and less politicized organizations with satisfaction.[33] To some extent, the emergence of political parties lifted the burden of mass organizing off Memorial and increased its capacity to focus on its unique goals, such as material aid and uniform benefits for Stalin's victims, historical research and publications, and exhibits on the history of Stalinism. But once Memorial lost the spotlight, it lost its ability to mobilize large numbers of volunteers.

---

30. See letter from Memorial Working Collegium rejecting the donation of an honorarium from a KGB supporter: "Eti den'gi nam ne nuzhny," *Moskovskie novosti*, 7–14 July, 1991.

31. Galina Zakharova, member of the governing board of the Mariupol' Memorial, to the author, 22 May 1991; also Aleksei Kiriushin, Tol'iatti Memorial, to the author, May 1991.

32. Valerii Savinkov, member of the governing board of the Barnaul Memorial, to the author, 30 March 1991.

33. Valerii Safranskii to the author, 6 May 1991.

## INTERNAL PRESSURES ON THE MOVEMENT

Despite Memorial's heterogeneous base, the organization suffered only one split—the one that produced the two victims' groups, the Assotsiatsiia and the Ob"edinenie. Both radicals and moderates found it easier to pursue their political agendas through other organizations. Memorial's inclusiveness made it easier to adopt overlapping memberships or to switch rather than fight. Subgroups emerged not out of strife but out of specific interests within their shared agenda. In Moscow, groups formed on the basis of interest (in human rights, oral history, archival work) or occupation (lawyers, doctors) and worked both independently in their specialty and together on larger projects.

Organizations may also experience tension over changes in leadership. Charismatic leaders may be lost, an increasingly independent leadership may switch goals, or emphasis may shift from mobilizing to articulating the organization's place in society.[34] Though Memorial never had a single charismatic leader, the death of Andrei Sakharov in December 1989 and the defection of luminaries to politics lowered its public profile. The election of democratic deputies hardly undermined Memorial's goals, but in some ways it did diminish the movement's clout. Complaints emerged that some candidates exploited their affiliation with Memorial during their election campaigns but neither helped the organization nor remained active in it after they won. "Once they're deputies," one activist said, "they don't come back."[35] Even those who supported Memorial often found their efforts frustrated by the inefficiency and weakness of their legislative institutions. Although Memorial never relied on a single charismatic leader, the defection or distraction of popular figures left the practical but less visible activists in charge.

As Memorial's role in the democratic movement waned and participation declined, its leaders did gain more independence from their original base of supporters. By 1990 they were more concerned with balancing the interests of organized subgroups than with involving the whole membership in mass meetings. As the organization contracted, leaders could turn from mobilizing to research, lobbying, charity, and so forth. Arsenii Roginskii, the head of the All-Union Working Collegium, proved to be a good consensus builder, and the organization remained cohesive, but the

34. Zald and Ash, "Growth, Decay, and Change," pp. 533–35.
35. Interview with Marina Zhzhenova, 4 June 1991.

shift from disruptive demonstrations to behind-the-scenes work lowered Memorial's public profile. The division into special groups, however, kept the organization from becoming uniformly more conservative or radical.

## THE END OF A WEAK CYCLE OF MOBILIZATION?

So-called mass movements and even popular mass demonstrations in the Soviet Union pale in comparison with such manifestations elsewhere. Only the Baltics and Caucasus witnessed demonstrations involving hundreds of thousands before 1990. For Moscow in 1987 a big demonstration involved fifty people. This standard grew exponentially over the next few years and peaked in 1990. The popular response to an opening up of the public arena contradicts political culture arguments, which expect traditional Russian attitudes toward authority to produce political passivity. And one should not expect waves of protest to encompass everyone; as Tarrow notes, cycles of protest "leave large pockets of citizens uninvolved, produce conflicts between groups of mobilized citizens, and usually awaken a backlash against disorder."[36]

Yet the question remains as to why the lowering of obstacles to political participation did not lead to greater antistalinist activism. If Memorial had a large base of passive support, why couldn't it mobilize that latent sympathy once authorities allowed the organization to register officially? Perhaps, along with the factors that contributed to a decline of interest in the purges, barriers to participation simply were lifted too late to benefit those groups that made up the USSR's first wave of independent protest. When the Party really removed barriers to political activity, the first small wave of protest had already begun to give way to a period of disenchantment with new social organizations. After all, not only Memorial but many early environmental groups, labor unions, and nascent political parties struggled to maintain their membership in the 1990s. Thus, though it emerged at the forefront of the democratic movement, Memorial suffered from the fact that it developed during a period of halfhearted reform.

The economic crisis that worsened during each year of the perestroika era severely affected antistalinist activism. Inflation eroded the organizations' meager savings and donations declined. Lack of funds reduced

36. Tarrow, *Struggle, Politics, and Reform,* p. 44.

Memorial's potential for activity across the board and forced local societies to make tough choices about which activities to pursue. The head of
the Barnaul Memorial reported that his group now devoted its scarce
resources to relatively inexpensive research programs.[37] But some local
groups found even cassette tapes and batteries prohibitively expensive.
The cost of travel, telephone service, and postage all increased dra-
matically, thus reducing communication between local branches of Memorial and the center. Moreover, the costs of paper drove most independent democratic newspapers out of business, leaving only the official press
as a source of information. And though the mass media diversified during
the perestroika period, it did not devote much coverage to civic activity
outside the arena of national politics.

Moreover, economic hardships reduced activists' free time. Many
sought second jobs (especially in the new privately owned enterprises);
they also spent more time either waiting in line to try to buy goods at state
prices or searching for bargains. As survival became more difficult, investments of time and energy in unpaid volunteer work were sacrificed. Pressure and tension over the state of the nation also affected perceptions of
what tasks needed urgent attention. Echoing the plaint of early denigra-
tors of Memorial, in 1991 activists began to recognize the powerful
distraction created by ominous economic decline and growing political
instability. One activist concluded his list of the obstacles confronting
Memorial in 1991 by noting, "The situation in our country is now critical,
and the horror of Stalinism fades in the face of possible catastrophe."[38] In
some nations economic crisis spurs waves of activism, but in the USSR it
fed the desire for order and stability, and a retreat from disruptive politics.

Economic distress was not the only change in Memorial's environment;
political reform was ongoing throughout the Gorbachev era. With the
Communist Party and the KGB intact, Memorial did not suffer a crisis of
mission. But it did get swept up in the reform process, and through elections strove for inclusion in the existing system. Electoral successes did
not compensate for the drop in social mobilization. Soviet legislators
faced numerous problems: first, they inherited weak and unwieldy institutions; second, many did not belong to the parties that supported them and
hence did not form natural alliances within the legislatures; third, many
candidates seemed to have taken their election as a license to behave as

37. Valerii Savinkov to the author, 30 March 1991.
38. Valerii Safranskii to the author, 6 May 1991.

they wished, without trying to poll or otherwise consult their constituents. Thus the election of sympathetic legislators did not produce substantial results for Memorial. The society had no impact on legislation until 1991, when Sergei Kovalev became head of the Human Rights Committee of the Russian Supreme Soviet. Memorial's input into specific legislation, however, should not be taken as equivalent to lobbying in the Western sense, because Memorial did not seek close relations with deputies other than those it supported in the 1990 elections.

Between 1989 and 1991 the Memorial Society evolved from a diffuse social movement into an instrumental organization with specific pragmatic goals and a clearly articulated structure. Memorial gained legal standing, a permanent headquarters, a solid core of activists, and sophisticated historical and charitable programs, but it also became more bureaucratized. Institutionalization appears to have been a mixed blessing to Memorial; while the society acquired stability and retained solidarity, it sacrificed some of its potential for mobilization and lost some of its most dynamic politicized activists.

Nevertheless, like all social movements, Memorial had both short- and long-term effects on society and politics. A study of the Solidarity movement in Poland after it was suppressed by martial law found that "Solidarity had a lasting influence through its empowerment of individuals, its reintroduction of citizens to the pleasures of belonging to an active community."[39] For many Soviet citizens, participation in Memorial provided the first taste of political freedom. The euphoria of early protests may have dissipated, but much of the popular sympathy and respect won by Memorial clearly remains. Though the society lost its early role as a leader in the democratic movement, its stance continued to serve some people as a barometer or litmus test on issues outside the group's specific domain. During the often confusing campaign leading up to the referendum on the union in March 1991, for instance, the volunteers who answered Memorial's telephones in Moscow reported repeated requests for advice about how to vote.

But having disavowed the form of a political party, Memorial could not compete in an arena in which parties became the preferred outlet for civic activism. Though Memorial's political activism declined, the organization did not entirely surrender its transformational goals. In an incomplete

39. Piotr Sztompka, "The Social Function of Defeat," in *Research in Social Movements, Conflicts, and Change*, vol. 10 (Greenwich, Conn: JAI Press, 1988).

transition to democracy Memorial could not abandon its broad goal of creating institutional safeguards against arbitrary rule, but it shifted its tactics to concentrate on educational methods to transform society. Through its research and propaganda work, Memorial continues to educate and sensitize the population to the history and consequences of human rights abuses.

# 9 THE END OF SOVIET RULE AND PROSPECTS FOR SETTLING ACCOUNTS

Metaphors of pain and healing crop up again and again in debates over coming to terms with past atrocities. Policies directed at investigating the past have been described variously as "lancing a boil," "healing an open wound," and "picking at a scab." The trauma caused by political persecution is not acknowledged or treated during the dictatorship, but liberalization brings talk of healing for both the individual and the society. Just as there are many symptoms of persecution, there are many diagnoses and prescriptions. Views of the consequences of exploring Stalinism depended on whether one saw the Soviet Union as on the way to a natural recovery or as still ill and in need of intervention.

Reformers thought that by explicitly repudiating the worst practices of past rulers, they could win the support and confidence of the liberal public while still operating within the system. They assumed that the reformist elite and the Soviet people shared goals that could be served by gradual reform. Sympathetic Western analysts concurred that the truth about the past could serve a "perestroika" of legitimacy of Soviet rule and hence promote Gorbachev's project of socialist reformation.[1] Such hypotheses

---

1. Stephen F. Cohen, "Introduction: Gorbachev and the Soviet Reformation," in *Voices of Glasnost: Inverviews with Gorbachev's Reformers,* ed. Cohen and Katerina Vanden Heuvel (New York: Norton, 1989), p. 28.

led many people to misinterpret Gorbachev's statement in favor of a monument to victims as a sign of his support for Memorial.[2]

We have seen, however, that by selectively rejecting the worst practices of the old regime and by downplaying the roots and remnants of repression, the regime alienated and antagonized people who were actively searching for the complex truth about the past. Yet through reform, the state opened the door for radicals who argued for a complete break with the past. Civic radicals could and did use the previous state-sponsored repressions to justify calls for deep institutional change and complete rejection of the old regime. The quest to uncover and commemorate past atrocities has universally led to contemplation and promotion of future-oriented preventive agendas. And, given the vacuum of organizations and alternative political programs in Soviet society in the 1980s, antistalinism had the potential to become the core of a new democratic ideology.

The first dynamic, an alliance for reform, did dominate for several years under Khrushchev, as socialist reformers successfully made destalinization one of their main planks. By ending the terror and freeing the survivors, Khrushchev earned the gratitude of millions in one fell swoop. Liberation or confirmation of death satisfied the most basic demands of victims and their families. Partial destalinization was facilitated by low expectations for reform, fear of political participation, and shared values on the part of the many victims who had been politically or social active before their arrest. Though the Soviet regime under Stalin had indeed devoured its own grown-up children, its survivors were not prepared to look for the roots of repression in their happy childhood. For true believers, criticism of Stalin did not need to reflect badly on Lenin.[3]

Reform followed so closely on the heels of repression, however, that Party leaders were acutely aware of the need to control the destalinization process. Khrushchev and his cohort sought to avoid queries about the status of reformers—were they heirs of Lenin or Stalin or both, and in what measure? A real investigation into the roots of the terror was fraught with danger for the Communist regime. If it tainted the Leninist period, it would destroy the historical basis for the Bolsheviks' legitimacy; if it

2. Geoffrey Hosking, for instance, reported that Memorial's goal of erecting a monument to victims of Stalinism was "crowned with success at the 19th Party Conference": *The Awakening of the Soviet Union*, enl. ed. (Cambridge: Harvard University Press, 1991), p. 73.

3. See, for instance Anna Larina, *This I Cannot Forget: The Memoirs of Nikolai Bukharin's Widow*, trans. Gary Kern (New York: Norton, 1993).

extended beyond Stalin and Beria, it would reveal the complicity of the new top leadership. Conservative intellectuals in particular feared the ideological ramifications of dwelling on the negative aspects of the past, and so they battled liberals over the limits of free expression and the nature of permissible discourse about Stalin.

Many members of Soviet society shared the leadership's ambivalence about delving into questions of accountability. Torn between a desire to restore justice and fear of examining their own consciences, some citizens found the return of survivors and the condemnation of the popular cult of Stalin unsettling. If the victims had been innocent, then those who voted at mass meetings for their punishment had participated in a lethal charade.[4] Others, however, sought to remedy their ignorance or to express their disgust with the purges. The lack of opportunities for independent publishing, organization, and protest, however, allowed the Party to curb public debate when it went further than the leaders preferred. But the thaw left a small radicalized sector of society, and for the next twenty years the Party engaged these dissidents in a relentless running battle.

In contrast to Khrushchev and the thaw, Gorbachev and his multifaceted reform program generated high expectations both in the West and in the East. When Gorbachev introduced the notion of "socialist pluralism," both the concept and the manner of its implementation had to be worked out. Gorbachev undoubtedly wanted to institutionalize a more participatory form of socialism, one that would allow the mature Soviet citizen to share in the effort to restructure the system. But what about the person whose concept of socialism, or of a good political and economic system, contradicted or outstripped the leadership's goals? Khrushchev had been unable to resolve the tension between his vision of a conflictless society and the unleashing of diverse interests, especially when pursued independently. When reform-minded officials seek allies among formerly disenfranchised sectors of society, they often attract unsolicited advice and unwelcome would-be participants. Social activity that escapes the limits of the reformers' tolerance tests their sincerity, flexibility, and intentions. Antistalinism tested Gorbachev's commitment to glasnost.

Gorbachev did not immediately recognize the need to craft a usable version of Soviet history to support his preferred mixture of change and continuity, but he publicly denounced Stalin's repressions after the press

4. See the character Nikolai Sokolov in Vasily Grossman, *Forever Flowing*, trans. Thomas P. Whitney (New York: Harper & Row, 1972).

raised the issue. Gorbachev was more openly critical of Stalin than his predecessors had been, but he still presented the Lenin years as sacred and the 1930s as a period characterized by socialist construction. The Gorbachev administration was prepared to acknowledge the purges and to permit a discussion of complicity, but it too attempted to manipulate the processes of commemoration and condemnation. The passage of decades could not destroy the corrosive potential of negative history on the regime's legitimacy. Ligachev correctly noted that there came a point at which talk about the past went beyond "healing" to "castigation" of the socialist system.[5]

Gorbachev's carefully balanced portrait of the 1930s satisfied neither conservatives nor liberals, and both sides took advantage of glasnost to contest his bland version of the period. Moreover, the regime's monologue could not drown out the new public dialogue on the past. The hidden truth had already become more interesting and alluring to the public than any official, propagandized version. Again Party leaders' pursuit of political stability and reconciliation clashed with intellectuals' search for truth and justice. Neither radicals nor reformers were interested in open prosecutions or harsh punishment of past offenders, but they split over the extent of institutional change necessary to prevent a recurrence of repression. Thus differences over the past shaped radical and reform agendas for the future.

Under reform communism public mobilization was limited, but it spurred an intellectual evolution toward rejection of the Communist system based on its inability to guarantee individual human rights—a process that has been characterized as the replacement of the concept of Stalinism with that of totalitarianism.[6] Consciousness raising begun by liberal intellectuals in the 1960s and followed up by dissidents in the 1970s came to fruition in the 1980s with the birth of Memorial and its linkage of commemorating victims with a broad democratic program. Memorial's supporters were instrumental in drawing connections between the mass terror of the Stalin era and the lack of accountability in modern Soviet-style socialism. Iurii Afanas'ev spoke for many when he protested, "We are not dealing with a deformed socialism but with an inhumane, regimented system whose foundations still have not been erad-

---

5. Yegor Ligachev, *Inside Gorbachev's Kremlin*, trans. Catherine A. Fitzpatrick, Michele A. Berdy, and Dobrochina Dyrcz-Freeman (New York: Pantheon, 1993), p. 285.

6. Jacques Rupnik, *The Other Europe*, rev. ed. (New York: Pantheon, 1989), p. 228.

icated. Perestroika must uproot all vestiges of Stalinism from our life. Therefore half-truths about the past will lead to half-measures today."[7] The theme of half-measures became popular among radicals in the 1980s precisely because they feared partial change could be reversed.

As journalists revealed more facts about Stalinism and Memorial protests spread, the impression grew among democrats that Gorbachev was doing too little too late. Liberals faulted Gorbachev for failing to take the initiative in repudiating Stalinism and for responding only grudgingly to demands from below. The Politburo Commission for Additional Studies of Documents Pertaining to Repressive Measures of the 1930s-1940s and Early 1950s epitomized the shortcomings of Gorbachev's in-system reform. With this commission, Gorbachev institutionalized a form of elite peer review of selected cases of top Party people who had been victimized, rather than addressing the calls for investigation and commemoration of the fates of ordinary purge victims.

Social movements have furthered the reform of many authoritarian regimes by exerting leverage through street politics and the force of numbers. Mass demonstrations emerged at the forefront of reform in Eastern Europe; but in the USSR, weak organizations formed tentatively. Adam Przeworski suggests that liberalization in the USSR did not lead to massive street demonstrations because Gorbachev developed a coalition with the people against the bureaucracy and transformed the Supreme Soviet "overnight into a fairly contestatory institution."[8] The case of Memorial shows Przeworski to be wrong on both counts. Gorbachev offended and alienated civic activists by publicly ignoring them, and the elections of 1989 created a legislature that entertained radical speeches but took no radical actions. Elections for the USSR Supreme Soviet were indirect, so that the Congress of Peoples' Deputies, which was heavily weighted toward the establishment, could weed out popular but radical figures. It is a myth that the first dynamic—an alliance of softliners and democratic activists on the national level—lasted beyond 1988. Faced with the Party's hostility and halfhearted reform measures, the democratic opposition radicalized rapidly and across the board and entered into extremely conflictual relations with official reformers.

---

7. Yuri Afanasyev, "The Agony of the Stalinist System," in Cohen and Vanden Heuvel, *Voices of Glasnost,* p. 102.

8. Adam Przeworski, *Democracy and the Market: Political and Economic Reforms in Eastern Europe and Latin America* (New York: Cambridge University Press, 1991), p. 59.

When we look at the concrete results of the campaign for destalinization under Gorbachev, we see that the greatest changes were cultural rather than institutional and that the most profound institutional change was the emergence of a lasting, albeit weak, public sphere. Otherwise change came either in ways that initially cost the regime little, such as the public rehabilitation of people victimized under Stalin, or in areas where civic initiative could make an impact: commemoration, oral history, material aid for survivors. The state did not initiate a systematic accounting for the purges, nor did it consider prosecutions or major reform of the security apparatus. Truth-telling was driven from below. But the surge of popular mobilization came at a stage in the reform dominated by official hostility, scarcity, and state monopolies on resources. The need to invent, rather than reclaim, public space explains in part why the path toward a civil society was so rocky. The shift from petitioners to protesters required time, and given the regime's ambivalence about conflict, civic empowerment did not translate into immediate political influence.

Nevertheless, demands that were turned aside during the thaw of the 1950s now found expression in the press, in protests in public squares, and in the formation of informal organizations. Political reform encouraged private citizens to claim competence in politics on many levels. Through legal and public rehabilitation of victims of persecution, the state redefined the community to include people once ostracized as political deviants. Survivors reentered society and regained the voices they had lost as "enemies of the people." They and their supporters then sought to prevent a recurrence of such horrors in part by staking out personal space—individual rehabilitation, memoirs, grave sites—and by carving out some public space through commemoration, reparations, and official acknowledgment. Part of the allure of membership in Memorial was the reversal of the status of pariah and inclusion in an instant community. But transformation of Soviet society resulted not only in the politicization of people who had been disenfranchised and stigmatized but in the creation of a new collective form—the independent civic movement. Individuals overcame both historical oblivion and social isolation to unite. And the collective expression of grief and anger became the base of the Memorial movement. As Afanas'ev observed, the act of creating civil society itself became a conscious effort to build a bulwark against a return to tyranny.[9]

9. Cited in *Sovetskii tsirk*, 4 February 1989.

## Prospects for Settling Accounts in Postcommunist States

Though Memorial empowered its members and became the conscience of the democratic movement, it did not fundamentally reshape the Communist regime. When conservative Communists struck out at Gorbachev and the reform movement in August 1991, Memorial put all of its meager resources into the defense of Yeltsin and the government of the Russian Republic. The failure of the conservative backlash must really be credited to the incompetence of the coup plotters rather than to the strength of the democratic movement, but that movement profited by it. The popular upsurge in defense of democracy climaxed in the toppling of the statue of Feliks Dzerzhinskii from its pedestal in front of the Lubianka.

Whatever its roots, the failure of the coup attempt of August 1991 heralded a major transformation in the state's symbols and political institutions. The dissolution of the Soviet Union and Yeltsin's banning of the Communist Party in Russia changed the playing field for politicians and activists alike. To what extent did the end of the USSR and the collapse of the Communist Party reopen the issue of examining the past? A brief glance at the immediate reactions to coming to terms with the past in postcommunist Russia will allow us to return to the broader comparative themes raised at the beginning of this book.

The most significant attempt to address the legacy of previous repressions was made by the Russian legislature in October 1992. Finally free from the problem of a "war of laws" with the more conservative USSR Supreme Soviet, the Russian parliament passed a long-awaited comprehensive law rehabilitating the victims of political repressions. The law embraced a broad time span—from 7 November 1917 to the present—and offered an inclusive definition of repression as

deprivation of life or freedom, commitment to forced treatment in psychiatric medical institutions, deportation from the country and deprivation of citizenship, eviction of groups of the population from their places of residence, exile, deportation to special settlements, forced labor in conditions of restricted freedom, and any other deprivation or limitation of rights and freedoms of people who were declared to be socially dangerous to the government or political structure for class, social, national, religious, or other reasons, as carried out by the decisions of courts or other organs sharing judicial functions, or by administrative command issued by organs of the executive power and responsible officials.[10]

The law stipulated numerous measures designed to restore justice and compensate survivors, including return of confiscated property, the right of return to one's former place of residence, financial compensation based on the number of months spent in incarceration or exile, priority access to housing and medical care, and free legal services for problems in respect to rehabilitation.

The deputies also voted to allow limited access to one's secret police files and to ensure the return of photographs, manuscripts, and other personal effects. The KGB has slowly begun to comply with the new law.[11] The government, however, has not followed through on another of the law's provisions. Though the parliament did not alter the statute of limitations to permit prosecution of the people responsible for distant human rights abuses, it did mandate publication of lists of victims and of people "bearing criminal responsibility on the basis of criminal law" for fabricating cases or gathering evidence by illegal means. But so far, no lists have been released.

Though the Russian government took quick steps toward official acknowledgment of victims, it found institutional reforms to displace remnants of the Communist regime more difficult and more controversial. Before the coup attempt democrats had introduced the term "departyization" to refer to the movement to evict Party organizations from workplaces, especially from army and police units. After the failed putsch, Yeltsin was careful to avoid actions that might be perceived as discrimination against individual Communists, but he swiftly addressed the fate of the Communist Party as an organization by banning it as a whole and nationalizing its assets.

In the resulting challenge before the new Russian Constitutional Court, conservative Communist Party members charged that Yeltsin's decrees banning the CPSU and its Russian branch and confiscating their property violated the separation of powers enshrined in the Constitution and the

---

10. "Zakon Rossiiskoi Sovetskoi Federativnoi Sotsialisticheskoi Respubliki o reabilitatsii zhertv politicheskii repressii," *Vedomosti s"ezda narodnykh deputatov RSFSR i Verkhovnogo Soveta RSFSR,* no. 44, 1991. The law denied rehabilitation to spies, defectors, terrorists, people who had committed violence against civilians or POWs or had collaborated with the Nazis, and common criminals.

11. Lucan Way, "Exhuming the Buried Past," *Nation,* 1 March 1993, pp. 267–68.

USSR law on parties and voluntary organizations, neither of which gave the president power to dissolve parties or expropriate their assets. Fearing that the ban on the CPSU would be overturned for procedural reasons, liberal deputies brought a countersuit asking that the Communist Party as an organization be declared unconstitutional. The president's advocates asserted that the CPSU was never a real political party, but rather part of state structures, as shown by the Party's role in making foreign and domestic policy, in selecting personnel for state posts, and in controlling mechanisms of repression. As part of the state, the Party was subject to the president's administrative orders.

Moreover, Yeltsin's supporters argued that "the organization calling itself the Communist Party" should be considered unconstitutional because both its ideology and its activity contradicted article 7 of the Constitution, which outlaws parties that have as their goal the violent overthrow of the Soviet constitutional system and socialist government or that inflame social, national, or religious passions. As evidence of the Party's violent and inflammatory tendencies, they pointed to its alleged participation in the coup attempt and its ideology, which elevated one class above all others. The Party's representatives defended its glorious past and argued that the Party that initiated perestroika and democratization should not be confused with the Party of the 1930s; the modern CPSU, after all, had abolished article 6 of the Constitution, which had enshrined the Party's leading role, and had become a parliamentary party.

The Constitutional Court combined these appeals and limited discussion to the activities of the Communist Party after the repeal of article 6 in 1990, thus severely limiting discussion of the purges. In December 1992 the justices issued a compromise ruling that overturned the nationalization of Party property and partially upheld the ban on the Communist Party. The Court ruled that leadership structures could be dissolved, but not local Party cells. Public interest in the fate of the CPSU was low during the trial. After all, Yeltsin's aim was not to prosecute or settle accounts with the Party or its former leaders but to break the Party's formal control over state structures, a problem that had all but resolved itself by the time of the court's ruling.

At the time of the verdict, it seemed Yeltsin had little to fear from a rebirth of the CPSU. Many top Party leaders had already resigned their membership and, like Gorbachev, refused to take part in the suit. As one commentator noted, the court was not delivering a death blow to the

Party but performing a postmortem on it; the Party had already decisively lost members and legitimacy by the autumn of 1991.[12] But Yeltsin's ukases did not ban the communist ideology, and some seven successor parties formed. By the parliamentary elections in December 1993, the Russian Communist Workers' Party had regained a popular following. After the election, in a tardy attempt to dispel nostalgia, Yeltsin rehabilitated the men killed in the 1921 Kronstadt uprising, in which revolutionary sailors challenged the direction of the Party and were massacred on Lenin's orders. Yeltsin's spokesman frankly admitted that the rehabilitation was intended to remind Communists "to look at the bloody trail you left and to draw a lesson."[13]

Yeltsin's decrees boiled down to the eviction of the Party as an organization, not some form of purge or even an official investigation of the old regime. Memorial historians recruited by the government to select archival material for the trial of the Communist Party did bring to light many new documents about a range of human rights abuses, but their work was no substitute for an official investigation of the terror. Moreover, while permitting victims and their heirs some access to their personal KGB dossiers, the Russian government and the KGB have expressed reservations about releasing compromising material even from the 1930s. A representative of the Russian KGB argued after the coup, "If we open all the archives, that will affect not just the relatives of the victims, but the relatives of those who perpetrated the crimes. . . . That could destabilize society."[14] As in Latin America, some officials worry that settling accounts might be more harmful than helpful to a fragile new regime.

Unlike Latin America, however, Russia has felt no international pressure to prosecute abusers of human rights. On the contrary, some human rights groups and foreign governments have been unsympathetic to the notions of decommunization and restitution. George Weigel points out that though the West required denazification in Germany and extensive screening in postwar Japan, it criticized the vetting of Communist officials and police informers by the Czechs and the trial of the Communist Party by the Russians. Weigel, to the contrary, defended the former Czechoslo-

12. Kronid Liubarskii, "Sud nad grazhdaninom Lui Kapetom," *Novoe vremia*, no. 29, 1992.

13. Quoted in Serge Schmemann, "Yeltsin Extols 1921 Rebellion, Denouncing Its Repression by Lenin," *New York Times*, 11 January 1994, p. 3.

14. Nikolai Stolyarov quoted in *Wall Street Journal*, 11 September 1991, p. 1.

vakia's screening law against due process concerns: "Considering the Communist repression and corruption to which [lustration] is a response, the law is remarkably lenient. It lays down none of the civil penalties involved in the de-nazification program . . . nor are there to be any criminal trials of the sort held at Nuremberg."[15]

Can one in fact extract lessons for Russia from the experiences of Eastern European nations? Let us consider for a moment the fate of attempts to settle accounts with those former Soviet-style regimes. Over time the rapid revolutions in Eastern Europe in 1989 produced numerous and varied measures aimed at decommunization and restitution to victims of repression. All of the East European nations focused on recent repressive measures and on the role of the former *nomenklatura* in hampering the consolidation of democracy.

Paradoxically, at the time of transition, East European democrats feared a Communist backlash; instead the spectacle of Communist officials and functionaries continuing to profit and dominate through their economic and political posts aroused popular resentment. The democrats took over parliamentary seats and high executive posts, but this altered only the tip of the Communist iceberg. Although former officials resigned their political posts, the Communist parties retained immense financial assets and properties, and the managers, administrators, and civil servants who had carried out the old regime's commands continued to hold their jobs. The specter of clandestine informers and collaborators remaining undetected in key posts alarmed many democrats. Thus the new states grappled with institutional reform, reparations to victims, and screening of collaborators—what Vaclav Havel diagnosed as a necessary second democratic revolution from above.[16]

Reform in the former Czechoslovakia, which took the most extensive steps toward decommunization, included an immediate overhaul of the secret police and a gradual restructuring and housecleaning in the judiciary, state-run economic institutions, and media. Though the new government did not ban the Communist Party, it did nationalize the Party's property and assets. In the months after the velvet revolution, the Czechoslovak parliament passed a law facilitating rehabilitation and offering limited cash compensation. The state also began to address the compli-

15. George Weigel, "Their Lustration—and Ours," *Commentary*, October 1992, p. 35.
16. Prague Radio, 13 October 1991, in *Federal Broadcast Information Service Daily Report on Eastern Europe (FBIS-EE)*, 15 October 1991, p. 13.

cated question of restoring private property confiscated after World War II to its former owners. Finally, in response to pressure from below, the parliament took steps to identify former collaborators, informers, and high Party officials in positions of responsibility and to bar them from high posts for a period of five years. Specifically it forbade secret police agents, collaborators, and Party secretaries from the district committee level upward to hold elective or appointive positions until 1996 in a range of state organizations, including the army, the state media, and the courts.[17] A variety of state and private institutions not covered by the law chose to screen their employees as well.[18]

The path of transition does seem to have had an impact on the settling of accounts in Eastern Europe. Negotiated transitions in Poland and Hungary produced slower progress toward opening up files and coping with former collaborators. Pacts instilled some patience with gradual change and blurred the distinction between "bad" Communists and "good" alliance partners. The speed and civic nature of the revolutions in Czechoslovakia and East Germany, by contrast, created high public expectations of radical change in personnel and institutions. When new governments hesitated to open files or expose informers, social organizations pushed successfully for action.

Ultimately, however, the debate over purging collaborators has proved inescapable for all of the postcommunist states, as the former *nomenklatura* neither retreated in disgrace nor were unseated by market mechanisms. In practical terms, because the democrats feel "we are not like them," the new rulers have been frustrated by their inability to unseat the old apparat quickly and fairly. The crime of collaboration is not one that lends itself to prosecution. Efforts to screen officeholders in Czechoslovakia and to change statutes of limitation in Hungary were condemned for violating due process norms.[19] While methods of screening continue to generate both great controversy and debilitating scandals for the new democracies, pressure persists to remove hidden collaborators who may be subject to blackmail and who arguably lack the appropriate character

17. *Rude pravo,* 5 October 1991, in *FBIS-EE,* 11 October 1991, pp. 14–15.
18. Lawrence Weschler, "The Velvet Purge: Trials of Jan Kavan," *New Yorker,* 19 October 1992.
19. The International Labor Organization condemned Czechoslovakia's lustration law, and the Hungarian Constitutional Court overturned the legislature's attempt to change the statute of limitations to allow prosecution of people involved in suppressing the 1956 uprising.

for public service.[20] The variety of policies adopted in Eastern European states should provide scholars of transitions with much food for thought as to how the approach to settling accounts actually affects the consolidation of democracy.

In comparison with Eastern Europe, Russia has made very few institutional and personnel changes. The KGB remains remarkably intact under a new name.[21] But Yeltsin, unlike Gorbachev, had an opportunity to deploy inverse legitimacy. He made the first move in this direction with the rehabilitation of the participants in the 1921 Kronstadt uprising. Even more telling was a statement made on that occasion by the head of the president's commission on rehabilitations—the architect of perestroika, Aleksandr Iakovlev: "All the repressions, camps, hostage-takings, mass deportations, executions without trial, even the execution of children, were not invented by Stalin. He was just the Great Continuer of Lenin's Task. It all began under Lenin."[22] Russian leaders no longer needed to look to Lenin for their "usable past."

But Yeltsin endured criticism for not acting swiftly and decisively to break up the old Communist system after the August coup. The former dissident Vladimir Bukovsky charged: "It was not enough just to seal the Party's headquarters and to confiscate its property. The other parts of the totalitarian machinery needed to be dismantled as quickly as possible, including the KGB. . . . Above all, the very essence of the Communist regime should have been delegitimized once and for all by a systematic exposure of its crimes, preferably in an open trial or a public inquiry."[23] Such a break with the Communist past would have required Yeltsin to end his alliance with the *nomenklatura* and totally restaff the highest echelons of power. And Yeltsin chose short-lived stability—perhaps because he overestimated both his own strength and the weakness of the opponents of reform.

In Eastern Europe decommunization has been driven from below. But

20. For a more extensive survey of efforts to settle accounts with the old regimes in Eastern Europe, see Kathleen E. Smith, "Decommunization after the 'Velvet Revolutions' in East Central Europe," in *Impunity and Human Rights in International Law and Practice,* ed. Naomi Roht-Arriaza (New York: Oxford University Press, 1995).

21. Amy Knight, "Russian Security Services under Yeltsin," *Post-Soviet Affairs* 9, no. 1 (1993): 40–65.

22. Quoted in Schmemann, "Yeltsin Extols 1921 Rebellion."

23. Vladimir Bukovsky, "Boris Yeltsin's Hollow Victory," *Commentary,* June 1993, p. 33.

thus far the lowering of barriers to mobilization in Russia has not produced a new surge of civic activism or significant new interest in the past. Aleksandr Mil'chakov claimed that the failed August 1991 coup stopped complaints about *Vecherniaia Moskva's* publication of execution lists because people recalled what awaited them with a return to the past. Indeed, one letter from the immediate postcoup period praised the newspaper and Mil'chakov while criticizing Yeltsin, Popov, and other liberal politicians, who despite their new power had still done nothing to commemorate Stalin's victims.[24] On the whole, however, renewed attention to the fragility of liberalization in the former USSR has not reinvigorated the antistalinist movement. Public displays of nostalgia for communism suggest that the halt in complaints about reminders of repression was purely temporary.

Like the *Historikerstreit* in Germany over the Holocaust, conflicting interpretations of the 1930s will continue to surface in Russia. The current economic and political crises have turned public attention to the need to stabilize the government and the market. But even in fragile democracies citizens may urge greater efforts to purge the system. When Chileans were polled about what they felt was lacking in their new democracy, for instance, the most popular wish was "that those guilty of human rights violations be brought to judgment." Nor will generational change necessarily diminish interest in past tyranny. In Brazil, an account of the terrorism of the right and left in the 1970s compiled by human rights activists not only became a bestseller but was most popular among the young, who had no memory of the harsh military dictatorship.[25]

In the former Soviet Union, lustration has thus far surfaced only in the Baltic states, where it has been hampered by the fact that departing representatives of the KGB took most of their archives with them. In Lithuania several top leaders of the independence movement were exposed as informers—apparently by deliberate leaks from the KGB. Only Latvia, which retained a card index of informers' names, has systematically vetted elected officials. A proposed law on lustration in Russia has failed to win popular or parliamentary support. Russians who favor lustration point to

24. Aleksandr Mil'chakov, "Mertvye preduprezhdaiut zhivykh," *Vecherniaia Moskva,* 16 March 1992.

25. "Chile: The Struggle for Truth and Justice for Past Human Rights Violations," *News from Americas Watch* (July 1992): 5; Lawrence Weschler, *A Miracle, a Universe: Settling Accounts with Torturers* (New York: Pantheon, 1990), pp. 71–74.

the experience of denazification in West Germany as a positive example. The banning of former Nazis from high office and restrictions on Communists, they argue, purified German society both morally and politically. Their opponents counter by pointing to the polarization of Lithuanian society caused by scandals generated by efforts to settle accounts or by focusing on the need to recognize "common guilt and common responsibility."[26]

To progress further, decommunization in Russia will require either a strong push from above or new demands from below. As long as Russia's democratic and market institutions remain weak, its politicians may join their Latin American colleagues in giving present stability priority over an exploration of past injustices. In the USSR, truth-telling and empowerment were inextricably linked. Whatever the course of future efforts to come to terms with the past in the former Soviet Union, it will involve a newly active and "recovering" public. Memorial continues to see promotion of knowledge about past abuses as the best way to build a democratic culture. It has not abandoned its chosen role of moral conscience and watchdog. But in the context of a faltering Russian democracy, Memorial activists may, like dissidents of old, become completely caught up in protesting a new cycle of human rights abuses. Memorial's human rights section spoke out against police brutality against reactionary demonstrators during the "October events" in 1993, and it did not hesitate to the campaign against Russian excesses in Chechnia.[27]

To end with a final medical metaphor, let us consider the conclusion of an Uruguayan therapist who worked with torture victims: "Rehabilitation from torture can occur only in a political and social context. The original point of the torture was to take various individuals who had been politically or socially active . . . and to gouge out their capacity for such activism: to leave them as if dead, unable to any longer aspire, let alone to act. The only true therapy for torture ought therefore to be revolution—overthrowing the system that tried to expunge that capacity for activism on behalf of those ideals."[28]

---

26. See column by Kirill Ignatov and "MN File"; Galina Afanasyeva, "The Law Buries Politicians, Politicians Bury the Law"; and Sergei Kovalyov, "Common Guilt, Common Responsibility," all in *Moscow News*, 28 January 1993.

27. "Zaiavlenie pravozashchitnogo Tsentra 'Memorial,'" *Nezavismaia gazeta*, 30 September 1993, pp. 1–2; "Pravozashchitniki sobiraiut informatsiiu," ibid., 14 October 1993, p. 1.

28. Quoted in Weschler, *A Miracle, a Universe*, pp. 240–41.

Despite incomplete institutional change, Russia has broken decisively with totalitarian rule. The dynamics of the thaw and perestroika—attempts to balance criticism and authority by the leadership and efforts to balance independence and survival by informal groups—will not be those that govern new struggles over coming to terms with the past. But other legacies of totalitarianism, such as weak organizations, a painful national history, and an entrenched *nomenklatura,* will continue to shape debates about commemoration and justice.

# APPENDIX

In the spring of 1991 I sent identical letters to forty branches of the Memorial Society across Russia, Kazakhstan, and Ukraine. I received twenty-three replies. Translations of my letter and a few replies provide a fuller picture of the experiences of Memorial activists in the provinces.

XXX Memorial Society
Dear XXX,

I am an American sociologist. At present I am engaged in researching the current attitudes of Soviet society toward the Stalinist repressions. Naturally, I am very interested in the activity of Memorial. Unfortunately, I am unable to visit your city, but I am very interested in the branch of the Memorial Society in your city.

If it would not inconvenience you, I would very much like to receive from you some information about your division of Memorial for my work. In particular, I would like to receive answers to the following questions:

- What is the history of the formation of your society?
- When was it founded?
- Does it exist at present?
- What is the size of your society?
- Does it engage in political activity, and if so, what kind?

- What kind of relations do you have with local authorities?
- Finally, what are your main problems and main successes?

I would be very grateful for any information. Thank you in advance.

KATHLEEN SMITH
University of California, Berkeley

## SEMIPALATINSK

. . . The history of the Memorial Society in Semipalatinsk begins in mid-1989. The group's primary goal was to challenge communist ideology on the basis of the examples of Stalinist repressions. The first group consisted of five people; I organized this group and am still its leader at the present time. By the beginning of 1990 we had eleven people and we decided to begin the registration process. In March 1990 the society was officially registered by the city council. Today we have around thirty people, of whom ten are fully active on the society's behalf and up to thirty take part in one time assignments. We also have collective members: a branch of the design institute, a small enterprise, the collective of an independent newspaper.

We devote a lot of time to propaganda for democracy and for universal human values to counterbalance totalitarian and communist ideology. For this reason we are constantly working with the smallish democratic forces—the local divisions of the SDA [Social Democratic Association] and SDPK [Social Democrats of Kazakhstan], the independent newspaper, and others. In fact, the majority of SDPK members are members of Memorial. Our main work in recent times has been support of the new democratically leaning deputies and participation in elections for the local legislatures. We organize small political meetings on current political events; we organize protests (on the Baltics, in defense of Yeltsin, and others).

The local authorities do not hinder us, but they treat us with definite prejudice and distrust. The KGB and the organs of the CPSU harass us. I and several other members of the society were summoned by the head of the KGB in regard to articles in the independent newspaper and they demanded that we stop organizing meetings and demonstrations. The Communists take any opportunity to try to slander us and humiliate us (and me as president).

By luck we managed to place a notice about our society's activity in the Communist paper (Irtysh). Several articles have been published in the independent paper and in the new city paper.

The society's successes consist in locating [the remains of] several repressed persons, at the request of their relatives, and we continue to work at this task. We are searching for dead Japanese, Poles, and French. We are searching for burial sites of the repressed. We have found three sites, two within the city limits (one almost at the center and one farther out). According to eyewitnesses, . . . [at these sites] they murdered people by shooting them in the back of the head and buried them in pits.

Our difficulties lie in the fact that by secret command of the CPSU, not one of the enterprises or organizations to which we repeatedly turn for aid will help us. Altogether we have collected 2,400 rubles, and 500 we transferred to Moscow. Now we have 1,700 rubles in the account, but this is not enough to go ahead with the work that must be done, as it costs 150–200 rubles to rent a bus to inspect a burial site. I and everyone else work on a voluntary basis. We have all had unpleasantness at work, although our work is good. Our dream is to erect a monument to the repressed in the city and that true democracy, which is not founded on communist ideology, will triumph.

Polls indicate that 80 to 85 percent of citizens condemn the repressions, 60 to 65 percent condemn Stalin, and no more than 15 percent condemn Lenin. So we still have a long way to go to reach democracy!

> N. ZHUKOV, President
> Semipalatinsk Memorial
> March 1991

## STAVROPOL'

. . . You know as well as I, of course, that our totalitarian government is not destroyed and that government structures don't want to show all their cards: who would want to give oneself away? The CPSU with its fighting detachment, the KGB (NKVD), especially comes out against revealing the Stalinist repressions. To hear them talk, though, it would seem that something is being done (that is, what can no longer be hidden from people).

Stavropol', as the president's homeland, is one of the last strongholds of totalitarianism now. Here the same old CPSU *nomenklatura* sits on the thrones, the same old guard around Gorbachev that existed before perestroika. Perestroika hasn't even started for us; any manifestation of democracy, including Memorial, is suppressed. To this day our Memorial does not exist de jure, only de facto, despite the fact that we first applied for registration in December 1988, not long after the Moscow Memorial was founded. Our society has about 30 members.

The Stavropol' Memorial has become a member of the Democraticheskaia Russia movement. Many Memorialists are members of the Popular Front of Stavropol' and of the Democratic Party of Russia. They take part in all political activities—in preparing and conducting elections, demonstrations, and meetings against the reactionary union government and local leadership and in support of B. N. Yeltsin.

The local authorities, as we say in Russian, "don't see us at point blank"; and, wanting to take all this business into their own hands, they immediately created a department on Stalinist repressions under the city Party committee and then under the city executive committee (where the same Communists are ensconced). But the repressed don't get any benefits there or even elementary support. In our region we don't even have a law that would put the repressed on the same footing as World War II veterans (though other regions do have such a law).

All data on repressions in Stavropol' are secret; they don't, of course, allow us into the archives (state, regional, or CPSU). And it is entirely possible that these materials have been destroyed. The authorities claim that there were no executions in the Stavropol' region, that people were transported outside its borders. But first of all, this doesn't change the substance [of the matter], and second, there are still people living who might have been witnesses but are so terrified that they're afraid to talk. Moreover, repressions went on in the perestroika period. There is not one democrat who has not suffered for his convictions: all have had mud thrown at them, they're driven out of work, fined to the hilt for holding meetings, put in jail. Which is better, physical or spiritual extermination?

With the makeup of the regional and city councils what it is today, we can't accomplish a thing. Some democrats are present, but their weak voices are blocked by the majority votes of the Communists. . . .

TAISIIA KAZACHEEVA
Stavropol' Memorial
Lecturer, Stavropol' Pedagogical Institute
Candidate in Philosophy
May 10, 1991

## TOL'IATTI

. . . As a sociologist, I was doubly pleased to know that my colleague from the United States was interested in the problems of social consciousness in the USSR, and in the relations of the Soviet people to the Stalinist repressions.

A few words about myself: a candidate in philosophy, I am head of the independent Omnibus sociological center in Tol'iatti, which conducts research on the social opinions held by the city's residents. I am active in the city's political life—I took part in the creation of a number of independent social organizations, including the Memorial Society.

I will try to answer all your questions.

1. The formation of the Tol'iatti Memorial society was directly linked to press reports about the Moscow group's call for the restoration of historical justice and truth in regard to the repressed. This was in the spring of 1988. A smallish group of intelligentsia (aged 25–35) began to collect signatures among the city's residents for the formation of Memorial, and put an announcement in the paper. They established contacts with the Moscow group and took part in the preparatory conference in October 1988 and in the founding conference in January 1989. On 15 February 1989 we held a meeting at which the Tol'iatti Memorial Society was founded. In May 1989 our organization was officially registered by the city executive committee. At the beginning we had about 20 members. But up to 50 residents of the city came to our meeting. Seven members, including one of the former repressed, formed the administration of the society. From the very beginning members of the "creative" intelligentsia—a sociologist, a journalist, a historian, a museum worker, a literary specialist, and other representatives of the humanitarian professions—were active in our society.

2. The society exists as before, but its activity has fallen sharply.

3. Now our membership has fallen to 10–15 people, yet there are on the order of 40 repressed people in the city.

4. Yes, we engage in political activity: we nominated our representatives to be deputies in the city council of people's deputies, and conducted meetings.

5. Relations with local authorities might be called normal; they became substantially better when new people came onto the city council. Repre-

sentatives of Memorial joined the city executive committee's commission on the affairs of rehabilitated citizens.

6. In the beginning the society's activists very broadly publicized the theme of the repressed—which at that time aroused great interest—in the local papers.

7. About our problems: the society is now in a serious crisis:

- Many of the society's activists have in fact left it: they began to engage in political activity in the new parties or in entrepreneurial activity, creating small enterprises, youth centers.
- Obviously people's interest in the problems of the repressed has waned.
- The repressed themselves do not aspire to take an active part in the society's work (the two main reasons are age and fear).
- The society does not now have any space of its own; meetings are held in the local natural history museum, whose director, Liudmila Alekseevna Kogdina, is the society's president.
- The society still does not have a bank account . . .

ALEKSEI KIRIUSHIN
Tol'iatti Memorial
May 1991

# INDEX